A DEMOCRACY OF CHAMELEONS

Politics and Culture in the New Malawi

Edited by Harri Englund

Afterword by Jack Mapanje

Copublished in Malawi by
Christian Literature Association in Malawi (CLAIM/MABUKU), Blantyre
ISBN 99908-16-49-2 (Kachere Book No. 14)

Indexing terms
Civil society
Culture
Democratisation
Human rights
Politics
Poverty
Malawi

Cover photo: The police use tear-gas to disrupt an opposition meeting in Blantyre in January 2001.

Photograph taken by Julius Bonex

Language checking: Elaine Almén

@ the authors and Nordiska Afrikainstitutet, 2002

ISBN 91-7106-499-0

Printed in Sweden by Elanders Gotab, Stockholm 2002

Didn't you say we should trace

your footprints unmindful of

quagmires, thickets and rivers

until we reached your nsolo tree?

Why does your mind boggle:

Who will offer another gourd

Who will force another step

To hide our shame?

You've chanted yourselves hoarse

Chilembwe is gone in your dust

Stop lingering then:

Who will start another fire?

Jack Mapanje, "Before Chilembwe Tree" (1981)

Dzana ndi dzulo takhalira kuphedwa	Yesterday, and the other day, we're being killed
Lero tikhalira kunamizidwa	Today we are cheated
Nanga titani poti anthu ndi omwewo	What can we do since it is the same people
Angosintha njira zotizunzira	They've only changed ways of torturing us
Ali ndi njira zawo	They have their own ways

Lucius Banda, "Njira Zawo" (1995)

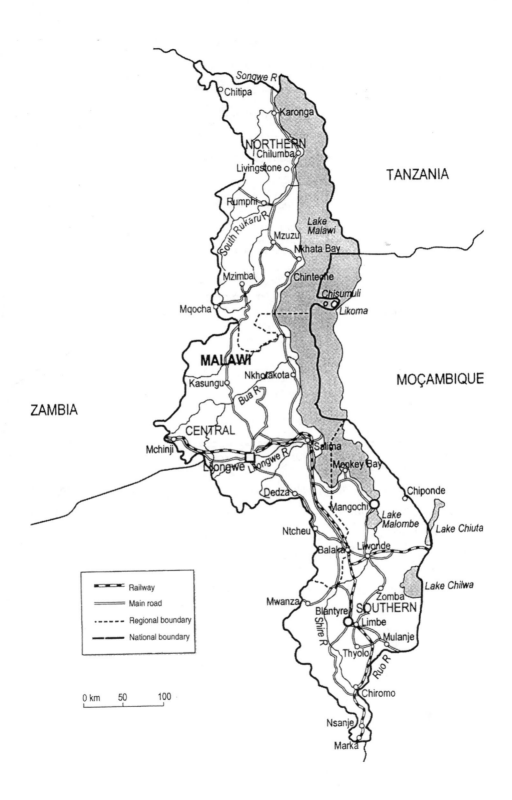

Songwe R

Chitipa

Karonga

NORTHERN

Chilumba

Livingstone

TANZANIA

Rumphi

South Rukaru R

Lake
Malawi

Mzuzu

Mkhata Bay

Mzimba

Chinteche

Chisumuli

Likoma

Mqocha

MALAWI

Nkhotakota

MOÇAMBIQUE

Kasungu

Bua R

ZAMBIA

CENTRAL

Mchinji

Salima

Lilongwe

Lilongwe R

Monkey Bay

Chiponde

Dedza

Mangochi

Lake
Malombe

Lake Chiuta

Ntcheu

Balaka

Liwonde

Lake Chilwa

Mwanza

Zomba

SOUTHERN

Blantyre

Limbe

Shire R

Mulanje

Thyolo

Ruo R

Chiromo

Nsanje

Marka

	Railway
	Main road
	Regional boundary
	National boundary

0 km   50   100

Contents

List of Tables

List of Abbreviations

ACB	Anti-Corruption Bureau
ADMARC	Agricultural Development and Marketing Corporation
AFORD	Alliance for Democracy
ATR	African Traditional Religion
CCAP	Church of Central Africa, Presbyterian
CLACA	Chitumbuka Language and Culture Association
CSRP	Civil Service Reform Programme
CSTU	Civil Servants Trade Union
DDC	District Development Committee
EU	European Union
FRELIMO	Mozambique Liberation Front
GDP	Gross Domestic Product
GOM	Government of Malawi
IMF	International Monetary Fund
J	Judge in High Court
JA	Justice of Appeal in the Supreme Court of Appeal
MBC	Malawi Broadcasting Corporation
MCP	Malawi Congress Party
MOH	Ministry of Health
MP	Member of Parliament
MPSR	Malawi Public Service Regulations
MYP	Malawi Young Pioneers
NAC	National AIDS Committee
NDA	National Democratic Alliance
NEC	National Economic Council
NGO	Non-Governmental Organisation
PAC	Public Affairs Committee
PAP	Poverty Alleviation Programme
PPEA	Parliamentary and Presidential Elections Act
PRSP	Poverty Reduction Strategy Paper
QC	Queen's Counsel
QUIM	Qualitative Impact Monitoring of Poverty
RENAMO	Mozambican National Resistance
SADC	Southern African Development Community
SAP	Structural Adjustment Programme
SDA	Social Dimensions of Adjustment
STD	Sexually Transmitted Disease
TEBA	The Employment Bureau of Africa
TRC	Truth and Reconciliation Commission
TVM	Television Malawi
UDF	United Democratic Front
UNDP	United Nations Development Programme
VAM	Vulnerability Assessment Mapping
WHO	World Health Organisation

Acknowledgements

The origin of this book can be traced to the *International Conference on Historical and Social Science Research in Malawi: Problems and Prospects*, held at Chancellor College in Zomba, Malawi, 26–29 June, 2000. Earlier versions of the chapters were presented at this conference, along with some 40 other papers on various aspects of Malawi's history, politics, economy, and culture. Major credit for this stimulating event is due to The Nordic Africa Institute which both provided the bulk of its funding and now publishes this volume. *Journal of Southern African Studies*, a co-organiser of the conference, has published a complementary selection of historical and social studies of Malawi in its first issue of Volume 28 (2002).

It is my conviction that the conference and the subsequent publications bear witness to the remarkable quickening of historical and social science scholarship in and on Malawi since the demise of Kamuzu Banda's stifling regime in 1994. Numerous are the Malawians who deserve praise for this auspicious political change. The studies in this volume are offered to nurture that fragile achievement through a responsible and balanced appraisal.

Among my personal debts incurred during the process from organising the conference to publishing this volume, two scholars stand out. Kings M. Phiri and John McCracken provided advice and made a considerable effort to ensure the success of the conference in 2000. An important contribution was also made by the Steering Committee at Chancellor College, comprising, in addition to Professor Phiri as its Chair, Blessings Chinsinga, Charles Chunga, Paul Kishindo, Anthony Nazombe, Naomi Ngwira, Martin Ott and Eston Sambo. I also wish to acknowledge the superb secretarial assistance rendered by the Centre for Social Research in Zomba. As for The Nordic Africa Institute, Nina Klinge-Nygård and C. Bawa Yamba went out of their way to provide moral and practical support when it was most needed. To all mentioned here and to the expanding fellowship of scholars working in and on Malawi, I say: *Mutu umodzi susenza denga.*

Lilongwe, April 2002
Harri Englund

Introduction

The Culture of Chameleon Politics

Harri Englund

Zinthu zatani?

Disgrace, public and sudden, befell Brown Mpinganjira, a self-proclaimed "democrat" and one of the key figures in Malawi's "second liberation" in the early 1990s. In November 2000, after steering the United Democratic Front (UDF) through two election victories since 1994, Mpinganjira was dismissed from President Bakili Muluzi's Cabinet on corruption charges. When Mpinganjira was Minister of Education, a "family friend" had allegedly bribed him on four occasions in order to be awarded lucrative contracts by the ministry. In December 2000, Mpinganjira was expelled from the UDF. He responded by founding the National Democratic Alliance (NDA), defined, in a terminology reminiscent of the era when only one political party was allowed to exist in Malawi, as a "pressure group".

For some, Mpinganjira's honour was restored almost as swiftly as he had been disgraced. He explained his dismissal as a consequence of his opposition to Muluzi's secret plan to undertake a third term in office, a plan at variance with the constitutional provision that allows a state president to stay in office for only two terms. The events in the early 1990s, moreover, had already become usable history in this bid to win the hearts and minds of Malawians. Both the local and international press participated in returning a democrat's aura to Mpinganjira. Barely three months after his dismissal, with the corruption charges still looming, Mpinganjira was touted as the "true founder" of the UDF, a hero whose fearless activism in the early 1990s was instrumental to the dismantling of Malawi's postcolonial autocracy.[1]

Mpinganjira's changing fortunes illustrate broader themes in Malawi's political pluralism. Allegiances among the political élite seem increasingly unpredictable and erratic. When the systematic challenge to Kamuzu Banda's authoritarian regime commenced, first as clandestine discussion and mobilisation in the late 1980s and then with the much-publicised pastoral letter of Malawi's Catholic bishops in 1992, the political divisions seemed clear enough. There were, on the one hand, the conservatives who clung to the ailing and ageing Life President, the "father and founder" of the nation, viewing multipartyism as an affront to both national unity and the Life President's unquestioned authority. Opposed to them were the democrats who, emboldened by aid donors' insistence on respect for human rights and good governance, staged protests and formed pressure groups. A referendum in June 1993 confirmed that the democrats were actually in the majority: Malawians chose a multiparty system of government. The pressure groups became political parties, with the UDF and the Alliance for Democracy (AFORD) at the helm of the ostensibly new breed of leadership. Despite its efforts to reform itself, the Malawi Congress

---

1. See e.g. "Brown Bites Back", *BBC Focus on Africa*, April–June 2001, pp. 28–29; "The Origins of the UDF", *Pride*, January–February 2001, pp. 31–32; "The Man in the News: BJ", *Pride*, January–February 2001, pp. 34–35; "'Living Dangerously?': Hon. Brown J. Mpinganjira", *The Lamp*, May–June 2001, pp. 22–23.

Party (MCP), the only party during the Banda era, has lost two democratic Parliamentary and Presidential elections to the UDF to date.[1]

After the first genuinely competitive multiparty elections in 1994, Malawians have been exposed to several bewildering shifts in their leaders' identities and allegiances. The tenets of liberalism in both politics and the economy are now shared by all the political parties. Their differences cannot be pinpointed with a reference to substantially divergent values and objectives. Everybody, it seems, is committed to multiparty democracy, human rights and the market economy. The parties' virtually identical manifestos attest to this, as does their respect for the new constitution that came into force in 1995 (see Kadzamira et al., 1998). A major distinguishing factor is, apparently, the parties' regional base of popular support. The three administrative regions of Malawi are now matched by three political parties: the Northern Region appears as the stronghold of the AFORD, the Central Region supports the MCP, while the UDF boasts a power-base in the populous Southern Region. Although politics is, in this regionally-defined pluralism, a matter of negotiating development aid for various localised constituencies, Malawi's political élite have not allowed regionalism to prevent several improbable alliances. The country's post-authoritarian political history has witnessed perplexing moments when the foes of yesterday have suddenly emerged as friends today. Such shifts have not been the prerogative of certain individuals only; entire parties have also changed their identities.

Consider, for example, how the three main parties have variously opposed and identified with each other since 1994. The leaders of the AFORD and the UDF did not mince their words when they condemned the MCP during the democratic transition. Chakufwa Chihana, the leader of the AFORD, described it as "the party of death and darkness", while Muluzi swore that he would never work with an MCP that included John Tembo, Banda's long-term henchman. After a short period of coalition government, the AFORD renounced its partnership with the UDF in 1995, only to enter into an opposition alliance with the MCP. Ordinary Malawians looked at the pictures of Chihana and Tembo smiling and shaking each other's hands, and wondered what had caused this sudden *rapprochement*.

Further shifts in allegiances, no less puzzling to the populace, have occurred in conjunction with conflicts among MCP leaders. Gwanda Chakuamba, whose ascendancy to the MCP presidency after spending thirteen years as Banda's political detainee is itself an enigma, clashed with Tembo over the MCP-AFORD alliance. After challenging Muluzi's legitimacy as the state president in the aftermath of the 1999 elections, Chakuamba was deprived of his position as the leader of opposition in the National Assembly by, among others, UDF leaders, the above-mentioned Mpinganjira amongst them. Tembo, hitherto the MCP's Vice-President, was elevated to this noble position, now hailed by Muluzi as just the kind of constructive and experienced politician that the young democracy needed. As if to complete this absurd drama, Mpinganjira, after his fall from Muluzi's favour, quickly allied himself with Chakuamba and Hetherwick Ntaba, another MCP strongman and the late Kamuzu Banda's personal physician. The three men addressed political rallies together, and Chakuamba and Ntaba came to offer moral support when Mpinganjira's corruption case was in court.

---

1. See Appendix for a breakdown of the election results in 1994 and 1999. An introduction to the political economy of Banda's regime is provided by Mhone (1992a). Classic academic critiques of the era include Vail and White (1989) and Kydd and Christiansen (1982). The 1992-94 transition is described, among others, by Nzunda and Ross (1995), Lwanda (1996), Schoffeleers (1999a), van Donge (1995) and Englund (1996a). Previous academic assessments of the "new" Malawi include Phiri and Ross (1998) and Ott et al. (2000). For extensive reviews of some of this literature, see e.g. McCracken (1999) and Forster (2000).

Zinthu zatani?, "What has happened?", became the cry of the UDF during the democratic transition. President Muluzi continues to open his rallies with this rhetorical question, followed by the crowd's response, *Zasintha!*, "Things have changed!". Few other than UDF zealots can avoid a sense of exasperation when the question *Zinthu zatani?* is posed a decade after it was first triumphantly sounded out. A charitable interpretation of the shifting allegiances in the new Malawi commends Malawian politicians for their capacity to compromise and to form alliances across the apparently entrenched regional lines. A less charitable interpretation questions the nature of democracy when leaders move in and out of their alliances with little consultation with their supporters. When a Malawian casts his or her vote for a particular political party or individual, he or she must be prepared, it seems, to observe baffling manoeuvres before the next opportunity to vote arises.

The Old in the New Malawi

The depth of the democratic reform also appears debatable when continuities in the relation between the political élite and the populace are considered. Those who are unfamiliar with the brutalities of the Banda era will do well to begin this book by reading its Afterword, penned by Jack Mapanje, Malawi's internationally acclaimed poet. As a member of the Writers' Group at the University of Malawi during the 1980s, he explored the limits of literary creativity and political critique in a postcolonial autocracy, only to languish in the notorious "Mikuyu Detention Camp" near Zomba. As Mapanje notes, a troubling continuity between the autocratic era and the current pluralism is the way in which youths are involved in politics. In Banda's Malawi, the Malawi Young Pioneers and the MCP Youth League had the notorious task of safeguarding discipline and obedience, often resorting to physical violence if there was any reason to suspect dissidence. In the new Malawi, the UDF's youth wing, confidently referring to itself as "Young Democrats", has been implicated in acts that have been anything but democratic. Public statements that can be interpreted as criticism of Muluzi's government have too often led to violent incidents. For example, after a group of Malawian Muslims had written a critical letter to Muluzi, persons in Muslim attire became targets of Young Democrats' wrath. One sheikh was beaten up after the opening of a parliamentary session in 2001 by youths who reportedly shouted, "Are you happy when the master (president) is insulted? This man insults the master" (*Kodi mumasangalala kuti bwana azitukwanidwa? Amatukwana bwana uyu*).[1]

Disturbing here is not so much the violence itself than the persistent perception of the state president as *bwana*, a master who is above criticism and whose power is partly based on violence and intimidation. Continuities between the old and new Malawi are all too obvious when we recall, with Reuben Chirambo, that during the Banda era "politics became a competition to please Banda by dealing harshly with his enemies" (2001: 219). Although many of the youths engaged in such acts are desperately poor, looking for favours from wealthy leaders, the political élite's own role in perpetuating intolerance must not be discounted. After a similar incident, now involving violence against a clergyman after a sermon that had criticised the government during the 2001 Independence Day celebrations, the Secretary General of the UDF argued that the youths had been provoked: "Never in the history of Malawi

---

1. Quoted in "Big Fight at Parliament", *Daily Times*, 13 June, 2001.

has a president been subjected to such preaching".[1] This statement not only begs the question whether Malawi's autocratic past offers commendable examples of how to treat a president; it also fails to admit that the depth of the democratic reform may be measured by the extent to which the state president can tolerate public criticism.

An astonishing feature of Malawi's political pluralism is the ease with which the political élite, particularly those who wield executive power, mix old and new, often quite literally in the same breath. An example is the comment which Clement Stambuli, Minister of Information, made in an interview with Television Malawi on 21 March, 2002. The interview took place in the aftermath of an attack on a journalist from *The Chronicle*—perhaps the most outspoken proponent of press freedoms in the new Malawi—by youths alleged to have been UDF Young Democrats.[2] Without as much as a full stop to separate his statements, Stambuli managed both to "condemn violence against journalists" and to urge the victims to ask themselves the question, "Why me?". Malawi has, he remarked, over one hundred journalists, but only a few of them have been the victims of physical violence. Although Stambuli did not openly justify violence, his double talk carried distinct messages to two different audiences—to foreign and local watch-dogs of Malawi's democracy and to Malawian journalists who, while pondering the question "Why me?", would be shepherded away from reporting on issues that the ruling politicians deem unsavoury. Intimidation and tolerance, old and new, exist side by side in Malawi's political pluralism. A key question is the relation between them; whether one is more consequential than the other; whether the rhetoric of change obscures the presence of the old in the new.

Although the Malawian political élite have never been in the habit of explaining themselves to their constituents, some politicians do occasionally provide insight into the passions that drive them. During a National Assembly session, for instance, a mischievous AFORD Member of Parliament posed the question to Tembo as to how his evident reconciliation with Muluzi was possible. Tembo pointed out that other Malawian politicians had already stated that in politics no one has permanent friends and enemies. He went on to elaborate: "The enemy of my friend is my enemy and the friend of my enemy is my enemy. Therefore, the enemy of my enemy is supposed to be my friend."[3] And what is the logic that underlies the formation of political friendships and animosities? In the same speech Tembo revealed that the MCP Area Chairman in his Dedza South constituency had been approached by officials from Mpinganjira's NDA. The chairman declined to join them, because they offered him only K7,000 (about US\$ 95). "He does not get K7,000 from me, but a lot more money", Tembo informed his fellow parliamentarians. Access to wealth, and the lack thereof, would seem to be the long and the short of it.

This volume, seeking to reach beyond Tembo's insight, offers more nuanced analysis to the debate on Malawi's political pluralism. The contributions in this volume explore a range of political, social and economic phenomena in the new Malawi in order to pose the difficult question: is there a culture of politics beyond mere greed? The contributors to this volume deploy *culture* as a useful tool to expand their purview of the "political" itself. Politics, patently, is more than the machinations of party leaders, encompassing other actors than simply political parties and state institutions. This volume brings to the spotlight forms of political discourse and practice that are rarely addressed in conventional political studies. They belong to

---

1.   Quoted in "CHRR Condemns Bishop's Attack", *Daily Times*, 12 July, 2001.
2.   See "UDF Young Democrats Attack the Chronicle", *The Chronicle*, 25 February–3 March, 2002.
3.   Quoted in "Tembo Hits Back", *The Nation*, 20 June, 2001.

domains as diverse as popular music, the clergy, ethnolinguistic associations, and "traditional" healers. When addressing more obvious topics of political studies—such as Malawi's Poverty Alleviation Programme, the work of judges in a multiparty system, or popular understandings of human rights—the chapters in this volume are likewise attentive to their cultural aspects, such as specific symbols and ways of conducting public affairs that may endure in spite of dramatic political changes.

This effort to reach beyond the most apparent realm of party politics derives partly from the prospect of increasing popular frustration with political parties in Malawi. There are indications that, after widespread excitement during the two general elections in 1994 and 1999, the intrigues of the political élite have begun to discourage participation in elections.[1] Scholars and other observers of the Malawian society need to be attuned to the concerns and frustrations of ordinary Malawians. Politicians' manoeuvres make the headlines, but the cost of their entertainment value is a distorted perspective on Malawian realities. It may be in the institutions highlighted in this volume that the most consequential—and the most constructive—politics is devised in the new Malawi.

Critique and Responsibility

The above remarks and the subsequent chapters indicate considerable discontent with the political and economic direction that the new Malawi appears to have taken. Much as the appearance of this volume bears witness to the positive aspects of the Malawian transition – to the fact that the contributors to this volume are able to engage in social research without fear of persecution – there is every reason to resist complacency. Yet the very precariousness of Malawi's democracy places the onus of evidence and accurate analysis on those who choose to be critical. The stakes are especially high in unstable democracies, and it should be made clear at the outset that this volume has been conceived from a non-partisan standpoint. If the UDF government appears to receive more punches than the Opposition, it is merely a consequence of its executive power. The primary task of this volume is to assist us in discerning the various challenges and promises of political pluralism in Malawi, not to act as an arbiter between its diverse custodians.

The imperative of responsible critique is also dictated by the international context in which Malawians pursue their new pluralism. In January 2002, the government of Denmark decided to terminate its development aid to Malawi, citing corruption and political intolerance as its reasons. Thus ended a "partnership" of many years and millions of Danish kroner. The full effects on the Malawian society are yet to be seen, but the most likely losers are the rural poor who had benefited from various agricultural projects, aspiring students whose education was greatly facilitated by Danish funds, and various non-governmental organisations. It is particularly surprising that the government of Denmark chose to express its concern over human rights in Malawi by ceasing to support non-governmental human rights watch-dogs in the country!

Such an abrupt and thoughtless move betrays, of course, the donor's own self-interest. The withdrawal of aid was effected by a new government in Denmark that came into power in December 2001. A populist right-wing coalition, it embarked on a campaign against anything that was outside narrowly-defined Danish interests, be

---

1. For example, the local government elections in November 2000 and several parliamentary by-elections have witnessed very low voter turn-outs, sometimes fewer than 20 per cent of the electorate casting their votes.

it the country's own immigrant population or its "partners" in less advantaged parts of the world. For the Danish government, any critique of Malawi's democracy was eminently convenient – it could be used to justify a blatantly selfish policy. Although social researchers cannot expect to have much control over the use of their findings in the public sphere, this example does remind us of the need to keep in mind the sometimes hostile international context in which poor countries like Malawi seek social and political transformation. Our critique should not contribute to the consolidation of the heinous boundaries between the South and the North, Africa and the West. Let the message of our critique be loud and clear; *disengagement is not the answer.*

It is also not the answer because of the way in which international aid is an integral element of Malawi's domestic politics. For example, Chakufwa Chihana, the leader of the AFORD, saw that his time had come when Denmark cut its aid. Chihana quickly abandoned the alliance with the MCP and made it known to Muluzi that he was available for a government of national unity in order to "win back donor confidence".[1] Chihana's sudden change of heart left his own party in disarray, with Muluzi and the UDF government benefiting from the further fragmentation of the opposition. Others representing the opposition in this dispute over aid hardly had a more insightful analysis to offer, bluntly putting all the blame on Muluzi's shoulders.[2] The Malawian media also kept the populace largely ignorant of the international context and fuelled the flames of the country's heated political debate.[3]

As always, the powerful claimed ownership of the truth. After allowing the debate to simmer in a manner appropriate to a democracy, the Ministry of Information intervened with a press release.[4] It noted, at the outset, the "difficult financial and budgetary circumstances currently obtaining in Denmark". Turning the tables, the Ministry stated that "the Malawi Government fully understands and empathises with the Danish Government for the very difficult circumstances in which it finds itself, and respects the choices it has made in order to find solutions". No longer was Malawi the poor relative begging for assistance, only to be rebuked by the rich relative for the mismanagement of funds. The press release sketched out two partners, two equally sovereign states, both embroiled in a financial crisis. The punch-line came later. The Ministry advised the Danes that "a weak democracy must be supported, and not abandoned. To disengage from Malawi at this time is abandoning the type of vision to (sic) which we had become accustomed to expect from the Danish Government". Moreover, the Ministry warned that "we will not respect a situation where a Friendly Government has decided to part ways with the truth at the expense of our country's name and its international image".

Whether anyone in Copenhagen noticed this press release is beside the point. It was designed as much for domestic as for international use. The Malawian government was able to portray itself as the true champion of democracy, while the Danish

---

1. "Aford to Meet Muluzi on Aid", *The Nation*, 4 February, 2002. See also "Chihana's Dream Fails to Materialize", *The Chronicle*, 4-10 February, 2002; "Aford Move Long Overdue", *The Nation*, 4 February, 2002; "After the Alliance: What Now Aford?", *The Nation*, 8 February, 2002.
2. "Muluzi Blamed for Aid Freeze", *Daily Times*, 1 February, 2002.
3. See e.g. "Travelling on a Steep and Slippery Slope: Can We, As a Nation, Recover from the Many Blunders", *The Chronicle*, 4-10 February, 2002; "Denmark Halts Aid", *Daily Times*, 30 January, 2002; "EU Denies Aid Cut to Malawi", *The Nation*, 14 February, 2002; "Danish Aid: What Next for Malawi", *The Nation*, 14 February, 2002; "EU Shares Danish Concern – Envoy", *The Nation*, 15 February, 2002; "Muluzi Denies Aid Cut", *Daily Times*, 15 February, 2002. Virtually the only article in the press that made any mention of the political change in Denmark was "Danish Aid Cut Scares NGOs", *The Nation*, 31 January, 2002.
4. "Ministry of Information Press Release: Danish Aid to Malawi", *The Nation* and *Daily Times*, 6 February, 2002.

government was noted to have lapsed from "the type of vision" that characterises democratic governments. The withdrawal of aid did nothing to subvert the UDF government's rhetoric. Inadvertently, it only provided the government with yet another opportunity to bask in the glory of democracy.

Understanding Chameleons

How to study politics and culture in the new Malawi? What is the impact of the old on the new in different domains and contexts of public life? Is Malawi a democracy? Or is it, as a hapless presenter on Television Malawi put it, "post-democratic"?[1] The apparently haphazard manner in which Malawian politicians forge alliances may be little else than a continuation of a culture of *chameleon politics,* a notion inspired by Jack Mapanje's poetry, written at the height of the Banda era, *Of Chameleons and Gods (1981).*[2] Heroes of yesterday may be villains today, depending on the dynamic of political friendship and animosity. As long as the political leadership changes its allegiances without transparent reasons, Malawi's political pluralism is a democracy in doubt, a puzzling combination of expedience and idealism, a democracy of chameleons.

New rhetoric serves to justify old ambitions for unlimited power. When this volume was being finalised, Malawians were approaching the next test to their democracy. The reason why the 1995 constitution prohibited, in its section 83(3), anyone from occupying the office of the state president longer than two consecutive five-year terms was obscured by the need to consolidate the networks of patronage that the Muluzi administration had created. Interesting here was not the predictable hunger for power but the rhetoric with which the constitutional change was demanded. Soon after his appointment as Minister of Justice and Attorney-General, Henry Phoya sought to "clarify" why there was nothing wrong with some people wanting to give Muluzi the opportunity to stand for the third term in office.[3] Phoya began with the widely held view that the new constitution had technical problems that needed amendment (see Ng'ong'ola's chapter in this volume). He used this technical approach to argue that the constitution did not take into account that some Malawians might want a president to serve more than two terms. "In such a situation", he is quoted as saying, "the majority will be denied their right to free political choice because of the provisions of section 83(3)."[4] In addition to the technical-legal approach, designed to dispel suspicions of un-democratic manoeuvres, Phoya joined the increasing chorus of UDF officials to assert that the government had no plans to amend the constitution in this respect. It was ordinary people, "the grassroots", who kept the issue alive. As such, the Members of Parliament—the democratically elected representatives of the people—were obliged to hear the cry of their people and to amend the constitution if necessary.

1. Tamara Mkandawire presenting the TVM News on 19 March, 2002.
2. The figure of the chameleon has appeared in other writings from postcolonial Malawi, both in political studies (Dzimbiri 1998 and 1999) and in poetry (Chimombo 1987 and 1993). It is beyond the scope of this Introduction to establish the extent to which this figure, which is primarily used to depict postcolonial politicians, resonates with tales and myths from Malawi's past. Chimombo (1988: 212), at least, is of the opinion that the chameleon (*birimankhwe* or *nadzikambe* in Chinyanja; its larger variety known as *kalilombe*) is a rare figure in Malawi's oral literature, unpopular when it does assume a role, appearing in creation myths rather than as a trickster.
3. See "Govt Supports Third Term Push", *The Nation,* 25 April, 2002; "Govt Open to the Third Term", *Daily Times,* 25 April, 2002.
4. "Govt Supports Third Term Push", *The Nation,* 25 April, 2002.

Phoya's reasoning was remarkable for the way in which it utilised the rhetoric of democracy—the unflagging respect for the constitution and the will of the people—to erase a protection against unlimited power that Malawians had fought for in the early 1990s. Chameleons may have changed their colour but not their motives. With the opposition in disarray and largely co-opted by the Muluzi administration, it was clear that the debate in the National Assembly would be more preoccupied with Muluzi's virtues than with the views of the people. The ingenious Chichewa/Chinyanja word for "fooling", *kupusitsa*, would once again capture the relationship between the political élite and the populace. *Kupusitsa* is a causative that properly means "to make somebody stupid or a fool". Just as Banda had "made Malawians stupid" by denying anyone else but himself the capacity to rule the country, so too would the post-Banda political élite "make Malawians stupid" by denying them a healthy turnover of the Executive. Even D.D. Phiri, a venerable intellectual turned into a partisan columnist, tried to dupe Malawians into believing that the best assurance against absolute power lay in individual psychology: "The incumbent president has a different temperament from that of our former president."[1] In a culture of chameleon politics, the masses are bound to learn that "appearances deceive" (*maonekedwe amapusitsa*). The question is whether they are able to outwit their rulers and pass this most recent test of their democracy.

The fact that many leading politicians in the "new" Malawi also held prominent positions in Banda's one-party state seemingly helps to explain continuities in political behaviour. However, the evocation of a "culture" of politics seeks to identify patterns and structures that are not reducible to the presence of particular individuals in politics. In this regard, genuine change does not commence simply with a change of incumbents. "Chameleon politics" refers to patterns that are common to postcolonial politics far beyond Malawi. A vibrant body of scholarship has emerged to address the complex realities of African postcolonies, their elusive achievements and enduring anxieties (see e.g. Bayart, 1993; Mamdani, 1996; Werbner and Ranger, 1996; Werbner, 1998 and 2002; Ake, 2000; Mbembe, 2001). For instance, the frequent shifts in personal and collective identities that appear so astonishing to outsiders draw upon histories of colonial rule and postcolonial repression. These histories furnish an amorphous repertoire of possible identities, their dynamic coexistence amply discrediting the conventional dichotomy between "tradition" and "modernity". Shifting identities are not the prerogative of the political élite. Chameleon-like leaders are challenged, often in subtle ways, by the equally intractable manoeuvres of those whom they are supposed to rule. Even in Banda's autocracy, as Mapanje writes in his Afterword, "one changed one's colours like the chameleon" in order to outwit the autocrat and his coterie. Combined with the all too evident economic decline, the current pluralism hardly dissipates the dynamic of hegemony and counter-hegemony in a culture of chameleon politics, with those in power forever mindful of new ways to lure others into pacts and submission.

These perspectives call into attention the circumstances under which political cultures emerge and are fostered. Those circumstances are profoundly *historical*, shaped by political and economic processes that are irreducible to the functions of particular nation-states. In his argument against the view that sub-Saharan Africa is only marginally involved in the current processes of economic and cultural globali-

---

1. "Democracy and the Third Term", *The Nation*, 23 April, 2002. Note also the way in which Phiri seeks to make critical perspectives on the third-term bid something foreign and un-Malawian: "Let us not allow foreigners with their money to turn us against one another. The third term question is our business, not the concern of donors."

sation, Jean-François Bayart (1993 and 2000) suggests "extraversion" as a concept for the long-term historical pattern by which the sub-continent has been inserted into the rest of the world. The exploitation and plunder of the sub-continent, more often than not willingly pursued by African leaders themselves, are nothing but the ways in which the relationship between Africa and the rest of the world has evolved during more than a century of internal and external colonisation. Through processes of extraversion, the external politico-economic environment has become an indispensable resource in the pursuit of power and authority in the internal politics of Africa. Extraversion is a more active mode of being subjected to external influences than outright dependency. For instance, every historical moment of Africa's exchange of ideas and goods with Europe, Asia and the Americas appears to have had its African collaborators, despite the often violent methods deployed by outsiders. The trans-atlantic slave trade may be the most notorious example of some Africans facilitating the subjugation of other Africans with a view to benefiting from what the external environment had to offer (see Thornton, 1992). What this tragic episode shares with the subsequent history is the active effort by Africans to mould their external environment into a resource for the internal politics of power and authority.[1]

Evidence on the shallowness of democratic reform in sub-Saharan Africa since the late 1980s is too compelling to make the current political pluralism an aberration in the long history of extraversion, or to permit mere cynicism about political change in the sub-continent. Much has changed, as this volume shows for Malawi, but much has also remained the same. The change in the external environment of African polities is only one aspect of so-called democratisation. The Cold War, which had contributed to the resilience of Kamuzu Banda's conservative regime, ended with a resurgence of old grievances over poverty and abuse. With an eye to the way in which aid donors, including the World Bank and the International Monetary Fund (IMF), expressed their post-Cold War fascination with "good governance", new democratic leaders, some of whom were not that "new" at all, steered popular aspirations to the direction of multipartyism and "rights talk" to which the donor community seemed most receptive.

The shallowness of the democratic reform has become evident in tandem with the new leaders' demonstrated capacity to continue with corruption and plunder. The "paraphernalia of democracy" (Englund, 2001a)—multipartyism, regular Parliamentary and Presidential elections, new constitutions, freedom of expression, a non-governmental sector—have ensured the flow of development aid that leaders may appropriate for their locally and regionally-defined orbits of power. In order to keep up with appearances, unlikely marriages of convenience emerge, such as when the former arch-enemies Muluzi and Tembo play out the roles of a "democratic president" and his "loyal opposition" for their mutual political survival. In its pastoral letter of April 2001, the General Synod of the Church of Central Africa, Presbyterian (CCAP) may have been more perceptive than it realised. It observed that "[Malawi's] democratic system is almost the only asset we have to attract donor money and foreign investment" (CCAP, 2001: 4). Compare this with Bayart's comment on Senegal, a pioneer in African democratisation: "It is no exaggeration to say

---

1.   It is important to caution against the kind of misrepresentation that Mamdani is guilty of when he dismisses Bayart's perspective for implying that "modern imperialism is...the outcome of African initiative" (1996: 10). Inequality is at the core of the notion of extraversion. The notion outlines the historically specific conditions for the contemporary expressions of power and authority in sub-Saharan Africa. As such, it may have more in common with Mamdani's compelling exposition of the making of "customary" power than he is able to acknowledge.

that the export of [Senegal's] institutional image...has replaced the export of groundnuts" (2000:226).[1]

If there is a discernible "culture" of politics in Malawi, it must, therefore, be seen as an historical phenomenon that structures, even as it is historically conditioned by, the relations between Malawi and the rest of the world. Any attempt to introduce a cultural perspective to the study of politics should be wary of the pitfalls that *culturalism* often involves. Some political scientists, for example, have periodically asserted the importance of studying values, norms and attitudes as foundations of a "political culture". Such a research agenda was widely adopted by students of newly independent nations during the 1960s and 70s (see e.g. Pye and Verba, 1965; Elkins and Simeon, 1979), only to resurface with the recent wave of "democratisation" (see e.g. Inglehart, 1988; Karlström, 1996; Hyden, 1999; Harrison and Huntington, 2000). Great caution should be observed, however, when these scholars present political culture as "an explanatory variable in its own right" (Hyden 1999: 20). When culture becomes an explanation rather than a phenomenon inviting historical elucidation, determinism easily creeps in. Such is the appeal of this unvarnished culturalism among some that Africa, for example, is thought to require not only a structural adjustment of its economies but also a "cultural adjustment" of its values (see Etounga-Manguelle, 2000)! Culture, according to culturalism, is a system of values that can be purposefully "developed" with a complete disregard of its historical conditions. Another common fallacy of culturalism is to assume that values and meanings are shared in society, creating a common political culture between the élites and the masses (see e.g. Chabal and Daloz, 1999).

After successfully navigating the pifalls and fallacies of culturalism, a cultural perspective into politics may, as mentioned, provide not only insight into long-term historical patterns but also expand the very definition of "politics". It invites us to explore the historically dynamic ways in which politics is *situated and shaped* by a whole range of discourses and practices in society. A crucial pre-condition for the success of such a perspective is a certain populism, an effort to accept the populace, in its full variety, as a worthy subject of political inquiry, as agents of discourses and practices which often counter or qualify the hegemonic rhetoric of political parties and their leaders. This kind of populism has both academic and political consequences. Academically, new phenomena inspire new hypotheses as the "field" of politics is allowed to expand. Politically, this empirical work can take us beyond a paralysing planetary perspective suggested by the notion of "extraversion". While it may be true that Malawi's democracy is in doubt because world democracy is in doubt, it hardly warrants inertia in Malawian policy-making. Much will be achieved when policy interventions based on critical analysis replace the self-serving rhetoric of the political élite.

Beyond the New Malawi

What could be a more appropriate starting-point for this volume's interrogation of the "new" Malawi than the issue of poverty? As Blessings Chinsinga shows in his chapter, the discourse on poverty is perhaps the most conspicuous way in which the difference between the "old" and "new" Malawi is currently demarcated. The issue, significantly, is not so much whether poverty has decreased with the advent of de-

---

1. Compare also with the concern over the international image expressed in the above-mentioned press release from the Ministry of Information.

mocracy. Rather, the UDF government uses the discourse on poverty to define its permissive political culture which, in contrast to the political culture of the Banda regime, acknowledges the existence of poverty in Malawi. President Muluzi rarely makes a public statement without mentioning his preoccupation with "poverty alleviation" and, more recently, "poverty eradication". Chinsinga examines the discursive and institutional foundations of Malawi's Poverty Alleviation Programme (PAP), a framework in which the notions of "local community" and "participation" feature prominently. Chinsinga finds at least two factors that expose the largely rhetorical nature of the current PAP. One is the negligible attention given to infrastructural improvements that would enable the programme to actually reach remote rural areas. As a consequence, institutional channels for "local participation" are likewise underdeveloped, the programme retaining a top-down character. Another factor which mitigates the attainment of the stated objectives is the economic policies of the new Malawi. Economic liberalisation stipulated by the donor community has well fitted the ideological outlook of the UDF élite, many of whom have long pursued considerable commercial ventures in Malawi. Trade rather than production has gained prominence under this ideology, but its severely circumscribed capacity to alleviate poverty has slowly begun to dawn on UDF leaders themselves.

The effects of economic liberalisation on Malawi's employed population are in the focus of Gerhard Anders' chapter. On the basis of fieldwork among civil servants, Anders highlights the predicament of those who have traditionally benefited from the most secure, if low paid, form of employment in Malawi. Under the guidance of the World Bank, the new Malawi has adopted a Civil Service Reform Programme, aimed at achieving "good governance" through efficiency and transparency. For ordinary civil servants, a shadow of "expenditure control" and "retrenchment exercises" has been cast over their lives. Anders shows some of the consequences of retrenchment in an economy which does not readily absorb redundant civil servants. A sense of insecurity haunts the citizens of the new Malawi, an insecurity that is heightened by the fact that the loss of a job is not merely an individual tragedy but often affects a whole range of relationships, indicating the futility of assuming a clear divide between "formal" and "informal" sectors of the economy. Moreover, civil servants' insecurity reaches cosmological proportions when the government begins to revise its long-standing commitment to support its employees' funerals. Discontent and insecurity are almost unbearable when, as Anders writes, "a civil servant cannot be sure any more whether he or she will be buried in a coffin provided by the government".

The next two chapters address more directly the behaviour of politicians and other assumed custodians of democracy in the new Malawi. Clement Ng'ong'ola brings to the fore disputes that accompany multiparty elections. His chapter shows the high profile which the legal profession has obtained in the new Malawi, with politicians frequently enlisting their services. Court cases give political disputes both publicity and an aura of respect for the rule of law, but Ng'ong'ola's critical question is whether judicial mediation represents, in fact, judicial meddling. By discussing a number of prominent cases in the new Malawi, he seeks to investigate the extent to which judges and lawyers fail to remain legal technocrats and succumb to various political passions. A disconcerting conclusion that arises from Ng'ong'ola's detailed analysis is that technically sound judgements may indeed be brought to serve political preferences, a situation made possible by what Ng'ong'ola calls the "hapless language" of the new constitution.

A similar observation on the limits of "the rule of law" in ensuring democracy is put forward by Edrinnie Kayambazinthu and Fulata Moyo, who examine incidents of hate speech in the new Malawi. The freedom of expression is one of the most cherished features of the new Malawi, but Kayambazinthu and Moyo's disturbing finding is that this freedom has been abused to amplify the voice of the ruling politicians at the expense of a genuine democracy of expression. The Malawi Broadcasting Corporation (MBC), for example, did not relinquish partisan reporting with the change of government; it serves the current ruling party by silencing critical voices at the same time as it grants UDF politicians time on air to castigate their political opponents. The doubtful extent to which more open media practices have been entrenched in Malawi was revealed to Kayambazinthu and Moyo when the MBC displayed considerable reluctance in granting them access to the recordings of the state president's and other UDF leaders' speeches. Slurs among competing political parties may be a feature of democracies everywhere, but as Kayambazinthu and Moyo argue, they assume a particularly volatile quality in a country with a coercive past and a regionalist-tribalist present. A recommendation that arises from this chapter is that the government should consider constitutional provisions to curtail hate speech.

Kayambazinthu and Moyo point out the striking discrepancy in the freedom of expression between the "old" and "new" Malawi. Whereas critical intellectuals and writers had to either avoid certain topics or express them in cryptic language under Banda's regime, the new Malawi appears to make an allegorical discourse on politics redundant. However, as Reuben Chirambo's chapter attests, there remains a vast domain of popular discourse which is rarely accorded the same attention as the speeches and behaviour of the political élite by the media and conventional political science. One perspective into this domain is afforded by popular arts, and Chirambo's focus is on the work of Lucius Banda, a musician who enjoyed tremendous popularity in Malawi during the 1990s. With lyrics that confirmed him as a "soldier" fighting the cause of the poor, Banda has been in the forefront of a new generation of popular musicians in Malawi who have addressed various social and political ills in idioms that are widely understood in society. Banda's work allows his listeners to contemplate how politicians' hate speech may merely mask leaders' mutual interests, while their supporters bear the brunt of intolerance and violence that hate speech incites. Banda's songs also resonate with popular ambivalence about Malawi's autocratic past, with unequivocal condemnation alternating with a sense of nostalgia. His success and critical messages have, however, been indisputable enough to attract the interest of the UDF, and Muluzi, cultivating his image as a "president who is not cruel" (*pulezidenti wopanda nkhanza*), has not missed an opportunity to embrace rather than persecute his critic. Despite the financial support which Banda appears to have received from Muluzi, Chirambo ends with a hopeful note that popular music will continue to provide an outlet for popular discontent in Malawi.

Apart from popular music, religion is another prominent aspect of the domain which potentially resists the hegemonic discourse of political leaders. Several publications have stressed the role that the Catholic and Presbyterian churches played in mobilising popular support for Malawi's democratic transition (see e.g. Newell, 1994; Ross, 1996; Englund, 1996a; O'Malley, 1999; Schoffeleers, 1999a). In his chapter for the present volume, Peter VonDoepp takes this discussion further by examining the discourses and practices of the local clergy in these churches a few years after the transition. His chapter makes an intervention into debates which depict "civil society" as an indispensable feature of liberal democracies. These debates assume, for example, that local-level non-governmental institutions, such as the church, are crucial to consolidating democracy. VonDoepp's research findings reveal, however, that it is important to see "civil society" as a complex field of actors and institutions, some of whom may not seek to distance themselves from the state at all, while others, such as local-level Catholic and Presbyterian leaders, may have other preoccupations than advocating socio-political issues. VonDoepp brings to our attention such factors as doctrine, organisational hierarchies and socio-economic position to explain the local clergy's limited activism. Indeed, his findings indicate that Catholic and Presbyterian leaders' concerns at the national level may have little resonance with the pursuit of spiritual and material security by the poor at the local level, a conclusion also suggested by the increasing appeal of Pentecostal and charismatic denominations in Malawi (cf. Englund, 2000).

While Christian churches facilitated the advent of multipartyism, the secular domain of politics in Malawi quickly became overshadowed by ethnic and regional antagonisms (see e.g. Kaspin, 1995; Chirwa, 1998a). Gregory Kamwendo takes up a corollary of this predicament—the emergence of voluntary associations which promote particular languages and ethnic identities, often understood as indices of distinct "cultures". As Kamwendo notes, of the ethnolinguistic associations that emerged in the early 1990s, the Chitumbuka Language and Culture Association (CLACA) appears to be the most resilient. The history of political tribalism in Malawi makes this understandable. Tribalism did not begin with multipartyism, and those teachers, intellectuals and civil servants whose origins were in the Northern Region had to endure the arbitrary powers of the Banda regime on the suspicion that they were its enemies. Despite the ethnic diversity in the region, Tumbuka identity came to capture the attention of both lackeys and dissidents under the Banda regime, while the Chitumbuka language, long promoted by missionaries and then devalued by Banda, assumed an emotional point of identification among Northerners. Although the activists of the CLACA are urban-based professionals, rather than "ordinary" Tumbukas, Kamwendo's evidence does not support the view that the association is simply an elitist contrivance designed to amass popular support for particular politicians, such as those in AFORD, a party that boasts a power base in the Northern Region. Rather, CLACA activists' passion for language and culture raises more difficult questions in understanding the new Malawi—how to nurture pluralism without being parochial, and how to achieve unity without tyranny.

Ethnolinguistic associations draw upon notions of "tradition", another issue under lively debate in the new Malawi. "Tradition" is, for example, summoned to assess the moral conduct of both individuals and cultural institutions. The final two substantial chapters address these debates for the light they shed on problems of health, sexuality and gender in the new Malawi. John Lwanda offers a brief history of the HIV/AIDS crisis in Malawi from a perspective which is more cultural than epidemiological. Although open discussion on HIV/AIDS, like on poverty, is cherished by the UDF leadership as one of the features that distinguishes the "new" Malawi from the "old", Lwanda argues that both the Banda and Muluzi regimes have evinced regrettable torpor in dealing with the epidemic. He identifies an enduring political culture in which "traditional" medicine is consistently side-stepped when health policies are formulated. This oversight is unfortunate for at least two reasons. One is the fact that government hospitals and health units provide inadequate care for the poor majority, while private clinics, and increasingly mission-based ones as well, offer services which are beyond the means of the poor. *Mankhwala achikuda*, literally "black medicine", thrives under these circumstances. Another consideration often missing in official strategies to combat the epidemic in Malawi are the many cultural practices that mould sexuality, variously advancing and curbing the spread of sexually transmitted diseases. Lwanda notes the irony of this oversight—Malawian elites solicit foreign aid against the epidemic and seek to "educate" their masses, while they privately subscribe to "traditional" beliefs, including witchcraft. For Lwanda, the HIV/AIDS epidemic in Malawi requires official recognition of this duality, a political culture which admits the modernity of Malawian traditions.

Both Kamwendo's and Lwanda's chapters raise the question of who the custodians of "tradition" are, and how the present pluralism encourages the assertion of various identities. The interplay between official and popular understandings is brought into a sharper focus by Ulrika Ribohn, who discusses the impact of the human rights discourse on popular opinions about women and culture. The discourse on human rights is probably the most taken-for-granted aspect of Malawi's democratisation, but little research has so far been conducted on the specific ways in which rights are understood and claimed among ordinary Malawians (but see Englund, 2000 and 2001b). Ribohn's study shows how official human rights discourses have inadvertently produced their popular adversary. By defining certain gendered "traditional" practices as threats to women's rights, official discourses— spoken by state officials, non-governmental organisations (NGOs), aid donors and the mass media—have received a response that asserts women as keepers of "tradition". Important in Ribohn's analysis is the observation that the two are interlinked; both official and popular understandings use "tradition" and "culture" interchangeably and, like all culturalism, make them abstract and ahistorical. Another salient issue is the eagerness of some women to participate in this definition of themselves as keepers of "tradition". Ribohn laments its consequences for attempts to uplift women's status in a male-dominated society, but also notes how women may thereby associate themselves with a morality that deserves respect. Ribohn introduces the notion of *ulemerero wa umunthu*, a somewhat academic neologism, to better convey the sense of human dignity, opposed to human rights, that underlies popular responses to official discourses.

Taken together, the chapters in this volume demonstrate how contradictory and competing understandings of democracy and development co-exist in the new Malawi. The imperative to reach beyond the self-serving rhetoric of ruling politicians is obvious; a more challenging task is to investigate in detail the range of practices and discourses in society, and to arrive at insights that take us beyond the rhetoric of the "new" Malawi. This volume takes up the challenge by opening up new empirical domains for such a project. This is partly facilitated by the fact that overviews on the Banda regime, the democratic transition and its aftermath are extensive enough to warrant inquiries that venture into hitherto little-studied terrains (see note on p. 12). Two analytical issues, as this Introduction has argued, are crucial to this project. On the one hand, the scope of the "political" must be allowed to expand to include various domains and popular discourses that are often overlooked in conventional political studies. On the other hand, the accompanying cultural perspective must be wary of culturalism and view the culture of politics from a historically nuanced perspective.

1. The Politics of Poverty Alleviation in Malawi

A Critical Review

Blessings Chinsinga

Setting the context

One interesting difference between the administrations of Kamuzu Banda and Bakili Muluzi is the purported intent of their economic regimes. The major emphasis of the former government was on estate agriculture as an engine of economic growth and development. This strategy of development was backed up by the 1967 Land Act which declared that all customary land was "vested in perpetuity in the President" (Sahn and Sarris, 1990:399). The Land Act was designed to reinforce a postcolonial agricultural strategy that distinguished estate farming from smallholder agriculture. The sectors differed in terms of land holding and types of crops which they could grow. While those engaged in estate farming were at liberty to cultivate a variety of crops without a limit, those within the smallholder sub-sector were legally prohibited from producing such cash crops as burley tobacco, tea and sugar.[1] Furthermore, the land market that was created following the 1967 Land Act provided only for one-way transferability of land. Land could only be transferred to the estate sector, usually with only a small compensation.

Most supportive agrarian policies, including policies in related economic spheres, were deliberately designed to serve the agricultural sector in a generally preferential manner. The visiting tenant system, which was utterly exploitative, was systematically tailored to ensure considerable profit margins for estate agriculture (Kydd and Christiansen, 1982; Sahn and Harris, 1990; Kishindo, 1997). It is in fact not surprising that the two ten-year statements of development policies during the Banda era clearly emphasised agriculture as a potential source of revenue that would eventually lead to financial autonomy in other sectors.[2]

The data in Table 1, incomplete as it is, nevertheless suggests that the estate sector grew much faster than the smallholder sector. The reason for this discrepancy was that the majority of the élites moved into the estate sector, facilitated by cheap finances obtained through excessive taxes on peasants. The Agricultural Development and Marketing Corporation (ADMARC) played a central role in implementing these policies. Even recent statistics, Structural Adjustment Programmes (SAPs) not-

---

1. The majority of those who were engaged in estate agriculture were often high-ranking party functionaries, senior civil servants, chiefs and high-ranking industrial and parastatal employees.
2. The statement of development policies outlined strategies to be pursued in various sectors in order to achieve satisfactory economic, social, political and cultural progress. The first statement of development policies spanned 1971–1980 whilst the second one was operational from 1987–96. Meanwhile, the ten-year planning cycle has been overtaken by the Vision 2020 planning innovation, which seeks to chart out the potential trajectories of development in all sectors of the economy whilst taking into account the aspirations, ambitions and fears of various segments of the population.

Table 1. Annual Growth Rate of Crop Production

Year	Estates		
	Tobacco	Tea	Sugar
1960–69	11.2%	3.7%	-
1970–80	20%	6.6%	22.2%

Year	Peasants				
	Tobacco	Groundnuts	Cotton	Rice	Maize
1960–69	-3.3%	6.5%	3.6%	-4%	11.1%
1970–80	3.4%	-4.8%	3.9%	5.3%	14.5%

Source: Kydd and Christiansen (1982).

withstanding, indicate that the situation has remained much the same. The small-holder sector has continued to be marginalised. In the pre-adjustment period, lasting until 1981, the smallholder sub-sector produced 84 per cent of agricultural output while the estate sub-sector contributed only 16 per cent. In the adjustment period, the share of smallholder agriculture declined to 76 per cent while that of the estate sub-sector increased to 24 per cent.

After the ousting of Banda's one-party regime, there has been a remarkable structural shift from agriculture to commerce as the desired hub of economic growth and development. The shift in the country's political economy was aptly captured by van Donge (1995), who contended that popular capitalism had slowly but nonetheless steadily assumed prominence since the UDF assumed the reigns of power. The change in focus is not a surprise since the majority of prominent leaders in UDF have their background in commerce and industry (see Lwanda, 1996).

The force and influence of commerce in Muluzi's economic policy were borne out by the dramatic upsurge of small- to medium-scale credit initiatives, touted as a means of fostering financial autonomy and hence poverty alleviation. The underlying goal behind the credit schemes was to alter the structural constraints of the country's financial sector. The argument was that the schemes would be instrumental in poverty alleviation since they would, inter alia, focus on indigenous resources, particularly labour which seems to be in abundance in the country (NEC, 2000). As a result, enormous financial resources[1] were channeled through the National Association of Business Women (NABW), Development of Malawi Traders Trust (DEMATT), Small Enterprise Development of Malawi (SEDOM), Women World Banking (WWB), the Promotion of Micro Enterprises for Rural Women (PMERW), Malawi Savings and Credit Cooperative (MUSCCO), Small and Medium Enterprise Fund (SMEF), Malawi Mudzi Fund and the Youth Credit Scheme.

All these credit initiatives were meant to be revolving funds, but they soon dried up. Hundreds upon hundreds of beneficiaries are reported to have deliberately defaulted in the name of democracy (Chirwa et al., 1996). At present, virtually nothing is heard of what has become of these credit initiatives. It would appear that the credit sector has been unsuccessful because of the lack of a coherent and robust policy to regulate its activities. Little has been done to ensure access to markets and to develop sustainable infrastructural support services for emerging entrepreneurs.

---

1. For instance, the Youth Credit Scheme was funded to the tune of 70 million Malawi Kwacha.

The paradox, however, is that during the same period that the country's economic policy stimulated entrepreneurship, the manufacturing sector progressively contracted. It expanded rapidly in the 1980s, but it has been on the decline since 1994. The sector has declined from 16 per cent in 1994 to 14 per cent in 1997 to about 12 per cent in 1999 (NSO, 1999). With the closure of several industries—for example, Brown and Clapperton, and Opitichem—the prospects for an early recovery look bleak. The trend for most companies is to shift from manufacturing products in the country to marketing products manufactured by their sister companies either within the region or beyond.[1]

It is important to note that these credit initiatives were implemented under the rubric of the Poverty Alleviation Programme, which has been the operative development philosophy of president Muluzi's administration since 1994. Its underlying vision is that every Malawian should have access to basic necessities in order to develop and exploit their potential to lead a productive, dignified and creative life through social, economic and political empowerment. The emphasis has, since the 1999 general elections, shifted from poverty alleviation to poverty eradication.

Poverty in Malawi

Poverty debates have been endlessly marred by the apparent lack of consensus as to what exactly constitutes poverty in the Malawian context. Part of the problem can be attributed to the lack of critical debate on policy issues during Banda's one-party regime. The state apparatus systematically cultivated a culture of submissiveness and docility. There was virtually no room for views that contradicted the officially articulated position. Poverty, according to Msukwa and his co-authors (1994), was one of the areas that lacked any critical and open debate. It was virtually a taboo to consider poverty as a public problem requiring urgent policy interventions.

For nearly three decades after independence, the official view of Banda's regime was that as long as every Malawian was well fed, lived in a house which did not leak and had adequate clothing, the question of poverty did not arise. Little wonder that the issue of poverty was hotly contested in the run-up to the plural electoral contest in May 1994 (Chinsinga, 1995). The thrust of the debate was whether the majority of Malawians had crossed the threshold of absolute poverty after thirty years or so of self-governance and administration. The Malawi Congress Party (MCP) regime was visibly at pains to admit widespread poverty at the household level. The impressive track record of growth at the macro level for more than a decade after independence contrasted sharply with the severity of want and deprivation among the populace. The majority of Malawians did not enjoy the benefits of the post-independence macro-economic prosperity.

The opening up of the political system has thus offered Malawi-based scholars and other intellectuals an unprecedented opportunity to take a fresh and critical look at the problem of poverty in the country. Inevitably, there are conflicting perceptions of the state of poverty, arising from the fact that various studies have generated different estimates of the incidence, prevalence and degree of poverty. The 1993 GOM-

1. See, for example, *Daily Times* of 7 February, 2001. In the business supplement, one of the contributors laments that Malawi is becoming a trading centre. The contributor observes that most companies have resorted to scaling down their processing plants, concentrating on the purification of already processed products with minimum labour so as to enjoy the local processing status. He concludes by saying that "dear Malawi shall shortly become a mere trading centre with all its needs being brought from neighbouring countries".

UN (1993) situation analysis revealed that about 60 per cent of rural and 65 per cent of urban residents lived below the poverty line which was estimated to be at US$ 40 per capita per annum. Using the same measure, the World Bank (1995) also estimated that about 60 per cent of the people in the country earned their living below the poverty line. The more detailed findings indicated, among other things, that 47 per cent of the population cannot meet basic needs, 52 per cent are very poor according to the criterion of US$ 40 per capita, and 32 per cent cannot afford to buy food which can satisfy the minimum calorie intake.

The study also confirmed that poverty is predominantly rural, although urban poverty is increasing, and the Southern Region has more poor households than its share of households (NEC, 1998). The Vulnerability Assessment Mapping (VAM) that was conducted in 1996 revealed that the people most vulnerable to poverty are in Nkhata Bay, along parts of the Mozambique border, and in the extreme southeastern portion of the shore of Lake Malawi. Recent estimates by NEC (2000) indicate that poverty affects up to about 64 per cent of Malawians.

The picture was different when Chirwa (1997) assessed the incidence of poverty in the country using the proportion of income which households spent on food. The incidence of poverty in the country was as high as 89.9 per cent. This translated into 49 per cent and 93.6 per cent incidence of poverty in the rural and urban areas respectively. A further breakdown of the statistics revealed that 65 per cent of the households in the semi-urban areas (district headquarters) were poor. An earlier study using the same measure but focusing exclusively on urban areas found out that the urban low-income population spent as much as 63 per cent of their overall budget on food (Chilowa and Chirwa, 1997).

The disparities in magnitude of the incidence of poverty emerge mainly because of differences in the methodologies used by each study; the divergences in the perceptions of welfare; the purposes and the frame of reference for those involved (Chilowa et al., 2000). The most important thing, however, is that all the studies reviewed underscore a widely shared consensus that the phenomenon of poverty in the country is not only an acute but also a growing problem.

The need for an official view of the problem of poverty in the country is pressing given the various perceptions of the incidence of the problem in the country. I subscribe to the definition of poverty in the 1993 GOM-UN situation analysis. Poverty is here taken as a condition characterised by serious deprivation of basic needs in terms of food, water, health, shelter, education, and a lack of means and opportunities to meet minimum nutritional requirements.

Recent statistics indicate that Malawi remains one of the poorest countries in the world despite undergoing significant economic and political reforms. The National Statistical Office estimated the country's per capita income at US$ 140 in 1994, which dropped to US$ 126 in 1998, and subsequently picked up to US$ 177 in 1999. The progress in human development has not been satisfactory either. In the last decade, Malawi's position has been among the last ten countries on the ladder of prosperity.[1] The 1999 World Development Report further confirmed the pathetic poverty situation in the country. It ranked Malawi as the eighth-poorest nation in the world out of 210 nations. Malnutrition rates in Malawi were—and are—among the highest in Africa. Infant mortality rate was 135/1000 live births in 1999. Child

---

1. The UNDP ranks countries in terms of their progress towards satisfactory human development at yearly intervals. A year after the Human Development Report was launched in 1990, Malawi was ranked 138 out of 176 countries. Since then, Malawi's performance has been steadily declining. It was ranked number 141 in 1992; 153 in 1993; 157 in 1994; 157 in 1995; 158 in 1996; 161 in 1997; 161 in 1998.

mortality was 234/1000 live births. However, according to Chilowa and his co-authors (2000), infant mortality rate has now been reduced to 133/1000 live births and the corresponding child mortality rate has also been reduced to 211/1000 live births. The total literacy rate is 41 per cent, of which 33 per cent are women and 67 per cent men, according to the estimate by the 1998 Southern African Development Community (SADC) Human Development Report.[1] The school drop-out rate among girls is 34 per cent. Life expectancy is also very low. It has declined from 48 years in 1990 to about 39 years in 1999, according to the 1999 United Nations Human Development Report. This trend is associated with the high HIV/AIDS prevalence rates in Malawi.

An Overview of Malawi's Economy

Any attempt to fully understand the current problem of poverty in Malawi has to be situated within the overall history of the country's economy since independence in 1964. Almost all accounts of the country's economy acknowledge the fact that the post-independence period can be divided into two broad phases. The first took place before 1979 when nearly every sector of the economy registered rapid growth, whilst the second one commenced around 1979 when almost every sector experienced tremendous decline followed by erratic recovery trends (Kaluwa et al., 1992; Mhone, 1992a; Chipeta, 1993; Chirwa, 1995; Chilowa et al., 2000).

During the period between 1964 and 1979, the country's economy registered high growth rates and enjoyed relatively favourable balance of payment positions. Savings as a proportion of GDP rose from the modest level of 0.3 per cent in 1964 to 19.7 per cent in 1979; industrial output expanded at the rate of 10 per cent per annum. The average economic growth was estimated at 6 per cent compared to only 2.9 per cent population growth rate per annum. Domestic exports rose from US$ 48 million in 1970 to about US $285 million in 1980. These impressive macro-economic variables were attributed to, among other things, favourable world demand; favourable climatic conditions; rapid expansion of large-scale agriculture; high levels of gross domestic investment; and low and declining real wages and labour costs in the agricultural sector (Chirwa, 1997; Chilowa, et al., 2000).

The impressive macro-economic trends as reported above began falling apart quite sharply in the late 1970s. The downturn persisted to the extent that the country's economy registered a negative growth rate for the first time since independence in 1981 (Chilowa, 2000). The GDP growth decreased to 0.4 per cent in 1980, plummeted to −5.2 per cent in 1981, then picked up to 2.8 per cent in 1982 and staggered around 4 per cent in both 1983 and 1984. Even though there were signs of recovery after the 1981 growth crisis, the subsequent growth rates were still below the rates which the economy achieved in the pre-1979 phase, and since then the prospects for a consistent recovery have been virtually non-existent.

The origins of a less than satisfactory economic progress since 1978 are partly attributed to the aftermath of the 1978–79 oil shock that affected the whole world. The decline was further exacerbated by the serious drought that hit the country in the 1980-81 agricultural season. All this coupled with the attendant sharp decline in the terms of trade; the rise in interest rates on international financial markets; the

---

1. The statistics on literacy should be treated with considerable caution. They can either under- or over-esti-
    mate the actual circumstances because of difficulties to maintain accurate databases. Moreover, there is a
    time lag between the time the data was collected and when it was reported.

closure of the Beira-Nacala trade corridor; the influx of refugees from war-torn Mozambique; and the declining levels of aid made the situation extremely difficult. The resultant economic hardships exposed several structural rigidities that underpinned the country's economy (Chilowa et al., 2000). These included the following:

— Slow growth of smallholder exports;
— The narrowness of the export base and increased reliance on tobacco;
— Dependence on imported fuel and on a declining stock of domestic fuel-wood;
— The rapid deterioration of parastatal finances; and
— Inflexible system of government-administered prices and wages.

The external and internal financial imbalances that occurred because of the constraints highlighted above were so serious that they necessitated urgent redress. The government, therefore, had little choice but to seek intervention from the World Bank and International Monetary Fund (IMF) in a bid to regain the lost economic glory. As a result, Malawi has since 1981 implemented a series of stabilisation programmes under the auspices of IMF and Structural Adjustment Programmes (SAPs) supported first by the World Bank and later by both the World Bank and the IMF. In the SADC sub-region, Malawi was the first country to adopt the World Bank- and IMF-sponsored SAPs. Since then Malawi has drawn on three different SAP loan facilities in addition to four sector-specific credit reform packages (Kaluwa et al., 1992; Mhone, 1992a; Chilowa et al., 2000).[1]

Despite being the pioneering country within the sub-region, Malawi is yet to show off the benefits for taking the lead in adopting the SAPs. The overall outcome has been disappointing. Several reviews emphasise that the SAPs have laid heavy social burdens on the vulnerable segments of the society, particularly women and children. The popular view in this regard is that the design of the SAPs did not take into account the potentially adverse effects on the poor in the short and medium terms. Public expenditure rationalisation has had a tremendous negative impact on the poor. Government expenditure declined from 36 per cent to 29 per cent of the GDP between 1987 and 1996, while at the same time the debt-servicing burden more than doubled. This meant that very few resources were available for other purposes, including social services.

On a somewhat positive note, the government's recurrent expenditure has substantially increased from 14.66 per cent in the pre-adjustment period to 23.87 per cent in the adjustment period. However, the increase in the recurrent expenditure notwithstanding, the shares of expenditure for the health and education sectors have fallen dramatically. The expenditure shares for education and health dropped from 15.5 per cent to 10 per cent and from 6.53 per cent to 3.17 per cent respectively during the adjustment period.

Market liberalisation has probably been the single most detrimental reform on poor households since they have traditionally depended on ADMARC for the purchase of maize. ADMARC's restructuring involved a management reform, closure of its uneconomic markets, liberalisation of the marketing of smallholder crops, among other strategies (Christiansen and Stackhouse, 1989). The decision to liberalise the marketing of smallholder produce culminated in the 1987 Agricultural Act which provides a legal basis for private traders to participate in the marketing of ag-

---

1. See World Bank (1990b), Kaluwa et al. (1992) and Chilowa et al. (2000). SAL I was implemented in 1981, SAL II in 1984 and SAL III in 1996. The four specific credit reform packages include the Industry and Trade Policy Adjustment Credit (ITPAC) 1998; Agriculture Sector Adjustment Credit (ASAC) 1990; Entrepreneurship Development and Drought Recovery Programme (EDDRP) 1992; and Fiscal Restructuring and Deregulation (FRDP) 1996.

ricultural produce. The closure of some uneconomic ADMARC markets, therefore, has contributed to the widespread food insecurity for poor households, especially in the remote areas that are hardly accessible to private traders.

The macroeconomic variables have not improved either. They have, since the implementation of SAP, never resumed the pre-1979 growth levels. The economy has, in the post-1979 period, on several occasions experienced boom and bust trends of recovery (Chilowa, 2000). For example, the GDP growth rate slumped to -7.2 per cent in 1992, rose to 10.8 per cent in 1993 and tumbled to -12.4 per cent in 1994. The pathetic GDP growth rates observed between 1992 and 1994, however, need a proper caveat. The dramatic fall registered during this period was, to a larger extent, caused by the reduction in agricultural production due to drought, political upheavals and the freezing of all non-humanitarian aid to Malawi by donor agencies. They wanted to force the leadership to adopt political and economic reforms that would foster the practice of good governance, democracy and the respect for human rights (Nzunda and Ross, 1995; van Donge, 1995; Phiri and Ross, 1998).

The sad reality, however, is that nearly two consecutive decades of faithful structural adjustment have not taken the country's economy back to the impressive performance of the 1970s. The SAPs have, according to Chipeta (1993) and Chilowa and his co-authors (2000), not only failed to alter the structure of production of the economy but, as already noted, economic growth has also been erratic.

The economic hardships engendered by the implementation of the SAPs, particularly public expenditure rationalisation, have forced the poor to seek numerous survival and adaptive strategies to alleviate their poverty. This lack of access to public social services has led households to resort to traditional medicine and treatment at home as far as health facilities are concerned (see Lwanda's chapter in this volume). Lack of adequate water facilities has forced households to revert to unsafe and unclean sources. The poor have found refuge in squatter settlements in which substandard houses and congestion are the norm. Chilowa and his co-authors (2000) have, through a three-year study, whose objective was to monitor social policy in the context of economic reforms, established, as reported in Table 2 below, some of the major coping strategies of the vulnerable segments of the society.

Table 2. Coping Strategies of the Vulnerable Segments of Society

Strategy	Rural	Urban	National
Begging	4.8	1.6	3.2
Assistance from relatives	67.6	45.3	56.5
Assistance from friends	40.7	50.9	45.8
Charitable organisations	1.4	3.0	2.2
Street vending	5.1	8.2	6.6
Past savings	13.2	28.6	20.8
Working for food	17.3	2.0	9.7
Prostitution	0.9	0.9	0.9
Selling used clothes	1.2	4.5	2.8
Buying second hand goods	13.9	17.5	15.7
Sending kids to relatives	3.9	18	2.8
Other	57.6	2.7	40.4

Source: Chilowa et al., 2000: 61.

Some of the observations in Table 2 are also echoed by other studies (Chirwa, 1997; Pearce et al., 1996). These studies report, among others, the following coping strategies for the vulnerable groups:

— Purchase of maize from ADMARC, local markets and other households in the growing season;
— Changes in the composition of meals with the tendency towards inferior foodstuffs;
— Greater reliance on the social networks of friends and members of extended families;
— Off-farm work either for food or cash;
— Sale of assets such as livestock and other domestic assets; and
— Migration to other countries and urban areas.

The tremendous negative impact of the SAPs on the social sector has been widely recognised all over the world. In Malawi, the acknowledgement of the need for "adjustment with a human face" led to the adoption of a special programme known as the Social Dimension of Adjustment (SDA) as early as 1990. This was in part influenced by the World Bank's (1990a) realisation that the wellbeing of an individual is an outcome of complex economic and social processes, which involve physical performance, labour input, income generation and consumption investment. The main aim of the programme was to develop the institutional capacity of the government in partnership with the civil society in order to meaningfully integrate social and poverty concerns in the development process (Kaluwa et al., 1992). It is not an exaggeration to say that the experiences with the SDA programme, coupled with the permissive political milieu, have substantially contributed to the adoption of the Poverty Alleviation Programme as the country's operative development philosophy.

At the international level, the last years of the 1990s saw the forceful return of poverty to the international development agenda. The comeback is closely associated with the work of the World Bank and UNDP. The 1990 World Development Report focused, almost exclusively, on the state of poverty in the world. The 2000 World Development Report took stock of the previous decade's experiences in the noble task of fighting poverty. Likewise, the UNDP inaugurated the Human Development Report in 1990. This annual publication aims at putting the people first; to wit, it proposes a "people-oriented" view of development. The Japanese development agency (JICA) also champions "human-oriented development" as the development strategy for the twenty-first century (Esho, 1999; Toye, 1999; Moore, 1999).

The most striking feature that has accompanied the return of poverty to the international development agenda is the proliferation of various national Poverty Alleviation Programmes (PAPs). They have, in fact, become the dominant characteristic of contemporary development strategies. Examples, among others, include the Bolivian Emergency Fund; the Economic Recovery Programme in Zambia; the Programme of Actions to Mitigate the Costs of Adjustment in Ghana; and the Poverty Alleviation Programme in Malawi. It is against this background that this chapter undertakes a critical review of the country's 1994 Poverty Alleviation Programme. The chapter seeks to establish the extent to which the PAP, which has after the general elections in 1999 moved into its second phase of implementation, represents a genuine commitment to address the problem of poverty in Malawi.

Overview of the 1994 Poverty Alleviation Programme

This section provides a brief overview of the 1994 Poverty Alleviation Programme. The overview sets the context for the rest of the chapter. The focus is on the institutional set-up, the content of the policy initiative, and the management and implementation of the programme.[1]

Institutional set-up

The PAP institutional matrix consists of the Presidential Council, National Steering Committee and Eight Task Forces

The Presidential Council
This is headed by the state president. The other members include the vice president, a number of cabinet ministers, religious groups, the Chamber of Commerce, the African Business Association (ABA), the private sector, academic institutions, traditional leaders, the three Regional Governors of the UDF party and independent members with vast experience in development issues. The Council is responsible for giving policy directions and guidance as well as assisting in sensitising the populace on the government's priorities.

The National Steering Committee
This is headed by the Secretary to the President and Cabinet. It has members from the civil service, non-governmental organizations (NGOs), the private sector and, where necessary, co-opted members from the donor community. The committee is, among other things, responsible for coordinating the activities of various task forces in order to avoid unnecessary duplication of functions and resources.

Task Forces
These are responsible for the actual implementation of the poverty alleviation programmes. They focus on agriculture, health, population, the informal sector, public works, social welfare and education. They, in liaison with local communities, assess the needs of the poor and assist in the planning and designing of poverty alleviation sectoral programmes.

Content of the PAP policy initiative

The PAP has been designed primarily with the intention of addressing the salient features of poverty in the country, which include household food insecurity and low productivity among smallholders, a weak institutional enterprise sector, limited access to essential social services and a shortage of management capacities for planning and implementing key poverty alleviation programmes. The objectives can be summarised as follows:

1) to increase agricultural productivity among resource-poor farmers;
2) to promote employment and income opportunities in the informal sector;
3) to improve the access of the poor to priority services; and
4) to enhance the capacities of the local communities in managing development .

---

1.   For details on the PAP policy, refer to GOM 1994.

The PAP policy initiative has four component programmes, each designed to address one of the four objectives named above. These programmes are:

1) Smallholder agriculture productivity programme

The objective of this programme is to enhance household food security especially among the resource-poor farmers through the increased application of on-farm technology, expanded coverage of extension services, increased access to farm inputs and labour saving technologies, better environment management and a more sustainable utilisation of fisheries and forestry.

2)Small enterprise development programme

The principal objective of this programme is to create alternative non-farm income opportunities in order to reduce poverty. Particular focus is given to the improvement of policy environment, entrepreneurial and technical skills development, access to credit, appropriate technology and marketing.

3) Social development programme

The programme aims at strengthening the delivery of social services (basic education, primary health care, low cost housing, rural transport and sanitation) to the poorest segments of the population. Emphasis is on the development of alternative delivery systems through increased community participation.

4) Management for development programme

The programme aims at creating efficient and effective management capacities for economic and social advancement. It envisages the formation of a competent and motivated leadership to steer and implement development activities at the local level as a critical factor in the implementation of anti-poverty programmes.

Management of the programme

The management of the PAP is entrusted to the Ministry of Economic Planning and Development. It is the secretariat for the whole programme. It liaises with the Office of the President and Cabinet and the Ministry of Community Services to ensure that appropriate institutions are established and strengthened. The ministry is further responsible for incorporating the PAP projects into the National Development Programme.

Identification and assessment of needs

The PAP policy initiative is being implemented through the hierarchy of the District Development Committees (DDC) institutional matrix in order to offer the local communities direct participation in the identification as well as implementation of programmes that affect them.

Forum for development

The forum is intended to facilitate the link between the DDCs and the various Task •
Forces through quarterly meetings in which the DDCs present their proposals to the Task Forces.

The forum for development serves as a basis for sectoral programmes formulated by the Task Forces. Once the sectoral programmes are formulated, they are submitted to the National Steering Committee for approval.

Implementation

The actual implementation of the approved projects is carried out by the relevant institutions identified by the various Task Forces. The Task Forces closely supervise and monitor the progress. They also keep the National Steering Committee informed through the production and submission of reports.

Appraisal of the 1994 poverty alleviation policy initiative

The primacy of the Poverty Alleviation Programme on the country's development agenda cannot be disputed. Poverty in Malawi is indeed widespread and deeply entrenched. Policy measures to fight poverty merit priority consideration. The PAP policy initiative, now in its second phase of implementation, is therefore quite laudable. One of its strengths is that it has at least broadened the scope of the anti-poverty programmes. Prior to its launching, the tendency was to equate poverty alleviation with infrastructural projects that were administered through the DDCs.

The question is, however, whether the policy initiative has been properly designed to facilitate the attainment of the desired targets of poverty reduction. I attempt to answer this question by examining some of the issues that may constrain progress. These include the institutional set-up, agrarian reforms and the SAPs.

Institutional set-up

It is a widely known fact that efficient institutional designs are particularly important in the success of any programme. This consideration is particularly crucial for PAPs in developing countries where the problem of poverty is often too deep and widespread to be solved by temporary relief (Esho, 1999; Ali, 1999). There are generally two major concerns. First, how can the programmes be designed so that they in fact primarily benefit the poor? Second, how can the initiatives achieve significant results with reasonable administrative costs given that resources are always limited?

In the contemporary official development discourse, the overall success of PAP policy initiatives is dependent on how participation is institutionalised. Nevertheless, the concept of participation itself, especially as it relates to grassroot development efforts, is as contested as it is fashionable because of the wide variations in the meanings attached to it. The official view is that development plans have to be based on the aspirations of the people if poverty is to be significantly reduced. As such, the ultimate goal should be to make communities masters or mistresses of their own destinies.

In addressing the issue of participation, there is, however, always the need to distinguish between *instrumental* and *transformational* participation. The former is a way of achieving certain specific targets (the local people participate in the outsiders' project), while the latter is an objective in and of itself (a means of achieving some higher objective such as self-help sustainability) (Mikkelsen, 1995). Thus much as the PAP policy initiative champions beneficiary participation as its guiding philosophy, the fact that the National Steering Committee retains the final say on which poverty intervention strategies are to be implemented makes the commitment to transformational participation rather superficial. The Steering Committee's mandate therefore leads one to conclude that the professed commitment to participation is less an effort at real empowerment of the poor than a managerial or, perhaps worse, rhetorical device.

The problem with the PAP policy initiative is that it is totally silent on the mode of participation that drives its implementation. In fact, no attempt has been made to define the notion of participation in the context of the programme and yet a large premium is placed on it. The concept of participation in this case is being used as a management strategy through which to mobilise local resources in order to implement a series of stand-alone, donor-inspired development projects.

All the task forces are mandated to review and prioritise poverty alleviation intervention strategies identified in the DDCs. This brief, likewise, does not augur well for the noble efforts to empower the target communities to ultimately graduate from their reliance on external forces to articulating their own priorities. Moreover, the task forces are the prerogatives of technocrats who are often alienated from grassroot realities. Ideally, the task forces could offer technical expertise without tampering with priority lists that emerge in the DDCs.

Another issue of concern is that the task forces are expected to achieve a nationwide coverage. This is clearly a tall order as the personnel involved are housed at the government headquarters in Lilongwe's Capital Hill. Remote districts are most likely to be disadvantaged. The unfortunate consequence is that the delays in responding to the pressing needs of the would-be beneficiaries may have a dampening effect on their enthusiasm. The failure would mean that the preparatory efforts (sunk costs) of the implementation of the PAP policy initiative would be virtually irrevocable.

Transaction costs are most likely to be very high because of the overlapping and vaguely defined mandates of the institutions. It is, for instance, stated that the programme is going to be implemented through the DDC institutional matrix and yet the task forces are mandated to undertake implementation through agencies that they may identify. The overall management responsibility is likewise entrusted to both the Presidential Council and the National Economic Council of Malawi (GOM, 1994). These conflicting mandates would, to a large extent, compromise the unity of direction upon which the ultimate success of ambitious programmes like this one often depends. The delays, as a result of the need to reconcile conflicting instructions or other administrative signals, would unduly impede the appropriate momentum of implementation.

Malawi has a multiparty system of politics. Yet membership in the various committees connected with the PAP policy initiative is heavily skewed in favour of the ruling UDF party. The UDF's dominance often means that its voice alone dictates the direction of the proceedings. Cases of the UDF being bent on pushing through its political agenda, however irrational, cannot be ruled out. This concern has, of course, to be situated in the broader context of African politics as espoused by Bayart (1993). The title of his book borrows a Cameroonian idiom—*Politics of the Belly*—to characterise the political and policy environment of many sub-Saharan African countries.

The expression is associated with the Cameroonian saying, "people know that the goat eats where it is tethered and those in power intend to eat". Thus with the tradition of completely competitive and fair politics yet to take root, PAP resources are highly susceptible to abuse. They may be used to facilitate, but more importantly to expand, the patronage network. After all, issues rarely play a decisive role in the electoral processes. Potentially, therefore, the PAP may be reduced to an arena of economic struggle for political dominance.

The concerns are more real when Bayart observes that multiparty politics in most African countries is simply a necessary and not sufficient condition for democracy: "Multiparty politics is nothing more than a fig leaf covering up the continuation and even the exacerbation of the politics of the belly from the prudish eyes of the West" (Bayart, 1993:xvii). As a result, the disbursement of the funds may not so much be based on sound and viable bureaucratic principles as on the vagaries of political expedience. Such observations have already been echoed elsewhere. Kangwere (1998), for instance, pointed out that the beneficiaries of the Poverty Alleviation efforts thus far are, in all fairness, disproportionately well-placed in the ruling political circles.

As a matter of principle, PAP policy initiatives must be primarily designed to assist particular groups and communities that are untouched by economic growth or adversely affected by it. The major problem of the PAP in this regard is its failure to clearly identify the various groups of the poor in the country and what their needs are. Apparently, there was no consultative process with the poor in order to establish the actual extent of poverty in the country. It would have been very important to establish who the poor are, where they live, what it is that they perceive as their problems, and how they think their problems could be solved. Rather than utilising or commissioning new research, a great deal of the planned policy interventions in relation to PAP was designed on the basis of the categories of the poor identified in the 1993 Situation Analysis (Chilowa, 2000; Chilowa et al., 2000).

Through Qualitative Impact Monitoring of Poverty (QUIM), established after the launching of the PAP, it is becoming increasingly clear that the poor classify themselves into three categories, namely, the very poor, the poor and the better off. The perception of wellbeing from the point of view of the people living in poverty is mainly a quantitative issue, revolving around how much a person owns in order to be able to cover his or her basic needs (NEC, 1998; NEC, 2000). Other means, including small-scale businesses and search for employment, are considered secondary. The basic problem is that this information is coming at a time when the PAP is in its second phase of implementation.

As a result of the lack of situation analysis at the time of the PAP's inception, there was much emphasis on offering general credit when in fact the major issue as far as the majority of the poor were concerned was the lack of agricultural credit. Of course, issues of money, capital, credit, credit facilities, and access to credit facilities feature prominently in QUIM exercises. However, the need for credit facilities for the promotion of small-scale business activities predominates in urban QUIM sites.

The experience with QUIM thus reinforces the view that special focus should be directed towards how the poor themselves perceive poverty and what solutions they envisage. Ideally, therefore, the findings of QUIM should feed into the implementation process of the PAP. The problem, however, is that there is a serious lack of implementation capacity for relevant policy instruments to achieve the desired strategic impact at the village level.

The PAP policy initiative and agrarian reforms

Agrarian reforms have been mooted as part and parcel of the institutional design of the efforts to realise the PAP policy initiative. However, the manner in which the land question has so far been handled does not indicate the government's commitment to redefine land rights in favour of those who have diminutive plots or who are virtually landless.

The land situation in Malawi makes decisive agrarian reforms a matter of urgency, especially since land is the major productive asset. About 85 per cent of the population depend on agriculture for their livelihood, and it contributes to about 35 per cent of the annual GDP. The primacy of land as a productive asset means that any tangible attempt at poverty alleviation has to address the challenge of agrarian reform.

After more than three decades without a comprehensive policy on land matters, Malawi now has a new land policy, approved by the Cabinet in January 2002. The process of preparing the new land policy benefited from the findings of the Land Reform Commission whose mandate was "to promote scholarly discourse, gather the opinions of the private sector, ordinary citizens and non-governmental organizations, and to organize their findings in such a manner as to aid the land policy reform efforts" (GOM, 2001: 13). It is debatable, however, whether the government has utilised the Commission's findings to a significant effect. Moreover, the government's commitment to consult diverse "stakeholders" will be measured at the next stage of the land reform when new legislation will be drafted and debated.

The 1967 Land Act distinguished three categories of land: private land, customary land and public land. "Public land" referred to "all land occupied or acquired by government and any other not being private or customary land" (Kishindo, 1994: 57). The 2001 land policy makes a fine distinction between government land and public land. In the new land policy, "government land" refers to land acquired and privately owned by the government to be used for designated purposes such as government buildings, schools, hospitals, public infrastructure, or land to be made available for private use by individuals and organisations. "Public land" refers to the land managed by agencies of the government and in some cases by Traditional Authorities in trust for the people and openly used by, or accessible to, the public at large. This means that common access land previously classified as customary land would now qualify as public land.

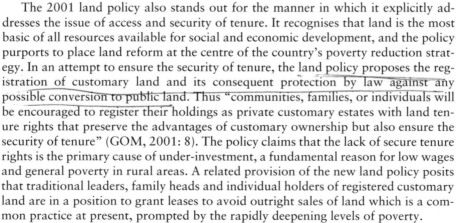

The 2001 land policy also stands out for the manner in which it explicitly addresses the issue of access and security of tenure. It recognises that land is the most basic of all resources available for social and economic development, and the policy purports to place land reform at the centre of the country's poverty reduction strategy. In an attempt to ensure the security of tenure, the land policy proposes the registration of customary land and its consequent protection by law against any possible conversion to public land. Thus "communities, families, or individuals will be encouraged to register their holdings as private customary estates with land tenure rights that preserve the advantages of customary ownership but also ensure the security of tenure" (GOM, 2001: 8). The policy claims that the lack of secure tenure rights is the primary cause of under-investment, a fundamental reason for low wages and general poverty in rural areas. A related provision of the new land policy posits that traditional leaders, family heads and individual holders of registered customary land are in a position to grant leases to avoid outright sales of land which is a common practice at present, prompted by the rapidly deepening levels of poverty.

The need to ensure the security of tenure for customary land should be understood as a strategic measure against the provision of the 1967 Land Act which, as already mentioned, only allowed for one-way transferability of land from the customary sub-sector to the estate sub-sector. This led to a loss of land in the customary sub-sector, more often than not at rates well below the market value. Yet much of the customary land converted into estate land has never been meaningfully utilised. The 2001 land policy estimates that about 28 per cent of the country's cultivable land, representing approximately 2.6 million hectares, lies idle in the rural areas, and much of it falls under the category of freehold land.

While the new land policy correctly recognises the extent of land problems in the country, it is, however, virtually silent on the radical strategies that have to be devised to rectify the problems. The silence of the policy regarding immediate strategies to relieve the problem of land pressure supports my observation above that many among the political élite have high stakes in the perpetuation of the status quo in land ownership patterns. Politicians, top policy-makers and prominent businessmen own vast tracts of land which they are not prepared to give up. The only radical reform designed to redress historical injustices is the provision that non-citizens cannot have freehold titles unless they are prepared to become Malawian citizens. The discriminatory nature of the new land policy against foreigners must, however, be understood in the context of the status quo in land ownership patterns. The issue of citizenship does not sufficiently address the historical and structural causes of unequal land distribution and ownership.

The urge for reform should not, in other words, disregard the politics inherent in redistributive policies. Quite the opposite; in most cases, agrarian reforms may engender unprecedented conflict, opposition and resistance. Yet the politics of redistribution notwithstanding, the implementation of radical agrarian reforms is potentially feasible; it all depends on the determination and political will of the governing élite. Without the reforms, the poverty alleviation initiative is unlikely to achieve the desired progress. The opening up of new commercial or technological opportunities to populations with unequal abilities to access them, for instance, can only widen inequality.

The comparative experiences with agrarian reforms of the states of Kerala and West Bengal in India are illuminating in this respect. Kerala has been able to achieve substantial poverty reduction. It is, in fact, a celebrated model of success in contemporary efforts at poverty alleviation. The paradox, however, is that Kerala has earned itself recognition in the international community as a success story despite its growth being anaemic (Herring, 1999). Its success is attributed to radical agrarian reforms, whose major thrust was the abolition of landlordism in the 1970s. It was the culmination of the reform efforts which had started as early as the 1920s with the Mappila rebellion and the dramatic revision of the Malabar Tenancy Act in 1929. The reforms created an almost level playing field and a fairly responsive system of governance and administration. Herring (1999: 16) described Kerala as "a social democracy on a sub-national scale with all the wants and messy politics of any democracy". The reforms have meant that anti-poverty values are embedded in actual institutions and guarded and reinvigorated by participation. Kerala's electorate is well informed, extraordinarily participatory, alert and assertive.

In contrast, West Bengal's agrarian reforms shunned serious rupture with the status quo. In pursuit of the reforms, its administration strove to maintain the coalition of various social classes in the existing equilibrium. The social structures associated with landlordism, which perpetuated poverty, therefore thrived unfettered. The land that was redistributed was of substandard quality. Even worse, the requisite services to develop it were not available (Boyce, 1987; Herring, 1999). The reforms were, on balance, incoherent, disjointed and heavily fragmented.

The lesson to be learnt from the experiences of Kerala and Bengal is that piecemeal reforms coupled with questionable political will constrain the chances of successful PAP policies. The success of institutional reforms is, to a great extent, dependent on historical junctures and political developments over time. The 1992–94 landmark political changes that Malawi experienced offered a rare window of opportunity to break loose from the inefficient institutional trajectories in numerous spheres. The sad reality is that this opportunity has not been put to proper use. Instead, the PAP policy initiative has degenerated into a source of rent subsidies for the bureaucracy and patronage for unscrupulous politicians.

The PAP policy initiative and SAPs

The majority of developing countries, Malawi included, have either been systematically induced or coerced to embrace SAPs as a result of persistently disappointing economic performances. SAPs have thus constituted a dominant policy framework for a vast majority of developing countries since the early 1980s. In most host countries, however, SAPs have generally exacerbated the depth and incidence of poverty (Sverrisson 1997; Ali 1999; Chilowa, 2000). The negative effects of SAPs have, by far, outweighed their positive effects. Unemployment has soared; prices of essential commodities have skyrocketed; and expenditures on social services, particularly health and education, have progressively contracted (Chilowa and Roe, 1987).

In fact, the findings of QUIM indicate that SAPs have had a significant negative impact on the welfare of Malawians. More specifically, ordinary people were able to relate their lived experiences to the SAPs policies of market liberalisation and the removal of subsidies. The information generated by QUIM would have been extremely useful in the initial design of the PAP. The ramifications of these policies could have been considered, leading to a better structure for poverty reduction and taking into account that people define their poverty mainly in terms of how they are coping in the agricultural sector.

The question is whether the PAP policy initiative has paid sufficient attention to the policy intent of SAPs in its institutional design. This is particularly important because SAPs, as has already been discussed above, have had a dubious impact, while at the same time realising that the success of programmes of this nature depends on the interacting social, economic and political variables. SAPs therefore constitute a very significant dimension of the economic environment for the PAP policy initiative. The major policy goals of SAPs are to contract the role of the state in socio-economic development and that the real values of goods and services should be determined by the market mechanism. Yet the adverse effects of SAPs have promoted the salience of informal safety nets in order to cushion the losers from the reform processes (Sverrisson, 1997; Ali, 1999; see also Anders' chapter in this volume). Potentially, therefore, the PAP policy initiative could at least enhance these reliable safety nets. It could cushion the adverse effects of SAPs through targeted expenditures and the expanded access of the poor to human resource development programmes. These programmes are intended to create a sense of agency among the people in poverty.

The PAP policy initiative in its present form cannot, however, serve as a plausible safety net vis-à-vis the policy inclination of SAPs. The problem is that it does not clearly stipulate how the earning capacity of the poor is going to be enhanced so that they ultimately become economically independent in the sense advocated by SAPs. The direct transfer approach which characterises the present poverty alleviation efforts becomes less effective over time. The state president has, for instance, disbursed funds for anti-poverty programmes not on the basis of bureaucratic principles but, rather, on political considerations. Even if the PAP policy initiative could serve as an instrument of targeted subsidy, it cannot, with this implementation strategy, realistically benefit the deserving poor. Political labels have invariably assumed precedence in lieu of the real poverty situation of the beneficiaries.

The non-bureaucratic implementation strategy is quite unfortunate especially in the light of the fact that the lifeblood of the programme is entirely donor dependent. A cause for concern is that donors aspire to contract the role of the state in socio-economic processes and to develop an autonomous financial capacity for the poor as embodied in SAPs. The *handing-out-of-alms* implementation strategy is likely to bring the initiative to a virtual standstill should donors, who have the tendency to fund stand-alone programmes and projects, decide to pull out.

The overall policy environment within which the PAP is being implemented is, therefore, a major cause for concern. There is a lack of an independent bureaucracy free from political pressure; inequality in the distribution of the benefits of economic growth, which has created special interest groups that protect their privileges at the expense of the majority; a lack of honest, highly motivated public servants sustained by merit-based recruitment and promotion, and competitive real earnings; the absence of formal councils for overall consultation and exchange of information and views between the government, on one hand, and labour, on the other; and the mismanagement and misallocation of human capital and revenue in the public sector (Chilowa et al., 2000).

Concluding Remarks

QUIM results have, inter alia, shown that both rural and urban poverty is on the increase despite the rhetorical commitment to poverty alleviation as the country's development philosophy. The increase in poverty is generally attributed to low production and high commodity prices due to market reforms and inflation; lack of access to farm inputs; declining yields; lack of access to credit; and declining employment opportunities (NEC, 1998; NEC, 2000). The poor have consistently drawn attention to these factors on all QUIM sites, which reinforces the fact that they define their poverty primarily in terms of agricultural productivity. In addition, the real GDP growth for the past four years has been lower than the recommended annual minimum rate of six per cent necessary to have a significant impact on poverty reduction.

Malawi's experience with the PAP policy initiative has, to a large extent, shown that the problem of defining and fighting poverty is more of a political than technical nature. The reason is that there are often variations in the perceptions of the problem of poverty by different stakeholders, including academics, politicians, planners, practitioners, expatriate technocrats, and the poor themselves. The major problem in this regard is how to define the concept of poverty, who the poor are and where they live. These very important considerations were overlooked when the PAP was designed. Likewise, the broader policy environment, especially in the context of SAPs, should also have been considered. These oversights coupled with a sheer lack of political will have presented enormous challenges to the success of the PAP policy initiative.

An issue worth critical reflection is whether in fact the country has a poverty alleviation policy or not. The linkage between various actors in the institutional matrix of the poverty alleviation programme implementation is not clear. It is, for example, not known who has to do what, when and how. Likewise, it is not known whose responsibility it is to ensure that the poverty alleviation policy is translated into concrete programmes of action. According to NEC (2000), very few institutions and organisations have translated the PAP into activities of their own. Whose responsibility is it, for example, to ensure that institutions and organisations embrace PAP?

The problem here is that the institutions that have been entrusted with various tasks relating to the PAP policy initiative lack the requisite implementation capacity. Much has been done in terms of policy, but there is still a lack of consistent and coherent implementation, with relatively little impact on the village level. Many programmes initiated under PAP have not gone beyond the pilot phase, thus not reaching the poorest sections of the country and those in the remotest areas. There is a serious problem with the filtering of information and action. At the national level much is known and planned for in terms of policies; at the district level some policies are known, some programmes and projects are implemented, but at the local level the impact is usually accidental. It is thus quite apparent that one of the obstacles in the implementation of the PAP is that communication structures between the communities and the outside are weak.

Not all is lost, however. The lessons to be learnt from the implementation of the PAP could be put to use as policy-makers are writing the Poverty Reduction Strategy Paper (PRSP). These papers are formulated within the context of the Heavily Indebted Poor Countries (HIPC) initiative of the World Bank and IMF, which links debt reduction with planned or ongoing poverty reduction. The data that have been generated through QUIM could, in addition to contributing to the ongoing consultative processes, be valuable inputs into the PRSP. Of utmost importance is *commitment* on the part of stakeholders at all levels of society. Otherwise we shall continue with donor-inspired initiatives which are often too incoherent and erratic to achieve the desired maximum strategic impact on Malawi's poverty situation.

2. Freedom and Insecurity

Civil Servants between Support Networks, the Free Market and the Civil Service Reform

Gerhard Anders

> Herewith you are being notified that your service will be terminated on grounds of redundancy. The last day of service is 31 January 1998. May I thank you for the services you have rendered to the government during the period you have been with us and to wish you all the best in your future undertakings. Monthly wages will be paid in lieu of notice. All outstanding debts will therefore be recovered from any payments due to you.

These are the words in a letter of notification delivered to Mr Kangame[1] on 19 January 1998. He had worked since March 1993 as a security guard for the Veterinary Department in Zomba, belonging, as such, to the Industrial Class of the Malawian civil service.[2] The Malawi Public Service Regulations (MPSR) provide only little protection to Industrial Class workers. Since Mr Kangame had been employed for less than five years, the due notice was only two weeks.[3] His dismissal was part of a retrenchment exercise implemented by the government under the Civil Service Reform Programme (CSRP) guided by the World Bank.[4] As a result of a study conducted in 1993, the World Bank had demanded that the number of Industrial Class workers be reduced significantly, the Industrial Class abolished and the remaining employees incorporated in the civil service establishment (World Bank, 1994:74).

Losing a job had an impact that went far beyond the loss of Mr Kangame's income. His wife had to stop selling *mandazi,* local doughnuts, since the couple could not afford to buy the necessary ingredients any more. Mr Kangame decided to grow cassava, which he planned to sell at the market. Cultivation of cassava is cheap since it does not require seeds or fertiliser. His relatives in the home village, where he lived, supported him: they assigned a plot to him and gave him cassava branches. According to Mr Kangame, they were rather reluctant to help since they were used to seeing him as a provider of support, not as a recipient. Because of his financial difficulties he could no longer buy cooking oil and fertiliser for his mother as he had previously. Instead, he was forced to do *ganyu*-work[5] in order to earn some badly needed cash for himself, his wife and his five children. The letter of notification signified his transformation from someone with status, if modest, to a person with the lowest status, a *waganyu*, who is not sure whether he will have enough food to feed his children the next day.

Mr Kangame's example illustrates the interdependence between public office and private life in Malawi and the far-reaching consequences changes in the realm of the public office have.[6] The term "private" suggests an individualised sphere as opposed

---

1. All names are fictive to protect the anonymity of my informants.
2. Employees of the Industrial Class are paid daily wages; they do not hold established posts. Industrial Class employees work as security guards, gardeners, messengers, receptionists, cleaners, etc. Their employment is decentralised and within the authority of individual departments.
3. GOM (1991) Malawi Public Service Regulations: 3:104 (1), (2b).
4. Circular of the Secretary of the Human Resource Management, 3 November, 1997.
5. Piece-work, income source of the poorest.
6. This dichotomy is based on Weber's definiton of bureaucratic power. See Gerth and Mills (1948: 197).

to the public realm. In the Malawian context this distinction is misleading and inadequate—civil servants[1] are embedded in an intricate web of social relationships with various rights and obligations. Kinship affiliations, patronage, friendship and membership in a church or some other association, are the co-ordinates of their social lives. Because the state fails to deliver even basic social services, people largely rely on their social networks for support in times of distress.

In Malawi, where only a tiny fraction of the working population is employed in the formal non-agricultural sector, even the lowest position in the civil service is a privilege. Civil servants have a special position due to their direct connection to the state. A job in the civil service is rare and highly valued. With it come a regular income, various benefits, social status and, potentially, access to the resources of the state. These factors determine to which networks a civil servant belongs and what his or her roles in these networks are.

The political and economic changes that Malawi has been going through since the early 1990s have created new opportunities but also a general feeling of insecurity. In order to maintain their position, civil servants have resorted to subsistence farming, private business and corrupt practices. However, these strategies have not led to independence from formal employment. Without the status, regular income, infrastructure and contacts that come with a job, it is very difficult to maintain private activities and social relationships at the same level. This precarious balance between the public office and the "private" sphere is jeopardised by the cutbacks of benefits and retrenchments, which are a part of the CSRP of the World Bank and the government.

The chapter is structured as follows. Firstly, I give a short overview of the history of the civil service in Malawi since colonial times. The second section surveys the conceptual background for my analysis. Thirdly, I briefly describe the research sites in Lilongwe and Zomba, and the methodology applied during fieldwork. The fourth section sketches civil servants' roles in support networks. Fifthly, I analyse strategies of diversification in the context of liberalisation and the economic crisis. In the final section, I assess the negative effects of the civil service reform for individual civil servants.

British Rule, Banda and the World Bank—Change and Continuity in the Civil Service

After independence, Malawi retained the structure of the British colonial civil service. Characteristic of the colonial civil service was the strict division between European expatriate officers and Africans. Until the late 1950s, only a few Africans served in the colonial service. Under the Localisation and Africanisation programmes during the last few years before independence the numbers of Africans increased, and by 1963 the most junior staff were Africans, while expatriates continued to hold senior posts. Even after independence, Africanisation was implemented very slowly when compared with other African states, many expatriates holding high positions in the civil service of independent Malawi (see Skinner, 1963; Baker, 1972). It is said that Kamuzu Banda preferred expatriates to Malawians because of the latter's know-how and their position outside the Malawian society.[2]

---

1. For the purposes of this chapter, I opt for a broad definition of the term civil servant, including Industrial Class workers, temporary employees, police officers, soldiers, teachers and health personnel employed by the government. Employees of state-owned enterprises are excluded since their conditions of service are more similar to the private sector.
2. Interview with Brian Walker, who worked in the Office of the President and the Cabinet (OPC) 1970–1986.

According to Brian Walker, who served in the Nyasaland colonial service and later in the Office of the President and the Cabinet under Banda, the first years of independence were characterised by high morale and motivation—"there was great pride in the service". But already as early as 1964 oppression and politicisation cast a shadow over the civil service. Under colonial rule people from the Northern Region, who traditionally had better access to superior missionary education, had dominated the African element in the civil service. Banda was suspicious of the Northerners and wanted to assert the Chewa identity as the national identity. In the wake of the Cabinet Crisis many civil servants, mainly from the North, were imprisoned, dismissed or went into exile. The political influence intensified in the following years to the extent that during the mid-1970s thousands of officers, many of them from the North, were arrested and dismissed.[1] At the National Statistical Office, for example, where the majority of the staff came from the North, all officers apart from two expatriates were arrested.[2] Until the end of his reign, Banda and the MCP exercised strict control over the civil service. The civil service became highly politicised, and merely suspected opposition against the regime could provoke dismissal or detention. Due to the oppression there was a culture of fear in the civil service, officers hoping to reach retirement age without attracting any attention.

During colonial times civil servants were not supposed to have private income sources. This changed soon after independence. In the early 1970s, Banda launched a somewhat clandestine "development programme" and encouraged top senior servants to acquire tobacco estates. To this end, the Commercial Bank offered soft loans to civil servants.[3] Through this development scheme Banda integrated the top officials who posed a potential threat to his position in his system of patronage. Yet patronage and the appropriation of the state's resources remained limited to a relatively small circle of MCP officials and senior civil servants; alternative or complementary networks found little political space to expand. For ordinary civil servants, the possibilities to set up a private business were limited. On the one hand, official directives that regulated conduct and discipline were usually enforced, leaving insufficient time to establish and run a business. On the other hand, the economy was strictly controlled and monopolised, reducing the scope for private business. Only after retirement would a civil servant invest his or her pension in a business, such as a maize mill or a small shop.

The division between senior grades, originally held by expatriates, and junior grades[4] has remained basically the same until the present day, although the new government has expressed commitment to a policy of salary compression to narrow the gap.[5] Accordingly, there have been substantial salary increases for junior officers,

---

1. On the creation of tribalism and assertion of Chewa as national identity, see the classic article by Vail and White (1989). See also Chirwa (1998a).
2. Interview with Brian Walker.
3. Personal communication: Brian Walker. See also Mkandawire (1992: 179) and GOM (1999a: 70).
4. For the purposes of this chapter I distinguish senior officers/top officials (Superscale), middle-ranking officers (e.g. junior professional, executive and technical officers) and junior officers (e.g. clerks, subordinate staff, primary school teachers and Industrial Class workers).
5. For details on the development of salary compression see World Bank (1994: 40). In reaction to the strike in 1994, the government established a commission of inquiry. In its report the commission underlined the need to increase the salary differential between senior and junior posts again in order to retain and attract highly-qualified staff; Report of the Commission of Inquiry into the Conditions of Service for the Civil Servants (GOM, 1995b: 8, 25, 42). The International Labour Organisation (ILO) commented on a draft of this report and observed that the salary differential was actually already quite high with a bottom-to-top ratio of 1:18 compared with the highest average of 1:9 in industrialised countries and 1:12 in Nigeria. The commission suggested to increase this differential to 1:28 (GOM, 1995b: Appendix III: 2). However, the recommendations on remuneration had not been fully implemented by October 2000. On the failed implementation of the report in the context of the civil servants' strike in 1997, see van Donge (1998a).

particularly in response to the junior civil servants' strike in October 1994.[1] Despite recent salary adjustments, civil servants regard their salaries as insufficient to meet their costs of living and to fulfil all their social obligations. Inflation has constantly eroded civil servants' salaries. In 1992, the real value of basic salaries was about 50 per cent below the levels of 1982 (World Bank, 1994: 37–39). Due to currency devaluations and a high inflation rate this trend has intensified since 1994. The government tried to counter the effects of loss of real income by annual salary adjustments. However, these adjustments have not been sufficient to compensate for the losses in real income.[2] Salaries are generally quite low: junior grades—including security guards, gardeners and messengers—earned about K1,000 per month in late 1999. Extension workers and primary school teachers earned between K1,500 and K2,000 per month. Even officers with higher qualifications, such as a diploma or a bachelor's degree, rarely earned more than K5,000 per month. Junior professional officers, such as secondary school teachers, for example, had a monthly salary of K4,000. The highest grades, in the so-called Superscale, earned roughly K8,000 per month.[3]

Apart from the salary, civil servants also enjoy various benefits, including institutional housing and travel allowances. The value of these benefits is substantial and might be many times higher than the salary. Especially for senior officers who regularly attend workshops and travel outside Malawi allowances are an important source of income.[4] Senior civil servants are also provided with telephones, mobile phones and vehicles. The unauthorised use of government facilities, particularly vehicles by civil servants, has become very common and is considered by many civil servants to be an extra benefit of government employment. These practices and corruption seem to have grown dramatically since the introduction of multiparty democracy in 1994. The fight against the spreading corruption has remained incidental despite strong rhetoric by the UDF government and the Anti-Corruption Bureau.[5]

After 1994, the new government has implemented far-reaching reform programmes under the guidance of the World Bank and IMF, focusing mainly on privatisation, deregulation and liberalisation. One component of the institutional reforms is the civil service reform. Consistent with the focus of the World Bank and IMF on promoting good governance, this reform aims at improving efficiency and transparency. Measures taken under the Institutional Development Project include a civil service census, public expenditure reviews, institutional reviews, privatisation, introduction of a meritocracy and a retrenchment exercise. These changes have caused considerable unrest among junior officers who fear losing their jobs.

Labour unrest, especially among junior officers, started already in May 1992 and culminated in the strike of October 1994. This strike was triggered by a series of

---

1. World Bank (1994: 33–43). Circulars of the Secretary of the Department for Human Resource Management *Revision of Salaries and Wages*, 20 October, 1994 and 25 October, 1994.
2. The salary increase for 1999 was 25 per cent; see Circular of the Secretary for Human Resopurce Management, *Revision of Salaries and Wages in the Civil Service*, Ref. No. HRMD/103/1/28/VII/56, 12 July, 1999. Urban inflation rate between November 1998 and March 1999 had been above 60 per cent, in April and May 1999 urban inflation was about 59 per cent, in June and July 56 per cent (see GOM 1999b: 46).
3. Circular of the Secretary for Human Resource Management: *Revision of Salaries and Wages in the Civil Service*, Ref. No. HRMD/103/1/28/VII/56, 12 July, 1999. In October and November 1999, K45 were about US$ 1. By early 2000 the currency rate was at K50 for US$ 1.
4. For travels in Africa US$ 180 per diem and for travels abroad US$ 240 per diem; Circular of the Secretary of the Department for Human Resource Management, Ref. No. PD/TO/15/II/219, 26 February, 1999.
5. Until February 2000, the Anti-Corruption Bureau (ACB) had investigated only a handful of cases. At the time of writing all of them were pending in the courts. By the same February the ACB could not report any convictions; see *The Anti-Corruption Bureau Annual Report for the period 1.3.1997-31.3.1998* and *The ACB News*, vol. 3 no. 2, February 2000. In general, only few civil servants have been convicted of corrupt practices.

strikes in the private sector. However, despite the political changes between 1992 and 1994, the civil servants' demands were limited to salary increases. After the strike of October 1994, the government substantially increased salaries for junior officers in an effort to appease them. Yet junior civil servants were not the only ones complaining. Both junior and highly-skilled professionals have criticised their narrow career perspectives and inadequate pay. In April 1997, civil servants went on strike again. This time the strike was mainly led by professionals in hospitals and the civil aviation department who demanded better pay (van Donge, 1998a: 13).

During Banda's time, any form of independent organisation of employees was forbidden, with the exception of the Teachers' Union of Malawi (TUM). During the 1994 strike civil servants were only informally organised. In subsequent years several trade unions were formed: the Civil Servants Trade Union (CSTU), the Customs Workers Union (CWU) and the Local Government Workers Union (LGWU). The CSTU led the negotiations with the government during the 1997 strike but was unable to realise most demands (van Donge, 1998a: 2, 10, 11). The trade unions have not yet managed to function properly as representatives of employees' interests. They have a very low degree of organisation and no membership administration. For example, it is said that the CSTU has no more than 800 members. They suffer increasingly from factionalism and internal power struggles and fail to play a decisive role in labour relations.[1]

How civil servants see themselves has changed considerably over the course of time. Africans who served in the Nyasaland colonial service were motivated and had a high work ethos, although many of them did not feel respected by their expatriate superiors and secretly supported the independence movement. During Banda's time the civil service had a high status and provided the small élite with guaranteed employment. However, the culture of fear had paralysed the civil service. Since the early 1990s there is a degree of freedom never enjoyed before. Nevertheless, civil servants feel less respected; employment with a development agency or an NGO is far more desirable than the civil service with low salaries, high levels of corruption and narrow career perspectives. The role models have changed drastically. The cunning and successful entrepreneur making use of the possibilities offered by a liberalised economy has replaced the diligent, obedient and loyal public officer of Banda's time. Many civil servants I talked with were doing business and emphasised that they were "business-minded".

At the dawn of the twenty-first century, Malawian civil servants were in a somewhat ambiguous situation. On the one hand, they did not have to fear for their lives any more and enjoyed considerable economic and political freedom; on the other hand, the economic situation was very unstable, the incidence of crime had increased sharply, and restructuring threatened job security. Civil servants who had served during Banda's time often expressed sentimentality for the good old times when the civil service was still respected, salaries not eroded by inflation and crime unknown. Despite its oppressive character, civil servants generally associated Banda's rule with a sense of material security that had been replaced by insecurity about the future.

---

1. In March 2000, four trade-unions including the CSTU broke away from the umbrella-organisation Malawi Congress of Trade Unions (MCTU) and formed the Congress of Malawi Trade Unions (COMATU). There were differences between the CSTU-president Banda and the MCTU-president Antonio. Then an internal power-struggle between Banda and the majority of the members erupted and the CSTU joined the MCTU again in the end of April 2000.

Conceptual Background: The Weak State, Informal Social Security and Legal Pluralism

The state in Malawi, as in most sub-Saharan African countries, has one distinctive feature. Unlike a Weberian bureaucratic machine or leviathan, it seems unable to enforce the rule of law and to implement public policies. It seems as if the state has fallen prey to particularistic interests. Except for externally funded development projects, the state institutions barely succeed in preserving themselves, only its employees having a connection with the state that transcends the occasional repressive measure or arbitrary handout. Authors such as Bayart (1993), Chabal and Daloz (1999:1-44), Médard (1982) and Migdal (1988) have classified the state in sub-Saharan Africa as weak; it is unemancipated from society because social networks operate beneath the surface of the official institutions and regulations. Politicians and civil servants regard the state primarily as a resource for patronage and self-enrichment. The appropriation of the state by informal networks frustrates enforcement of the rule of law and implementation of public policies. The state institutions often function merely as empty shells for the thriving informal networks.

Many Malawians I spoke with stated that "civil servants only feed themselves and their dependants". To deal with a state that fails to deliver services to the majority of the population means that in practice a relationship with a civil servant is vital in order to gain access to the resources of the state. Civil servants have succeeded in appropriating a significant share of those resources and in redistributing part of it within their social networks. Hence the "rules of engagement" with civil servants are a complex interplay of official rules and rules of kinship, ethnic and patronage networks. This situation is different from the operation of the state in a Western context where similar or comparable networks might exist, but where the official institutions maintain a certain degree of autonomy from society and regularly deliver services or benefits according to the official rules.

An approach that acknowledges the reality of the postcolonial state and the inadequacy of the conventional dichotomy between the formal and the informal, state and non-state, requires an inclusive definition of social security. Hence social security does not refer only to the support provided by the institutions of the state "against the economic and social distress that otherwise would be caused by the stoppage or substantial reduction of earnings resulting from sickness, maternity, employment injury, unemployment, invalidity, old age and death; the provision of medical care; and the provision of subsidies for families and children" (International Labour Organisation, 1984: 2–3). Social security can also be a feature of social networks. People belong to various networks that are based on kinship, ethnicity, residence, religion, friendship, patronage, job and status. Individuals or groups of individuals who need social support due to distress caused by the insecurities of their existence depend on their social networks. People have social security arrangements based on multiple relationships that tend to be of a reciprocal nature. The social security function is not separate from other aspects—relationships are generally multifunctional. Empirically, even institutions of the state may have a social security function that deviates to a large extent from state norms; the resources of the weak state are channelled into the informal networks, which have invaded its institutions.

Social relationships are reciprocal, and people usually act simultaneously as providers and recipients in regard to their specific social security arrangements. In the course of a life cycle, the emphasis on either providing or receiving help will usually change. A junior civil servant might primarily depend on support at the beginning

of his/her career. When he/she advances
sourceful networks and turns from a re
serves as an investment for the future wh

The various social relationships are re
might define rights and obligations very di
tomary or folk law and religious law coexi
cific social field. This situation can be de
Beckmann and Strijbosch, 1986; Griffiths, 1
tutions and official rules are creations of the
dependent, the new states adopted the colon
changes. Patently, a bureaucracy geared to m
tan centre is at odds with informal networks se
enous social groups. The colonial administrati
mainly for its exploitative purposes and failed ....uing public
morality.[2] The norms regulating social relations ....med mainly by kinship and
patronage, remained largely unaffected by Western public morals.[3] After the departure of the colonial rulers, these networks and their respective norms have captured
the official institutions and statuses, now devoid of the public morality of the colo-
nisers (Chabal and Daloz, 1999: 11–16). As a consequence, the informal norms of
kinship and patronage relationships will often determine whether and how official
rules will be applied, forming a complex patchwork of official rules, kinship rules
and rules of patronage.

Methodology and Research Sites

I obtained the information that forms the basis of this chapter by conducting informal and semi-structured interviews with Malawian civil servants and ordinary
Malawians between October 1999 and October 2000. Most of the research was carried out in the capital, Lilongwe, and in Zomba, the colonial capital and still one of
the largest towns in the country. All ministries have their headquarters in Lilongwe,
where a large proportion of their staff are concentrated. Civil servants' access to benefits and contacts is easier at the headquarters than in the districts. The ministerial
headquarters absorb a large proportion of the budget. Therefore civil servants prefer
a post at the headquarters to a post "in the district". Research in Lilongwe concentrated on Capital Hill, the hub of the ministerial headquarters, several schools and
the township of Biwi. Zomba, the other research locality, was the seat of the colonial
government and served as Malawi's capital until 1974. The town hosts Chancellor
College, the largest constituent college of the University of Malawi, the headquarters
of several government departments and a large army base. Research in Zomba focused on the National Statistical Office, Geological Surveys, the General Hospital
and the district administration.

The two towns are very different, reflecting Malawi's past and present. In Lilongwe, several new buildings are under construction in the City Centre, the business
part of town, to house government departments and development agencies. Belief in

1. Cf. the "functional" approach of von Benda-Beckmann and von Benda-Beckmann (1994). See also von
    Benda-Beckmann et al. (1988).
2. On the modest origins of the colonial civil service in the late 19th century, focused mainly on public security
    and revenue collection, see Baker (1988).
3. See Hyden (1983: 39) with references.

and progress seems to be common, it is the place where
more vibrant, there are expensive hotels and night-clubs, de-
and foreign diplomatic missions are based in Lilongwe. Zomba,
quiet town that breathes the air of decay and past glory. Its physical
still dominated by the colonial heritage, with most government offices
ated buildings that previously housed the colonial administration. Many
with institutional housing live in houses dating from the early twentieth cen-
, while in the town only little construction work can be observed. The main reason for these visible differences is money, or rather the lack of it. Lilongwe is now
the entry point for development aid and the national centre, while Zomba has been
cut off from direct access to vital resources and has been degraded to a provincial
centre in shoes too large to fit.

I interviewed about 150 civil servants; with 60 of them I conducted intensive
semi-structured interviews which usually lasted between one and two hours. With
about 20 informants I had several interviews and about ten became acquaintances
and friends whom I met on a regular basis. Informants in the civil service were from
all salary grades; Senior Officers on the Superscale, Professional Officers, Senior
Technical Officers, Technical Officers, nurses, primary and secondary school teachers, not forgetting cleaners and watchmen of the Industrial Class. Most of the informants worked for the Ministry of Health, the Ministry of Education, the Army, the
Veterinary Department, Zomba District Administration, the National Statistical Office, Geological Surveys, the Ministry of Gender and the Ministry of Works. About
50 per cent of my informants were women. It was the rule rather than the exception
that people were married and had children. Often both spouses were employed by
the government. Accessibility and availability were not always easy. The culture of
fear under Banda had left its traces in the offices of the government. The closer I got
to the headquarters and the top the more difficult it was to find people who would
talk freely. Many were afraid, associated me with donor agencies or simply had little
time to spare between office, social obligations, farming and business.

Since my research sites were in the Central and Southern Regions, most informants came from these regions, although a sizeable number, especially in the senior
grades and the professional grades, came from the Northern Region. It is important
to note, however, that some of those who stated that they came from the North had
grown up or were even born in the Central and Southern Regions, because their parents had already moved there. Generally kinship organisation in the North is patri-
lineal, while the South and the Centre are predominantly matrilineal. Informants
often stressed these differences and had clear ideas about the culture of other groups.
These differences were not as clear to me when I compared these statements with the
information I obtained. I had, however, the impression that people's perceptions
were based on an idealised image of, for example, Chewa and Tumbuka "cultures"
rather than on social realities in Lilongwe or Zomba. Therefore, I will not address
the issue of ethnicity in this chapter, the complex issues in regard to ethnicity in the
Malawian civil service requiring more space than is available here.

Civil Servants between the State and Social Networks

Civil servants in Malawi are not only holders of a public office; within the "private"
sphere they maintain a whole range of social relationships. These networks are an
important source of social security. Social status, regular income, benefits and access

to the resources of the state which come with employment in the public sector are important factors in the social support networks of civil servants.

Benefits like institutional housing provided by the government can have an important social security function for relatives in the home village. Most of my informants had one or more children of relatives living with them, hoping to have better access to education and career options in town. That children stay with relatives for some time has always been the norm, but with the impact of HIV/AIDS it has become a necessity for many orphans who are entirely dependent on support from relatives.

> Mr Chazunda, a Professional Officer in Grade 7 of the Superscale, lived in a house leased by the government. The house was in Area 18 in Lilongwe where most residents are high- and middle-ranking civil servants. It had four bedrooms and was quite comfortable. He only paid ten per cent of his basic salary—about K800 in 2000— for this house, which would cost about K15,000 on the free market. Since there was ample space in the house, several relatives lived in the household. When I visited them, three relatives were living in the household: a teenage nephew attending secondary school in Lilongwe and two nieces, one in her teens, and the other nine years old. All of them were expected to do household chores, but the older niece actually worked as a nanny and a housekeeper, although Mr Chazunda did not regard her as a worker. She was one of the three teenage daughters of his wife's older sister, who lived in a village in the vicinity of Lilongwe. These three daughters took turns living and working in the household of Mr Chazunda, usually staying for a couple of months. He supported all the children staying in his household and paid their school-fees; the younger niece even attended an expensive private primary school together with his own daughter. He also paid school-fees for two other nieces staying in the village.

Access to government property and contacts within the civil service are often crucial when civil servants organise support for relatives.

> Mr Kondowe was a junior clerk at the National Statistical Office in Zomba, while his older brother was a police officer in Chikwawa, in the south of Malawi. Their divorced mother lived alone in Nkhata Bay in the north of Malawi as a subsistence farmer. Mr Kondowe and his brother supported her with regular remittances. When she got seriously ill the older brother organised a police vehicle. Both drove to Nkhata Bay to collect their mother. They brought her to the Queen Elizabeth Hospital in Blantyre, the best government hospital in the country. It also had the advantage that it was midway between Zomba and Chikwawa, keeping her closer to her sons. Hospitals in Malawi are notoriously overcrowded, and it is not easy to receive treatment. Yet the older brother could make use of his connections to make sure that she was admitted to the hospital in Blantyre.

Kin relations are not the only important social networks in times of distress; for their own social security, civil servants often rely on voluntary networks. Whether someone belongs to a specific congregation or association depends to a large extent on social status, and people of the same social strata tend to group together in the same residential areas, associations and congregations. Spatial segregation of the main towns is also a social fact, and it is easy to identify the residential areas of junior, middle-ranking and top-ranking officers in Zomba and Lilongwe. If someone dies, neighbours are expected to contribute firewood and food to the funeral ceremony. There is a strong moral obligation to attend the funeral ceremony; attendance in itself constitutes an important form of social support. It is also in the interest of neighbours to attend funerals in order to maintain good links with fellow neighbours. At a time of high mortality rates caused by the HIV/AIDS pandemic many people also anticipate their own death or the death of a family-member. A secondary school teacher in Zomba told me that she was afraid that no one would come to attend a funeral in her family, if she did not attend the funerals of neighbours and friends.

Church congregations often visit and help members who are ill and who lack the support of relatives, who live far away from the home in town. However, the church as an institution plays only a marginal role in regard to social support for civil servants since the status of even the lowest civil servants is too high to be eligible for charity. The church is more important as a gateway to a social network tied together by shared beliefs.

> A senior female professional, for example, told me that once she had planned to buy a minibus with the money that she had earned from a consultancy. Unfortunately, her older brother, himself a civil servant, became very ill. She used a large part of the sum earned through the consultancy for the treatment of her brother. Yet she had agreed to purchase the minibus. Friends from the same congregation—wealthy businesspeople—helped her out of her predicament and lent her the money to buy the minibus.

District associations and Social Welfare Clubs constitute a more institutionalised form of support networks. After democratisation in 1994, many associations were established in the main towns with membership based on the district of origin (see also Kamwendo's chapter in this volume; Englund, 2001c). These associations are loosely defined by ethnic and kinship criteria. The associations often function as revolving funds, which help members to finance and organise funerals and weddings. Wealthy members, especially politicians, donate large sums of money to enhance their status among their clients.[1] A number of district associations are also engaged in charity and donate money to health care in the home district. The Friends of Kasungu in Blantyre, for example, had plans to build a new mortuary at the district hospital of Kasungu. Social Welfare Funds at the workplace are an institutionalised form of solidarity among colleagues. At most departments and schools there are so-called Social Welfare Funds, which operate as revolving funds that disburse money for funerals and emergencies. This growth of institutionalised solidarity does not imply better social security. Many of these funds face difficulties because of inflation and the increasing number of funerals due to the impact of the HIV/AIDS pandemic.

Protection by a patron is generally necessary in order to get access to benefits and resources. It is irrelevant whether these are benefits to which a civil servant is entitled. The MPSR contain provisions on terminal benefits, death benefits, emergency advances, provision of a coffin and transport.[2] In practice payments are often delayed, people often having to wait for months and even years for their payments. In many departments, participation in workshops, promotion and transfers also depend on a patron-client relationship with the superior officer. As for the unauthorised use of benefits and resources, the intervention of a patron is even more crucial.

Some of the demands for support do not concern the living but the dead—support for the organisation of funerals constitutes a very important form of social security. In Malawi, funerals are a major issue in the relationship between the employer and the employee (see Otanez, 2000).

> Mr Mashanga, a senior civil servant, employed a housekeeper. They were very close; the housekeeper worked for him for many years. One day, the mother of the housekeeper who

---

1. The president, Bakili Muluzi, for example, is a member of the Friends of Machinga in Blantyre, and the vice-president, Justin Malewezi, is member of the Friends of Ntchisi in Blantyre, a fact regretted by members of the Friends of Ntchisi in Zomba who cannot boast such influential members.
2. GOM (1991) *Malawi Public Service Regulations*: 1: 826, 1: 718–722, Supplement 1: 192.1, 192.2.

had lived on the compound died unexpectedly of malaria. Within only a day he had arranged two vehicles from the office to transport the body to the home village in Nsanje, in the far south of Malawi, where the funeral would take place. According to the MPSR,[1] the government provides a coffin and vehicles to transport the body and the guests to the place of burial in case of the death of a civil servant or his family. Although Mr Mashanga's housekeeper had worked for him a long time, he would not qualify as a member of Mr Mashanga's family. Mr Mashanga, however, could not refuse to help his housekeeper, because as patron his responsibilities went far beyond the duties of a mere employer. In order to get the vehicle he needed the consent of his boss. He could count on understanding in the office, because the obligations arising from a funeral are too important to be dismissed by referring to the official regulations "that only exist on paper", as he told me.

However, the strength of patron-client relationships in the civil service does not imply that the official regulations are irrelevant. They *are* applied—albeit in a selective manner. Without the help of Mr Mashanga's boss, the official rules would have been applied, preventing the use of the government vehicle for the transport of the deceased "family member".

New Insecurities—Threats or Opportunities?

In the early 1990s, the government started to implement a new generation of Structural Adjustment Programmes under the guidance of the World Bank and the IMF. An important aspect of these reforms was the liberalisation and deregulation of the economy. The reforms gained momentum when the new democratically elected government took office in 1994. However, democracy and free market economy came with a price. The liberalisation of the economy also exacerbated the economic crisis which the country had been suffering from since the 1980s. Economic growth has been stagnant, with inflation hovering around 30 per cent since the currency had been floated in 1994 (GOM, 1999b:46; see also Chinsinga's chapter in this volume). In 2000, the prices for tobacco, the main cash crop, collapsed, and the trade deficit increased even further. Despite the new freedoms there is a general feeling of disappointment and growing insecurity about the future. Prices are no longer fixed, subsidies have been abolished, inflation is high, jobs are less secure, crime is on the rise, and business promises both quick profits and high risks.

Liberalisation of the commercial and agricultural sectors entails more freedom to participate in the economy. The introduction of the free market is visible everywhere; in Lilongwe, Zomba and Blantyre privately-owned minibuses fill the streets, private schools with often dubious credentials are mushrooming, and the side-walks are lined with stalls where vendors sell anything from drinks to stamps. Rural areas have also been touched by the free market, where everybody can cultivate tobacco and sell it.

During the Banda era, the material security of civil servants came at the price of repression and fear. The rules concerning conduct and discipline[2] were usually enforced and private activities were not encouraged.[3] This made it nearly impossible for a civil servant to engage in private business. This strict discipline started to collapse in the early 1990s, when Banda's regime started to lose its tight grip on the civil

---

1. GOM (1991) *Malawi Public Service Regulations*: Supplement 1:192.1, 192.2.
2. GOM (1991) *Malawi Public Service Regulations*: 1:201.
3. Except for the few hundred top civil servants who participated in Banda's "development" scheme, see above.

service and labour unrest in the civil service grew, without similar discipline being restored ever since. Absenteeism, corruption and unauthorised use of government property have increased dramatically. Superior officers are often unable and unwilling to enforce the rules, because they themselves most blatantly disregard them. The decrease in discipline in the civil service has created space for private business activities among officers who sometimes use their offices as the headquarters for their commercial enterprises. The boundaries between the public office and "private" income-generating activities have become increasingly blurred.

In the civil service, "business" has become a buzz-word, with virtually everyone setting up or planning to set up a business. It is impossible to give an exhaustive list of businesses of civil servants, but examples for relatively large-scale businesses include bus companies with minibuses or pick-ups, private schools and fishing boats, while medium-scale businesses might be breeding poultry, selling second-hand clothes, running a restaurant or a bar or a shop or a maize mill, while small-scale business can include the sale of *mandazi* (local doughnuts), *samosas* (local pastries), soft drinks, potato chips or *freezies* (water ice). The scale of a business operation very much depends on the amount of the money invested. A bar can be a hut with a thatched roof in a village where an extension worker sells *Chibuku* (local beer made of maize and millet), or it can be a bottle-store in town with a sound system, bottled beer, soft drinks and food, owned by a senior civil servant. The scale reflects the social status and wealth of the civil servant. High-ranking civil servants run large-scale businesses that require substantial investment and know-how, while junior civil servants are engaged in small-scale business and petty trading, which require only small investments. Very rarely did I find a civil servant actually working him- or herself; usually relatives or employees would work in the business, and the officer would manage and supervise the business. Yet many civil servants devote a considerable amount of time to managing their businesses, many running more than one business.

Despite its growth in recent years, business is not entirely new to civil servants. After retirement, it has always been common to set up a business. Retirement age is 50, but after 20 years of service it is already possible to retire from the civil service. Pensions are usually paid as a lump sum payment. This arrangement allows the civil servant to start a second career in self-employment at a relatively young age. For many civil servants, especially in the middle ranks, the prospect of this lump sum is the main motivation to stay in the civil service. Even before retirement the public office and private business are never entirely separated. Planning for the time after retirement starts at an early stage when the officer is still in service.

Mr Moyo, a retired senior executive officer who had served in the Office of the President and Cabinet (OPC), was quite successful. In 1969, he bought property in Lunzu, about 20 km north of Blantyre, where he wanted to settle after retirement. In the early 1970s, he built a house which he let until retirement in 1981. This was a smart move. In the 1970s, the government developed the area, and Lunzu became an important trading centre along the new road between Blantyre and Lilongwe. Prices for property went up while many businesses were established. When he retired in 1981, Mr Moyo moved into his house and used the lump sum to build a shop on his property. He started a tailoring shop with four employees. The business went well until 1992 when he could not compete with cheap imports of second-hand clothes from Europe and had to give up the business. Later he bought two more shops from people who had to sell cheap during the economic crisis. Now he lets out all three shops providing him with a monthly income of about K15,000.

The difference between Mr Moyo's business endeavours and those of the contemporary "business-minded" civil servants is a shift in focus. In the past the emphasis used to be on the preparation for the time after retirement from the civil service. Since the changes in the mid-1990s, the focus has shifted to the present. There is, of course, still the hope that business will help one to prosper in the future, but now business is often necessary to maintain the standard of living that is threatened by the erosion of salaries by inflation.

Liberalisation, privatisation and democratisation have not succeeded in improving the economic conditions for the majority of the population. Instead, there are indications that the reforms may have widened the gap between the élite and the rest (see Chinsinga's chapter in this volume). Even urban-based employees of the formal sector are threatened by this process of polarisation. Junior civil servants, in particular, suffer from the erosion of salaries and rising prices. In the past they could always count on a regular salary, meagre compared to other countries but generally sufficient to get by as the prices were strictly controlled and the currency fixed. In recent years there has been a growing gap between the top layer of the civil service who benefit from the new possibilities and middle-ranking and junior civil servants who struggle to make ends meet. The top officials accumulate wealth by doing "big business", while junior officers try to keep their head over water by selling *Chibuku*, snacks or soft drinks. This widening gap is also reflected in the recent shift to the cultivation of maize on every available plot in order to provide the household with food. Of course, subsistence farming has always been practised by teachers and extension workers in rural areas, but now even middle-ranking civil servants in Lilongwe and Zomba rent gardens, *minda* (sing. *munda*), where they grow maize. It is clearly a survival strategy for those who have difficulties to make their living. Under the pressure of inflation it is no longer possible to rely exclusively on the salary. Business and the cultivation of maize are strategies to spread the risks.

> Mr Tsoka is an example of a middle-ranking civil servant in trouble. He is a Senior Technical Assistant at Zomba General Hospital. His allowance included, he earns K3,000 per month. He lives with his wife and his two children in a house leased by the government. His wife works as a primary school teacher and earns about K1,500 per month. Before 1994, he did not have to grow maize or to do business since his and his wife's salaries were sufficient. They were even able to support a younger sister of his wife who stayed in their house while she attended secondary school in Zomba. The currency devaluations in 1994 and 1998, the kwacha losing 80 per cent of its value, and the constant inflation have made Mr Tsoka very insecure, and he feels he can no longer rely exclusively on his salary. He started, therefore, to rent a garden in order to grow maize. The yield is sufficient to supply his household with enough maize for the season. Once a month he goes to the lakeshore where he buys fish, which he sells wholesale in Zomba. The business provides him with about K3,000 of extra monthly income. He would prefer not to do business since his work at the hospital is very demanding, but he needs the extra money to maintain his family's standard of living.

It is important to keep in mind that business and farming have never been purely individualistic in character. They have to be seen in the context of the social networks and their social security function which were sketched in the previous section. A wide circle of people benefit directly or indirectly from a business or the cultivation of maize and vegetables. Civil servants employ relatives in their businesses, they send remittances to the home village, and they give maize to friends or relatives who do not have enough food. In turn, they might depend on a loan from a friend or help from relatives to set up or run a business.

In the previous section I already suggested that the government job is an important variable in civil servants' social relationships. The same holds true for business and farming. Civil servants hope to reduce their dependency on the salary, but only a few succeed in achieving complete independence from the sphere of the public office. This dependency on the position in the civil service has various aspects. Primarily, the regular salary can be used to invest in a business or agricultural inputs such as land, seeds, fertiliser and labour. Allowances for workshops and official trips are also important. Especially for senior officers, who receive US$ 240 a day when they travel abroad, allowances are an important source of income, but even a messenger or Technical Officer who goes to the "field" outside the district capital receives K900 per diem. Allowances are usually paid out as a lump sum. This means that an officer has a considerable amount of cash at his or her disposal, which can be invested in a substantial commercial enterprise or the purchase of land. Another important aspect of the job is access to infrastructure. Government vehicles, for example, are often not only used to help relatives but also to run the business or to transport maize from a garden to a storage room or a granary (*nkhokwe*). In addition to this material aspect, employment gives access to information and contacts. Employment in the civil service is a means to get in touch with a patron who can offer the necessary protection for one's business.

Often it is not possible to raise the necessary capital for a business by legal means, and it seems that the recent rise of corruption is interrelated with increased business activities by civil servants. *Katangale* denotes any illegal or dubious deals linked to the sphere of work and covers corruption, embezzlement, theft, fraud and unauthorised use of state resources. The kind of *katangale* a civil servant is involved in depends on his/her post and rank. Obviously in a highly hierarchical civil service, where all decisions are taken at the top, superior officers have more possibilities to enrich themselves than a mere constable or clerk. Examples include an executive officer who rents his own car on behalf of the office, allowances for fictive field trips, fraudulent award of government contracts against the payment of a commission, bribes for the distribution of a deceased's estate, store clerks selling stationery, headmasters selling exercise books to private schools and drivers using government vehicles for *matola*, the commercial transport of passengers. Such practices have spread from top to bottom with disappointed junior officers imitating their superiors – usually with less success. Corrupt practices are even more dependent on the job than business or farming. Without access to the resources of the state and a network of patronage it is impossible to engage in *katangale*.

Effects of the Civil Service Reform

Since 1994 the new government has been implementing a Civil Service Reform Programme (CSRP) under guidance of the World Bank (GOM, 1995; 1996; 1997; 1998; 1999b). Consistent with the recent focus of the World Bank and IMF on promoting good governance (see e.g. World Bank, 2000a; 2000b), this reform is aimed at improving efficiency and transparency. Thus far, the implementation of the programme has resulted only in expenditure control and the retrenchment of Industrial Class workers. The other components of the reform, such as privatisation and the establishment of a more performance-driven civil service with a new salary structure, are yet to be addressed in a systematic manner.

The implementation of the reform has widened the gap between the few top officials who have access to the resources of the state and junior officers who are threatened by unemployment and the loss of benefits. The officers of the Superscale enjoy generous benefits and have not been affected by retrenchment and the cutbacks in benefits and services. Junior and middle-ranking officers, on the other hand, do not enjoy benefits to the same extent as the senior officers and suffer from the cutbacks. Worse still, many Industrial Class workers have already been dismissed or are going to be made redundant soon. Many junior civil servants are disappointed and angry about ministers and senior officers whom they accuse of enriching themselves at their cost. There have been several strikes, and morale which was already low is getting worse under the influence of the civil service reform.

Retrenchment

The most obvious and drastic negative consequence of the CSRP is the loss of a job. In a study on the civil service, the World Bank advised the government to abolish the Industrial Class and consequently dismiss redundant workers (World Bank, 1994:74). Within the framework of the Institutional Development Project II, two major restructuring operations took place in 1995 and 1997, leading to the dismissal of approximately 20,000 Industrial Class workers out of a total number of about 50,000. The objective of the exercise was to reduce the number of Industrial Class workers to 16,000, who would be incorporated in the establishment of the civil service.[1] This means that about 14,000 more workers are going to be laid off.

Support for the employees who are made redundant is virtually non-existent and is usually limited to the payment of a small lump sum payment. For civil servants holding an established post, the MPSR provide for the payment of a gratuity equivalent to one month's salary multiplied by the number of years of service and, under qualifying conditions, an additional pension. For Industrial Class workers the situation is much worse. When the employment of an Industrial Class worker is terminated, only due notice has to be given, or the equivalent to the wages in lieu of due notice has to be paid. Due notice is a rather short time—for a worker who has been employed more than six months but less than two years it is one week, for employment of more than two years but less than five years it is two weeks, and for more than five years it is one month.

Retrenchments have been implemented in a very short period of time. In November 1997, some departments had to reduce their support staff by half within six weeks, and in 1995 the retrenchment exercise was supposed to be completed in two weeks.[2] Neither the government nor the IMF and the World Bank had designed a social plan for dismissed employees. Payments of terminal benefits were often delayed for several months or even years, and whether terminal benefits are received depends again to a large extent on the grace of a patron. Workers who had been made redundant had to resort to collective action—and sometimes to violent protest—to force the government to pay the benefits they were entitled to. In South Africa, by contrast, Industrial Class workers who are going to be made redundant receive training for three years to enable them to start their own business in their occupation. Beyond the payment of meagre lump sums, the Malawian government does not assume any responsibility for the unemployed. The only state institution

---

1. Circulars of the Secretary of Human Resource Management, 8 January, 1996 and 3 November, 1997.
2. Circulars of the Secretary of Human Resource Management, 8 January, 1996 and 3 November, 1997.

that has contact with dismissed workers is the Labour Office in the district capitals but vacancies have become a very scarce commodity indeed.[1]

Salary advances

All ministries and departments operate loan facilities for salary advances for specific purposes like an emergency and the purchase of furniture or a car. Interest on the loans is very low—at about three per cent—and the conditions of repayment are very generous compared to private moneylenders or commercial banks.[2] Since the government has introduced the cash-budget system to improve budgetary discipline, it has been virtually impossible to obtain salary advances. Cash-budget means that a department cannot spend more money than allocated by the annual budget. The high inflation rate has depleted the funds even more. For civil servants outside the ministerial headquarters—such as primary school teachers—these loan facilities were never really accessible, but now even for officers at the headquarters it is extremely difficult to get a salary advance.

In the absence of salary advances people resort to so-called welfare committees in offices or schools, and revolving funds for condolence money and emergency loans or grants have been established in recent years to compensate for the loss of the government loans. For example, an army officer told me that since the cash-budget system had been introduced the army did not pay emergency advances any more. He established, therefore, a loan facility in his unit to help soldiers with financial difficulties. Every soldier contributed to the fund, and the officer decided on applications for loans. He charged an interest of ten per cent and punished defaulters by deducting the money owed from the salary.

Many funds have collapsed, however. Two factors have been responsible; firstly, funds shrink with the high inflation rate and, secondly, the demand for advances is growing due to the economic crisis, the absence of other loan facilities and the high mortality rate. Especially junior civil servants who cannot draw upon a resourceful network are often forced to resort to an informal system of borrowing money, *katapila*, which charges an interest of at least 50 per cent. Commercial banks are not an option for junior officers, because they demand collateral and also charge an interest of 50 per cent.

Money troubles—death benefits, coffins and leave grants

The main perk of government employment—apart from the regular income—is the various monetary and non-monetary benefits. During Banda's time, civil servants could rely on these benefits, but in recent years many of these once cherished benefits are no longer considered to be vital by the government and its donors. As a consequence, expenditure control has resulted in cutbacks and cash flow problems. For example, the payment of death benefits to heirs is often delayed, cheques are not cashed any more, and travel warrants have been replaced by leave grants.

1.   The whole economy is affected by restructuring and downsizing. For example, in 1994 the state-owned Malawi Railways dismissed 1,000 workers. After privatisation, another 300 workers were made redundant. The state-owned Shire Bus Company dismissed 480 workers in June 2000.
2.   GOM (1991) *Malawi Public Service Regulations*:1:701-708 (Part A: Advances of Salary Generally), 1:710–715 (Part B: Education Advances), 1:718–722 (Part C: Emergency Advances), 1:725–731 (Part D: Bicycle Advances), 1:733–745 (Part E: Motor Vehicle Advances).

Mrs Chipoka was married to a Technical Officer at the Agricultural Development Division in Machinga. They had lived in an institutional house. Unexpectedly, her husband died in May 1999. In June, she was evicted from the institutional house and since she had not yet received any money, she had to rely on support from her son, a secondary school teacher in Mangochi. She moved in with him. November came and she had still not received the death benefits. In December, her financial situation got worse, and she went to Lilongwe to demand the money in person and to contact old friends of her husband to ask them to speed things up. Finally, in fact, she got half of the money. However, by January 2000 she still had not received the other half.

Mrs Chipoka's case seems to be the rule rather than the exception. Payments of death benefits[1] to dependants are often delayed for months. Widows have to go through considerable trouble to get at least part of the death benefit paid out by the Administrator General's office.

The MPSR stipulate that the government should provide a coffin and vehicles for the transport of the deceased civil servant or a civil servant's "dependants".[2] This provision is generally considered by civil servants to be one of the essential benefits of their job.[3] In the past the Ministry of Works had workshops which made coffins for deceased civil servants. In the course of the privatisation and contracting-out exercise all workshops were closed. Now the government issues so-called Local Purchase Orders. A private carpenter who makes the coffin is supposed to cash this order at the Treasury Cashier's Office. However, the treasury cashier often refuses to cash the cheque since all available funds have already been spent. Such is, at any rate, the information given by the cashier; it is also possible that the money has been embezzled. According to several teachers in Lilongwe, only a few private workshops still accept these orders since their owners are senior civil servants or politicians who are able to cash the Local Purchase Orders because of their good contacts with the Ministry of Finance. This is extremely disturbing in a country where the duties of an employer in the event of an employee dying are a major issue in labour relations.

For visits to the home village, the government used to issue travel warrants for the civil servant and the family. In 1991, the government stopped this practice and started to pay an annual leave grant of K700. With rising prices for public transport it has become difficult for government employees posted at some distance from their home area to maintain ties with their kin.

Mr Munthali, a Senior Technical Officer from Rumphi in the Northern Region, told me that in the past he, his wife and his two children would go several times a year to his home village. In recent years he could only go once a year, often only by himself. He could not afford the trip for the whole family—the return ticket would cost more than K1,000 per person.

Junior and middle-ranking civil servants, in particular, complained about the loss of these benefits, which were very important for their social security and the maintenance of social relationships with relatives at home.

---

1. GOM (1991) *Malawi Public Service Regulations*: 1: 826 (2).
2. GOM (1991) *Malawi Public Service Regulations*, Supplement 1:192.1, 192.2.
3. In Malawi employees generally expect their employer to pay for or provide a coffin, transport of the deceased and the guests of the funeral to the place of burial, and sometimes even food and drinks at the funeral. This expectation usually applies not only to the employee but also to an ill-defined circle of "dependants" and family members. See Otanez (2000) on the issue and practice of "dropping dead bodies".

Polarisation and Alienation between Seniors and Juniors

All these changes have intensified the feeling of insecurity among middle-ranking and junior civil servants. Many of them live in the constant fear of restructuring and retrenchment. The implementation of the civil service reform has reduced much-appreciated privileges even to the point where a civil servant cannot be sure any more whether he or she will be buried in a coffin provided by the government. Primary school teachers have to wait weeks for their salaries, and widows have to wait months for the payment of death benefits. As a result, morale in the civil service is becoming increasingly lower, and there is growing alienation between junior and senior officers. The strikes since 1994 have often been instigated by junior officers who complain about low salaries and bad conditions of service with few career prospects. They accuse ministers and superior officers of selfishly enriching themselves, while the junior civil servants' already meagre salaries are under pressure from inflation, and they are threatened by retrenchment. All junior civil servants whom I asked to draw their department as an animal would draw a lion or a leopard ready to strike with its claws.[1]

This negative image differs from the perception of senior civil servants in the highest grades—the Superscale—often appointed by the president. These officials belong to the small and influential élite of politicians, officials, managers, estate owners and businesspeople, who use their privileged position to take advantage of the new democratic freedoms. It is usual that they received a part of their education abroad. By virtue of their education and privileged position, they adapt more easily to a flexible and unpredictable environment where initiative and risk-taking are rewarded. Most of them live in an institutional house, have a car and own property, houses and business enterprises. Their salary is often insignificant for them since they receive allowances as high as US$ 240 per diem for foreign trips. To them the government job serves mainly as a stepping-stone to lucrative trips and contacts.

The alienation between top officials and junior civil servants indicates a transformation of the parallel structure of the civil service. In the past junior civil servants could rely on a regular income and a safe position. As long as they enjoyed protection by their patrons, they did not mind self-enrichment by their superior officers. Now, however, the bosses seem to have terminated the silent agreement between junior and senior civil servants. The withdrawal of protection by patrons is seen as a betrayal, and junior civil servants do not feel bound by loyalty any more. This feeling already surfaced during the strike in August 1993 when civil servants demanded that Principal Secretaries should be excluded from salary increases since they already enjoyed generous benefits (World Bank, 1994: 50).

Conclusion

In this chapter, I have wanted to show that the distinction between public office and private sphere does not do justice to civil servants' social realities in Malawi. The public office is embedded in a web of informal social networks. These networks constitute an important source of social security. The state fails to provide universal social services. This does not imply that the state is irrelevant for informal social security. On the contrary, the resources of the state are being appropriated and re-

---

1.   Thanks to Kevin Quinlan, Blantyre, who suggested to use this technique.

distributed by civil servants. Thus civil servants' support networks and extra-office activities depend on employment by the government.

The economic reforms that have been implemented since the early 1990s have contributed to the acceleration of the economic decline. Civil servants in general have responded to the new situation by diversification in order to compensate for the losses inflicted by the economic crisis. They have turned to business and subsistence farming. For most civil servants, however, these strategies are fuelled by a growing sense of insecurity. Despite their attempts to become independent from their employment, they remain dependent on their regular salary, the benefits and the access to the resources of the state. To gain that access by illegal means has become a popular option—*katangale* provides increasing numbers of officers with an extra income, which they can invest in their commercial enterprises. Every change in the civil service has repercussions on their private projects, which, in turn, are linked to their social networks. It is only the senior officers, belonging to Malawi's social élite, who experience economic liberalisation as freedom.

The civil service reform has widened the gap between the rank-and-file and the top officials. Retrenchments, cash-flow problems and the reduction of benefits do not exactly ease the feeling of confusion and insecurity among junior civil servants. Cutbacks have not hit the top officials, with trips and other benefits often draining the budgets of ministries to the point that telephone bills cannot be paid. Junior officers used to tolerate self-enrichment by the élite since they could rely on their protection. This feeling of loyalty has been replaced by jealousy and discontent against "the bosses who only feed themselves".

3. Judicial Mediation in Electoral Politics in Malawi

Clement Ng'ong'ola

Introduction

By the time when research for this chapter was conducted, one referendum, two sets of Presidential and Parliamentary elections, and numerous Parliamentary by-elections had been held under Malawi's transformed political system since 1993. The administration and management, or mismanagement, of these processes has been well chronicled in several accounts.[1] This chapter grapples with a slightly different, not so well documented, aspect of electoral process management in Malawi. It is concerned with judicial mediation, or meddling, in the disputes that inevitably arise after the conducting of elections.

This is only one aspect of a larger issue that should fascinate and engage historians, social scientists and other students of political change in Malawi. As the brief sketch of the constitutional and legal background to electoral process management will confirm, the Judiciary and the legal profession has had more than a passing interest in the political transformation of the country. Kamuzu Banda, during the period of his long rule, fermented a political culture of extreme disdain and intolerance for the rule of law, legality and the ways of the legal profession. The legal profession naturally eagerly participated in the dismantling of that political and constitutional order, and arrogated to itself an indispensable role of acting as "guardians" of constitutional rights under the new order. The performance of the legal profession in its new role requires constant monitoring and evaluation. The sustenance and survival of the new political and constitutional order is probably inextricably linked to the discharge of its mandate by the legal profession.

This chapter attempts to assess the performance of the formal courts—the High Court and the Supreme Court of Appeal—from some of the key cases arising from the 1994 and the 1999 Parliamentary and Presidential elections. There are at least two questions that the assessment will provoke, but may not successfully answer. First, many of the High Court and Supreme Court judges had unpleasant personal or professional experiences under Banda's political rule. To what extent is this an underlying factor in the disposal of cases involving Banda's party, the Malawi Congress Party (MCP), or some of his erstwhile supporters? The second issue is that most of the judges and some of the senior counsel appearing before them received their legal training in London or Malawi, in environments in which manipulation of law to promote certain constitutional, political or social values would not have been an emphasised aspect of the curriculum. They were trained mainly as legal technicians, to search for the law from known sources, and to interpret and apply it to the problem at hand, often regardless of other ideals, values and issues also raised by the problem. The revamped legal order has placed most of the legal profession on a steep

---

1. On the 1993 Referendum and the 1994 Elections, see, for example, Dzimbiri (1994); Posner (1995); Newell (1995); van Donge (1995); and Ng'ong'ola (1996). On the 1999 Elections, see Ott et al. (2000)

learning curve, to assimilate different techniques of legal reasoning and new constitutional jurisprudence. To what extent is this a factor in the disposal of election disputes?

The Constitutional and Legal Background

As will become apparent, various aspects of the constitution for the Second Republic feature prominently in election disputes and other cases with a political dimension. It is therefore necessary to begin this analysis with an appreciation of the salient features of the constitution and the legal backdrop against which it was developed.

Earlier Constitutional Arrangements

Malawi was granted independence from British colonial rule on 6 July, 1964. This was under a "Lancaster House" type of constitution that, on paper, permitted political pluralism and competition for political office through regular elections, and incorporated a "Bill of Rights" securing mostly first-generation civic and political rights. On the ground, the domination of the political landscape by Banda's MCP was such that the country was de facto a one-party state, and Banda, by virtue of his Life Presidency of the MCP, was the unquestioned and unchallenged ruler of the country.[1]

After the much-discussed crisis in the first post-independence Cabinet in September 1964 (see e.g. Baker, 2001), the process began of consolidating in law Banda's domination of the political landscape. First, public security exceptions to the fundamental rights were invoked to promulgate draconian legislation for the incarceration and seizure of property of perceived political opponents.[2] The "Bill of Rights" itself was subsequently expunged from the Republic Constitution of 1966.[3] It was replaced by a statement of "Fundamental Principles of Government" which tamely acknowledged "the sanctity of the personal liberties enshrined in the United Nations Universal Declaration of Human Rights", and the relevance of the "the Law of Nations", but allowed Government to pass legislation in contravention of the principles "in the interest of defence, public safety, public order or the national economy".[4]

The 1966 constitution also formally declared Malawi a one-party state,[5] and an amendment in 1970 formally declared Banda Life President.[6] It also declared that the President shall have the "supreme executive authority of the Republic", with the power to appoint Ministers and other executive officers as he saw fit, and to act "in his own discretion without following the advice tendered by any person".[7] The legislature was effectively placed under the control of the executive through provisions

1. For details on some of the earlier constitutional and political arrangements see Williams (1978); and Hodder-Williams (1974).
2. See, for example, Preservation of Public Security (Amendment) Regulations, GN 156 of 1964; Preservation of Public Security (Amendment) (No. 3) Act, No. 61 of 1965; and the Forfeiture Act No. 1 of 1966. For a commentary on the latter see Roberts (1966).
3. Attached as Second Schedule to the Republic of Malawi (Constitution) Act, No. 23 of 1966.
4. Section 2, as amended by Republic of Malawi (Constitution) Amendment Act No. 6 of 1968.
5. Section 4.
6. Republic of Malawi (Constitution)(Amendment) (No.3) Act No.35 of 1970. He took the oath for the office in 1971
7. Sections 8 and 47

entitling the President to dissolve it at any time,[1] or when it passed a vote of no confidence in the government or insisted on passing a Bill that he would not assent to.[2]

The Judiciary was the only wing of Government that was not made subservient to Banda under these early constitutional arrangements. The framers of the constitution did not, however, expect the Judiciary "to question or obstruct the policies of the Executive Government, but to ascertain the purposes of those policies by reference to the laws made by Parliament, and fairly and impartially to give effect to those purposes in the courts when required to do so".[3] It did not take long before the Judiciary was shackled after being adjudged to have failed the Executive.

In 1969, the High Court acquitted hurriedly apprehended suspects in the "Chilobwe axe murders" for lack of sufficient evidence.[4] Incensed politicians saw in this a major flaw of a judicial system inherited from colonial rule that was enamoured of procedural technicalities. They demanded the creation of courts that would be better able to deliver "substantial justice" without paying "undue regard to technicalities". They also demanded that these must be courts better placed to take proper cognisance of traditional or customary elements of some troublesome cases, and courts in which professionals steeped in foreign law would not have a decisive influence over the course of justice.[5]

Parliament obliged. The Local or "Native" Courts of the colonial era were transformed into "Traditional Courts" with an independent structure and parallel jurisdiction to that enjoyed by the formal courts.[6] "Traditional" leaders and personnel lacking in formal legal training were selected to preside in cases which, in due course, for Malawians of African descent, included all capital and other serious offences in the Penal Code, such as murder, treason, sedition and theft by a public servant. Legal representation was strictly forbidden. The Traditional Courts became the preferred fora for the processing and certain conviction of perceived opponents of the Banda regime in one sham trial after another. An enfeebled Judiciary[7] and a cowed legal profession were reduced to helpless bystanders in this sad parody.

General Attributes of the 1995 Constitution

In addition to the painful experiences of the one-party era, the manner of its making left indelible birthmarks on the constitution for the multiparty era. It is generally conceded that the constitution was too hurriedly framed between 1993 and 1995.[8] It should be recalled that the process started under a government that had lost the moral, if not legal, authority to oversee the exercise after the loss of the referendum on the introduction of political pluralism. Key drivers of the process were political groups and personalities who initially had no clear mandate to act as constitutional brokers for the people of Malawi. The interim constitution of 1994 has the dubious distinction, among constitutions, of being enacted in one day. All parliamentary pro-

---

1.   Section 45.
2.   Section 35
3.   White Paper on the Republican Constitution of Malawi, No. 002 of 1965.
4.   *Republic v Nakulenga and others*, Criminal Case No. 73 of 1969, (unreported), discussed by Brietze (1974).
5.   See Malawi Government, *Hansard, Official Proceedings of the Malawi Parliament*, (7th Session, 1st Meeting, 17 November 1969, Government Printer, Zomba), 56–57.
6.   Local Courts (Amendment) Act No. 31 of 1969. For an unduly sympathetic discussion of these developments, see Chimango (1977).
7.   Experienced expatriate judges of the High Court resigned *en masse* earlier on when it became apparent the jurisdiction of the Traditional Courts would be increased to cover capital offences. See Davidson (1973).
8.   For more detailed discussions on the making of the constitution, see Mutharika (1996); Ng'ong'ola (1996); Banda (1998); and Kanyongolo (1998).

cesses were completed and the Presidential approval given on 16 May, 1994. The disbanded single-party Parliament had to be recalled solely for this purpose. The constitution came into force "provisionally" on 18 May, 1994, one day after the conducting of multiparty elections, and "definitively" entered into force a year later.[1] In the interim, a constitutional committee of the new Parliament complied with its mandate to collect proposals on amendments from citizens and convened a constitutional conference to finalise the document.

There was generally broad consensus in this politically heady environment on what was required to banish the ills and excesses of Banda's rule. Among other notable features, the 1995 constitution underlines its own supremacy in the hierarchy of legal norms. There is a comprehensive human rights chapter,[2] and several institutions mandated to deal with grievances against the State and constitutional infringements.[3] It attempts to effect a rigid separation of the "status, function and duties" of the Executive, Legislature and Judiciary,[4] and to set Parliament and the Judiciary as counterweights to the exercise of executive power. The Judiciary is also restored to its pedestal as the supreme authority on the interpretation and application of the constitution and other laws. The constitution is also specific on the holding of Presidential and Parliamentary elections on a particular day every five years. The ability of Parliament to amend the constitution and to tamper with some of these essential attributes is also severely restricted.[5]

There was, however, insufficient time for national consensus building on the dividing issues, such as qualifications for the office of President; the need for and viability of a second chamber; or the right of constituents or a political party to recall a duly elected member of the National Assembly before the end of the Parliamentary term. There was also insufficient time for scrutiny of the details on some of the issues on which there was consensus, or of the language in which the constitution was generally drawn. With due respect to those entrusted with the work, the constitution is in parts drawn in language that is inelegant, imprecise and susceptible to interpretations that may not have been intended by the framers or the stakeholders. This will become evident from the provisions highlighted below on the conduct of elections, and from the review of the election disputes referred to the Judiciary for mediation.

Elections and the Constitution

Provisions of the constitution to which reference may be made on the subject of elections are in Chapter III on "Fundamental Principles"; Chapter IV on Human Rights; Chapter VIII on "Elections", and Chapters VI and VIII on "The Legislature" and "The Executive".

The "Fundamental Principles" are not as direct as one would have expected given the relevance of elections under the new political order. Section 12(i) in part states that "all legal and political authority of the State derives from the people of Malawi". Section 12 (iii), more fully but still obliquely, indicates that "authority to

---

1. See Section 212(1) of the Republic of Malawi (Constitution) Act, No. 20 of 1994, and Republic of Malawi (Constitution) Act No. 7 of 1995.
2. Chapter IV, sections 15 to 46.
3. These institutions include the Ombudsman (Chapter X); the Human Rights Commission (Chapter XI); the Law Commission (Chapter XII) and the National Compensation Tribunal and Fund (Chapter XIII).
4. Sections 7–9.
5. Section 196 requires a referendum for amendments affecting "the substance or effect of the constitution" and a majority of at least two-thirds of the total number of members of the National Assembly entitled to vote for all other amendments.

exercise power of State is conditional upon the sustained trust of the people of Malawi", and that trust "can only be maintained" through transparent government and "informed democratic choice".

The most relevant provision in the Human Rights Chapter is section 40. It secures for "every person" rights to form, join and participate in the activities of a political party; to campaign for a political party or cause; to participate in peaceful political activity intended to influence the composition and policies of Government; and freely to make political choices. It also secures rights to vote, in secret, and "to stand for election for a public office", and financial support for political parties recording more than a tenth of the national vote in parliamentary elections. These rights are buttressed by the traditional civic rights or freedoms related to association, conscience, expression, press and assembly reflected in sections 34 to 39 of the constitution.

Although, as noted above, several provisions refer to "fundamental rights or freedoms" in the constitution, there are no rights in Chapter IV classified, graded or identified as "fundamental" or not so fundamental. If the "human rights" secured must be ranked or graded, the more appropriate distinction would be between rights that are or are not capable of admitting derogation, restriction or limitation in terms section 44(1) of the constitution. Except for "the right to freedom of conscience, belief, thought and religion and to academic freedom", rights associated with political activities and elections do not feature on the list of "non-derogable rights". These are, to use the highly inelegant terminology the constitution has popularised, "derogable" rights. Restrictions or limitations "prescribed by law, which are reasonable, recognised by international human rights standards and necessary in an open and democratic society", may be placed on the exercise of these rights. This is the yardstick by which to measure the constitutionality or legality of any law that appears to derogate from the "fundamental rights or freedoms" related to political activity.

Chapter VII of the constitution does not in fact strictly deal with elections. It provides for the establishment, composition, broad functions and powers of the Electoral Commission, and describes "the franchise". Among the notable provisions that have featured in election disputes are section 75(1), which provides that the chairman of the Electoral Commission "shall be a Judge nominated in that behalf by the Judicial Service Commission"; section 76(2), which indicates that the duties of the Commission shall include delineation of constituency boundaries and determination of electoral petitions and complaints; section 76(4), which requires the Commission to exercise its powers and functions and duties "independent of any direction or interference by other authority or any person"; and sections 76(3) and (5), which indicate that decisions of the Commission are subject to appeal or judicial review in the High Court.

From the Chapter on the Legislature, the first notable provision is section 49(1), which indicates that "Parliament" shall, unless otherwise provided, consist of the National Assembly, the President as Head of State, and a second "indirectly elected" chamber called the Senate. Contrary to the wishes of some of the stakeholders and framers of the constitution, the establishment of the Senate was initially postponed until after May 1999.[1] A constitutional amendment has more recently abolished provisions on the establishment of the Senate.[2] The repeal of section 64 on recall of

1. Section 210(1)
2. See Constitution (Amendment) Bill No.1 of 2001.

members of the National Assembly in 1995 also dismayed many within the community of civic pressure groups.[1]

Two other notable provisions from this Chapter to feature prominently in election disputes discussed below are sections 65(1) and 67(1). Section 65(1) empowers the Speaker to declare vacant the seat of any member of the National Assembly "who was, at the time of his or her election, a member of one political party represented in the National Assembly other than by that Member alone but who has voluntarily ceased to be a member of that party and joined another political party represented in the National Assembly". This is the convoluted, technical description of the phenomenon in Malawian politics that should more simply be termed "crossing the floor" of Parliament.

Section 67(1) indicates that the National Assembly shall stand dissolved "on 20th of March in the fifth year after its election, and the polling day for the general elections for the next National Assembly shall be the Tuesday in the third week of May that year". A proviso further states that if it is not practicable for polling to be on this day, it "shall be held on a day, within seven days from that Tuesday, appointed by the Electoral Commission". For the 1999 elections, however, as will be noted below, a constitutional amendment was required to provide for polling "on a day not later than 15th June, 1999, appointed by the Electoral Commission".[2] This is not only proof of the constitution's inelegance, but also of its tendency to over-regulate. The mischief anticipated by the makers of the constitution would have been pre-empted by a provision requiring the Electoral Commission to call for general elections within a specified period towards the end of the five-year term of the National Assembly.

In Chapter VIII on the Executive, sections 80(2), 80(4) and 83 have given rise to notable legal and political disputes. Section 80(2) provides for the election of a President by "a majority of the electorate through direct, universal and equal suffrage". Section 80(4) indicates that the President shall be elected concurrently with the First Vice President whose name shall appear on the President's ballot paper. As will be noted below, these provisions may not be in complete harmony with comparable provisions under the principal Act of Parliament on electoral law. Section 83 states that the term of office for a President shall run until a successor has been sworn in. Thus, although Presidential and Parliamentary elections must be held concurrently every fifth year, the President's term may run for an unspecified and uncertain period if the swearing in of a successor is held up.

Electoral Laws outside the Constitution

The principal Act to which the constitution refers for details on electoral law and procedures is the Parliamentary and Presidential Elections Act (PPEA) of 1993.[3] This Act is supplemented by the Political Parties (Registration and Regulation) Act, 1993,[4] and the Electoral Commission Act, 1998.[5]

The registration of political parties under the Political Parties Act is an important initial activity in Malawi's electoral process. Although the process accommodates persons contesting elections as independent candidates, it is generally assumed that

---

1. Repealed by Act No. 6 of 1995
2. Amendment No. 11 of 1999
3. No. 31 of 1993
4. No. 15 of 1993
5. No. 11 of 1998.

political parties will be the principal actors. Even the constitution assumes persons associating in the form of political parties will be the principal beneficiaries of the political rights and freedoms secured by section 40. An extreme manifestation of this assumption appears in section 17(2) of the Political Parties Act. It states that a political party or any combination of persons "shall not electioneer, or authorise any person to Act on its behalf, in connection with an election in which political parties contest unless it is a registered political party". This comes close to suggesting that "electioneering", an activity not properly defined in the Act, is only for registered political parties.

Section 5(4) of this Act is also controversial. It states that a person shall not be considered as a member of a political party for purposes of the Act unless he is a citizen and has attained the voting age for general election purposes. It is notable by way of contrast that a non-citizen ordinarily resident in the country for seven years qualifies for the franchise in terms of section 77 of the constitution.

The Electoral Commission Act of 1998 was carved out of Part II of the PPEA. A separate Act was passed to recreate the Electoral Commission as a statutory corporation with its own personality or standing in law. The Commission was also given a management organ and empowered to receive and keep funds additional to allocations from the Consolidated Fund. Some of the notable aspects of the reconstituted Commission include the power of the President to appoint the members, but "in consultation with leaders of the political parties represented in the National Assembly"; the designation of the Chief Elections Officer as the Chief Executive of the Commission and head of the management team; and the addition of functions related to voter education and research to the main responsibility of conducting all elections to be held in the country. The restructuring of the Electoral Commission in this manner was obviously intended to improve its ability to deliver free and fair elections under the constitution. The Commission has been adjudged to have significantly, but perhaps not substantially, failed to deliver on its first assignment, the 1999 presidential and parliamentary elections (see Malawi Electoral Commission, 1999; cf. Kadzamira, 2000; Patel, 2000).

After the excision of provisions on the Electoral Commission, the PPEA covers in great detail other standard aspects of the electoral process such as delineation of constituencies, voter registration, candidate selection, the actual conduct of the poll, determination of results, complaints and appeals, and election offences and penalties. The Act also covers international observation of the process. A review of all these aspects of the Act cannot be accommodated within the scope of this chapter. It will suffice to note that the Act generally proposes a "simple plurality" or "first-past-the-post system" for both the National Assembly and presidential elections. For the presidential poll this has contributed to the controversy surrounding section 80(2) constitution.

It should also be noted that the PPEA was passed before finalisation of the 1995 constitution. It was amended at least twice before the 1999 poll,[1] but this was still not sufficient to bring it into complete harmony with the constitution. According to the doctrine or principle of constitutional supremacy advocated in the constitution, the Act must give way on points of conflict. Some of the inadequacies and inelegancies of the constitution have, however, confounded the application of this principle by the courts.

---

1. Parliamentary and Presidential Elections (Amendment) Act No. 16 of 1994, and Parliamentary and Presidential Elections (Amendment) Act No. 10 of 1998.

Election Results and Electoral Politics in the Courts

Elections in Malawi are now keenly contested and generate much public excitement. But, contrary to popular belief, the results have so far not generated alarming levels of litigation given the numbers of candidates and constituencies contested for.[1] There was no petition against the results of the Presidential poll in 1994. The results of the parliamentary poll were contested in about four High Court cases, two of which were in the end not so consequential.[2] Recurrent by-elections in between the two general elections increased the scope for litigation, but, again, the notable cases in terms of the development of electoral law and procedures were very few.[3] The arena for electoral politics then shifted to the National Assembly. At least three precedent-setting cases were taken to the Supreme Court of Appeal in which the underlying issue was the division of seats in the National Assembly and the struggle for the control of chamber after the 1994 poll.[4] During the preparatory period for the 1999 elections, four cases with profound legal and political implications reached the High Court.[5] At the time the research for this chapter was conducted, the High Court had disposed of at least two of the seven cases known to the Electoral Commission in which the results were under challenge.[6] All these cases can best be analysed following the sequence of election activities such as voter registration, nomination of candidates, campaigning, conduct of the poll and post-poll activities and consequences.

Candidate Selection

In *Re Shadreck Kusinyala*[7], a candidate in a by-election, was disqualified because his nomination was not supported by at least 10 voters registered in the constituency as required by section 37(2)(b) of the PPEA. The Registrar of the High Court dismissed the suggestion that only the High Court could debar the candidate. He suggested that the Commission acted constitutionally, in line with its mandate in section 76(2)(d) of the constitution to ensure compliance with the constitution and any other Act of Parliament such as the PPEA.

---

1. In 1994 there were 4 candidates in the Presidential poll and 614 candidates contesting 177 seats in the Parliamentary poll. In 1999 there were 5 Presidential candidates and 657 Parliamentary candidates for 193 constituencies (see Malawi Electoral Commission 1994: Appendix XII; and General Notice No. 103, *Malawi Government Gazette Extraordinary*, Vol. XXXVI, No. 44, 20 August 1999).
2. See Malawi Electoral Commission 1994: Appendix VIII. The important cases were: *Gwanda Chakuamba v Electoral Commission*, Civil Cause No. 1062 of 1994; and *Grace Chikweza v Electoral Commission*, Civil Cause No. 1061 of 1994. The not so important cases were: *A. Malengamzoma v Electoral Commission*, Civil Cause No. 966 of 1994; and *J.M. Chikwesele v Electoral Commission*, Civil Cause No. 967 of 1994.
3. See *J.J. Chidule v Electoral Commission*, Civil Cause No. 5 of 1995; *Rolf Patel v Electoral Commission*, Civil Cause No. 84 of 1996; In *Re Nomination of Shadreck Kusinyala*, Civil Cause No. 1170 of 1996; and *Kapolo Msungeni Manda v Electoral Commission*, Civil Cause No. 1921 of 1996.
4. *Attorney General v Mapopa Chipeta*, MSCA Civil Appeal No. 33 of 1994; *Attorney General v Malawi Congress Party*, MSCA Civil Appeal No. 22 of 1996; and *Fred Nseula v Attorney General*, MSCA, Civil Appeal No. 32 of 1997.
5. See Malawi Electoral Commission (1999: 21). The cases are: *Dr Charles Kafumba and Others v Electoral Commission and the Malawi Broadcasting Corporation*, Civil Cause No. 35 of 1999; *Attorney General v Gwanda Chakuamba and Chakufwa Chihana*, Civil Cause, No. 25 of 1999, and *Attorney General v Gwanda Chakuamba and Chakufwa Chihana*, MSCA Civil Appeal No. 7 of 1999; and *Gwanda Chakuamba v Electoral Commission*, Miscellaneous Civil Application No 29 of 1999.
6. See Malawi Electoral Commission (1999: 23). The two cases are: *Iqbal Omar v Samuel Rodger Gama and The Electoral Commission*, Miscellaneous Application No. 28 of 1999; and *Gwanda Chakuamba, Kamlepo Kalua, and Bishop Mnkhumbwe v Attorney General, The Malawi Electoral Commission and The United Democratic Front*, Civil Cause No 1B of 1999. This latter case had already been to the Supreme Court as *Attorney General and Others v Gwanda Chakuamba and Others*, MSCA Civil Appeal No 20 of 1999, on preliminary procedural matters related to discovery of election documents.
7. Civil Cause No.1170 of 1996

In *Chidule*,[1] a Returning Officer rejected the nomination of a candidate because he was not registered as a voter in the constituency for which a by-election was called. He was registered in another constituency. This was believed to be contrary to section 38(1)(c) of the PPEA, which required from every candidate in an election evidence that he or she was "registered in the constituency". The High Court noted that section 51(1)(c) of the constitution required evidence that the candidate is "registered as a voter in a constituency". The Court opined that there was a slip or a mistake in the drafting of section 38 (1)(c). The draftsman could not have deliberately intended to contradict the constitution. If there were no such slip or mistake, then section 38(1)(c) would be invalid under the doctrine of constitutional supremacy. The candidature of the applicant was duly restored. The Act was of course passed before the constitution, and section 38(1)(c) is consistent with other provisions in the Act, such as section 37(2)(b) referred to above. If there was a slip, it was in the drafting of section 51(1)(c) of the constitution. The draftsman should have referred to "the" constituency instead of "a" constituency. The constitution must however prevail under the revised legal order, and section 38(1)(c) was accordingly amended in 1998.[2]

The Running Mates

Strategists for the two opposition parties, the MCP and the Alliance for Democracy (AFORD), obviously took careful note of the results of the 1994 poll in their preparations for the 1999 poll. They decided to contest the 1999 presidential poll as "an alliance", with the President of the MCP, Gwanda Chakuamba, as the presidential candidate, and the President of AFORD, Chakufwa Chihana, as his "running mate". It was decided that the symbols for both parties should appear on the ballot paper, obviously for the benefit and guidance of supporters of both parties. The Electoral Commission at first prevaricated and desisted from pronouncing on the legality of the arrangement. The Supreme Court ruled that it was part of the Commission's mandate under section 76(2)(d) of the constitution to determine legality of the proposal and the eligibility of the candidates.[3]

The Commission referred to three provisions: section 80(4) of the constitution, indicating that the First Vice President shall be elected concurrently with the President, and his name shall appear on the same ballot paper as the presidential candidate who nominated him; Section 49(1)(c) of the PPEA, indicating that the nomination form for a presidential candidate shall, where the candidate is sponsored by a political party, specify that fact and indicate the name of the party and its distinctive symbol; and section 76(b) of the PPEA, indicating that the ballot paper for each presidential candidate shall legibly and clearly print his name or an abbreviation thereof, and his election symbol or that of his political party. The Commission determined these provisions did not envisage the printing of a ballot paper on which different parties using separate or different distinctive political symbols would sponsor the presidential candidate and his running mate. It indicated that it would not accept nominations of a presidential candidate whose registered political party is different from that of his running mate.

1. Miscellaneous Civil Cause Application No.5 of 1995.
2. Amended by section 7 of Act No 10 of 1998.
3. *Attorney General v Gwanda Chakuamba and Chakufwa Chihana*, MSCA, Civil Appeal No. 7 of 1999.

The running mates appealed to the High Court in terms of section 76(3) of the constitution.[1] The Court saw no requirement for political party affiliation in any of the provisions cited by the Commission, or in any of the eligibility rules in section 80 of the constitution. The Court held that the Commission would not be justified in rejecting the nomination of the running mates on account of their different party political affiliation or symbols to be printed on the ballot paper. The Court acknowledged that there appeared to be a lacuna in the law. The PPEA underlined qualifications for nomination as a presidential candidate, including, where applicable, political affiliation. It was silent as regards the running mate. But the Court concluded that to "start restricting the constitution in the face of the silence of the Act would be overzealous judicial activism".[2] Since both the constitution and the PPEA never anticipated this type of candidature, a minor quibble on this technically sound judgement is that comments should have been offered on the compatibility of the candidature of the running mates with the ethos of the new constitutional and political order.

Voter Registration

In *Kapolo Msungeni Manda*, an *ex parte* application was lodged on behalf of 87 petitioners for an injunction restraining the Commission from proceeding with a by-election.[3] The petitioners alleged that officers at different centres had refused to register them as voters for various reasons. The injunction was sought three days from the date of the poll, but a period of 20 days had passed between the acts complained of and the lodging of a formal appeal with the Commission. The High Court refused to grant the injunction. It held that the application was not urgent in these circumstances. The Court also observed that postponing elections in the interest of only 87 potential voters could do more harm. The Court suggested that the petitioners could seek the nullification of the results afterwards, if they were not satisfied with the conduct of the Commission.

One troublesome aspect of this case was the suggestion that infringements of electoral laws and procedures committed so close to the polling date could be tolerated, as long as the results could be challenged and nullified afterwards. The other was the constitutionality of denying a potentially deserving applicant access to appropriate legal redress. These concerns notwithstanding, the National Assembly amended the PPEA in 1998 to reflect the position taken by the Court. New subsections added to section 114, on complaints and appeals, stated that "no application shall be made to the High Court for an injunction or for an order restraining the holding of an election" within 14 days of the date of the election, but the High Court shall have the power, subsequently, to declare the election void if satisfied that "there are good and sufficient grounds".[4]

These issues came back to the High Court in the run-up to the 1999 poll in *Gwanda Chakuamba (representing himself and other stakeholders) v The Electoral Commission*.[5] In terms of section 67(1) of the constitution, the 1999 elections were due on Tuesday, May 18. The Commission, as entitled to under that provision, shift-

---

1. *Gwanda Chakuamba and Chakufwa Chihana v The Attorney General*, Civil Cause No. 25 of 1999.
2. P. 9 of the transcript.
3. Civil Cause No. 21 of 1996. For an analysis of national and local politics during this controversial by-election, see Englund (2001a).
4. Sections 114(6) and (7), introduced under section 18 of Act No. 10 of 1998.
5. Miscellaneous Civil Application No. 29 of 1999.

ed the polling date to May 25. The Commission's management of preparations for the poll, especially voter registration, as the Court agreed, was, to say the least, very tardy. It found itself in a situation where voter registration had to be extended to May 14. This left only 10 days for inspection of rolls and registers for voters. This was an abridgement of the period of not less than 21 days between close of registration and polling required under section 29 of the PPEA. Chakuamba petitioned the High Court for declarations and orders that this was unlawful; that many eligible voters would not be registered by election date; that proceeding with the poll as scheduled would be an unconstitutional infringement of the right to vote; and that the Commission should request or implore the State President to reconvene the National Assembly under section 67(4) of the constitution to consider statutory abridgement of the voter registration verification period or a constitutional amendment to shift the polling date. Chakuamba also sought an injunction to restrain the Commission from proceeding with the poll as scheduled. For this he sought an order declaring the amendments to section 114 of the PPEA noted above as unconstitutional.

In an earlier case, Chimasula Phiri, the presiding Judge, was inclined to the view that last minute interventions should not be allowed to derail the electoral process.[1] This time he agreed that amendments to section 114 of the PPEA compromised the rights of voters. They were inconsistent with sections 41(3), 46(2) and 46(3), the access to justice clauses in the human rights chapter of the constitution; and section 76(3) on the right of appeal to the High Court against determinations of the Electoral Commission in electoral processes. He was also of the view that the amendments did not further "the explicit or let alone implicit values of the constitution". Applying the doctrine of supremacy of the constitution enshrined in sections 10 and 5, he declared the amendments invalid.

Although he declined to declare that proceeding with the elections as scheduled would be unconstitutional as many eligible voters would not be able to vote, Chimasula Phiri J. agreed that abridgement of the 21 day voter registration verification period was unlawful, and the Commission would not be able to discharge its constitutional and statutory duty to deliver free and fair elections. He granted a "conditional injunction" restraining the Commission from proceeding with the poll until after the expiry of 21 days, unless Parliament reconvened to pass a law abridging this period. He also declared that it was the duty of the Commission to apprise the President so that he could form an opinion as to whether a grave crisis or emergency had occurred calling for the reconvention of Parliament to pass legislation as advised.

As it turned out, Parliament reconvened, not to amend section 29 of the PPEA to abridge the 21-day period, but to amend section 67(1) of the constitution so that the date of the poll could be shifted to 15 June 1999.[2] This is the irony of the case. It

---

1. *Rolf Patel (representing the Peoples Democratic Party) v The Electoral Commission*, Miscellaneous Civil Cause No. 84 of 1996. The High Court in this case granted an injunction on the basis of an *ex parte* affidavit alleging widespread violence and intimidation in preparations for a by-election. The injunction was granted pending an appeal by the petitioner against Commission's decision in terms of section 113 of the PPEA. Ndovi J. discharged it two days later. It transpired that the petitioner had not lodged a written complaint and the Commission had not decided on matter as envisaged by section 113. Ndovi J. also observed that section 76(2)(d) of the constitution did not in fact require the lodging of complaints for the Commission's determination in writing. The requirement for a written complaint in section 113 of the PPEA could thus be invalid under the doctrine of constitutional supremacy. Section 113 further suggested that the Commission was a higher body for the determination of complaints not "satisfactorily resolved at a lower level of authority", but there was no indication of these lower level authorities. Ndovi J. sheepishly left these issues for definitive pronouncement by the Supreme Court.
2. Amendment No. 11 of 1999.

was easier, and politically more expedient, to pretend that there was a constitutional crisis calling for the reconvention of Parliament so that the constitution could be amended. The supremacy of the constitution, which the Court sought to uphold in respect of the amendments to section 114 of the PPEA, could not be upheld in respect of the choice between amending section 29 of the PPEA and section 67(1) of the constitution. Commentary on this development must conclude with the following contrasting observation, made by Chimasula Phiri J. in April 1999, when dissolving an interlocutory injunction order on nomination of candidates for the elections:

> Possibly for the avoidance of doubt, let me clearly state here that there are other democracies of the world where it has been established that the polling date should not be left to the President to decide because he may abuse his powers to the detriment of other presidential aspirants. For example in the USA the date for the new president to assume office is fixed and the parties plan their erection (sic) strategies with certainty. Malawi too opted for a fixed day as Tuesday of the third week of May in election year. There is no evidence to suggest that the political parties are unaware about this fixation of polling date. I urge our politicians to respect the constitution. It must always be born in our minds that this is not a political party constitution but a constitution of the country. It is quite clear from the exhibits of the applicants that all is not well at the Electoral Commission. However, the solution does not lie in breaching the constitution but otherwise dealing with the Electoral Commission itself.[1]

Campaigning

One campaign issue that has bedevilled elections in Malawi is biased coverage by the national radio broadcaster, the Malawi Broadcasting Corporation (MBC), of the campaigns by the incumbent President or ruling party.[2] In *Kafumba and others*[3] the plaintiffs complained to the Commission about live and repeat broadcasts of President Muluzi's speeches in the 1999 campaign, a facility not extended to the other political parties. They gave the Commission five days from 18 May 1999 to correct the situation and then appealed to the High Court in terms of section 76(3) of the constitution on 31 May 1999. There was no dispute that MBC's conduct, the second defendant in the application, contravened the constitution, the PPEA, as well as section 45(1)(f) of the Communications Act. The point of departure was whether the Commission had also failed in its duties and was not likely to deliver a free and fair election campaign. From the affidavits tendered on behalf of the Commission the High Court was satisfied that no case had been made against it. It had taken appropriate arrangements to ensure free and equal access to the MBC, and it was "on the right track" towards the delivery of a free and fair campaign. This, with hindsight, was probably too benevolent a conclusion. But the main lesson from this case is that campaign irregularities, whether arising from violence, intimidation, advertising, broadcasting or other aspects, are not likely to outweigh other considerations in the validation of election results.

---

1. *Brian Mungomo and Goodwin Mvula v The Electoral Commission*, Miscellaneous Civil Application No. 23 of 1999, p 5 of the unedited transcript.
2. See, for example, *A.W. M'nthambala v Malawi Broadcasting Corporation*, MSCA Civil Appeal No. 6 of 1993 on the coverage of the Referendum campaign.
3. Miscellaneous Civil Cause No.35 of 1999.

Irregularities in the Conduct of the Poll

Election results are more likely to be impugned by irregularities in the actual conduct of the poll. In *Chikweza* and *Gwanda Chakuamba*,[1] Election Officers in two constituencies in the 1994 poll were adjudged to have failed to comply with sections 93, 94 and 95 of the PPEA on recording of the polling process, handling of ballot papers and other documents, and compilation of district results. The Commission determined that the irregularities were sufficiently serious to cast doubt on the apparent result and ordered what it called "a re-run". The High Court dismissed petitions lodged by the candidates initially pronounced as winners in the two constituencies and allowed the by-elections to proceed. These cases are also notable for the moot point whether the Commission had the legal power to order a re-run or a by-election. The Court found the necessary authority in the part of section 113 of the PPEA stating that the Commission "shall take necessary action to correct the irregularity and the effects thereof upon confirmation of its existence". This was arguably incorrect. The Court itself should have the declared the election of the candidates void on grounds of non-compliance with the Act in the conduct of the elections in terms of section 114 (3)(d) of the PPEA.

The Missing Votes

In *Iqbal Omar*,[2] the comparable case in the 1999 Parliamentary poll, the High Court took full and proper cognisance of the range of options available to it when considering an election appeal under section 114 of the PPEA. The case involved an extreme and remarkable example of "inadvertence" in the handling of election results. Counted votes from one out of 14 polling centres in a constituency were not taken into account when computing the results. The results (form) apparently "went missing" in the premises of the Returning Officer after counting on 16 June, 1999. A party functionary in the presence of the Returning Officer found them on 18 June. They were excluded from the final count presumably because their authenticity was by then questionable. Without the votes from that centre the petitioner lost the election by about 74 votes. With those votes he would have won by about 293 votes. From the available evidence, the Court concluded that the voting process and the counting at the centre had been properly conducted. The impropriety was the failure to return the results. The election of the candidate could be declared void for non-compliance with the Act in the conduct of the poll in terms of section 114(3)(d) of the PPEA. The Court however felt that the proviso to that section was applicable. A Court need not declare the result void under this section if it is satisfied that the failure to comply with the Act would not have affected the result of the election. The Court upheld the appeal. The petitioner's results stood, after taking into account the missing votes.

This is the questionable aspect of the decision. The Court would appear to have first determined under section 114(5) that the declared loser of the poll had in fact won. It then appears to uphold that result under the proviso to section 114(3)(d), as if it was the result emanating from the Commission against which the petition was lodged. In the interests of transparency, and avoidance of perceptions of partiality, the Court perhaps should have declared the Commission's result void under section 114 (3)(d) and ordered a by-election, the expense of the process notwithstanding.

1. Civil Cause No. 1061 and No. 1062 of 1994.
2. Miscellaneous Application No. 28 of 1999, Lilongwe District Registry.

The President Shall Be Elected by a Majority of the Electorate

From a political as well as constitutional perspective, the most important case to date on the 1999 presidential poll is *Gwanda Chakuamba, Kamlepo Kalua and Bishop Mnkhumbwe v The Attorney General, The Malawi Electoral Commission and The United Democratic Front.*[1] The case concerned a purely legal or technical irregularity in the conduct of the poll. The plaintiffs, three of the presidential candidates in the poll, complained that the Commission unlawfully determined the winner of the poll under section 96(5) of the PPEA instead of section 80(2) of the constitution.[2] Section 80(2), it should be recalled, states that the President "shall be elected by a majority of the electorate through direct, universal and equal suffrage". Section 96(5) states that "in any election the candidate who has obtained a majority of the votes at the poll shall be declared by the Commission to have been duly elected". The petitioners referred to section 202 of the constitution as authority for the suggestion that section 96(5) was appropriate only for the 1994 presidential poll. Section 202, in the chapter on transitional issues, states that the first President "after the date of commencement of this constitution shall be the person successfully elected in accordance with the Act of Parliament then in force for the election of a … President". The petitioners contended that in terms of section 80(2) a candidate must secure votes "equal to 50 per cent plus one of those entitled to vote, or registered to vote" in order to be duly and lawfully pronounced as elected. The Commission had pronounced as winner a candidate who had secured only a majority of the votes actually cast in the poll.

Mtambo J. in the High Court first considered whether section 80(2) and section 96(5) purposefully created different mechanisms for determining presidential election results. He did not see in section 202 any acknowledgement of the suggested different mechanisms. Section 202 simply sought to clarify, for the avoidance of doubt as it were, how the first President was to be elected under the new constitutional order. He concluded that there was in fact no difference in meaning or mechanisms between section 80(2) and section 96(5). The word "majority" in section 80(2) carried its ordinary dictionary meaning of "the greater number or part of something". The word "electorate" meant "persons registered as voters in an election considered as a group". The words "through direct, universal, and equal suffrage", according to the Court, indicated that the "electors" must actually have voted. The word "suffrage", qualified by the words "direct, universal and equal", meant the "right to vote in political elections". A vote would count only if it had been exercised in an election. The President was therefore to be elected by the greater number of votes cast in the poll. There was no irregularity in the manner in which President Muluzi had been declared winner of the 1999 poll.

The Court professedly came to this conclusion by applying the first rule of statutory interpretation under which words must be given their ordinary meaning. But the result was in fact more consistent with the application of other special rules of interpretation the Court took cognisance of and claimed it would have applied in the alternative. These rules call for interpretation of particular constitutional provisions in a broad, purposeful manner, which integrates and harmonises provisions, and seeks to avoid absurdities and unworkable situations. The Court attempted to har-

---

1. High Court, Lilongwe District Registry, Civil Cause No. 1B of 1999.
2. A second irregularity complained of was that a "Justice of Appeal" had been appointed to head the Electoral Commission instead of a "High Court Judge. This ground, advisedly in my view, was not pursued in argument.

monise sections 80(2) and 96(5). The Court was openly concerned with the absurdities the petitioners' contentions might lead to. There are no provisions in the constitution on re-running presidential elections. The political divide in the country was such that it would have been difficult, certainly for any of the candidates in the 1999 poll, to obtain support from 50 per cent plus one of all registered voters. The prospect of perpetual re-runs could not be discounted, and the incumbent, in the meantime, would have had to remain in office without a mandate from the electorate. As the Court noted, "the outcome of all this would be to subvert the democratic purposes of the constitution". These arguments were more compelling.

The full bench of the Supreme Court, on appeal,[1] addressed two issues on which the seductive legal reasoning of the trial court seemingly faltered. The first issue was the trial court's generous interpretation of the word "electorate", which was not confined to the true ordinary, dictionary meaning of the word. The Court reiterated the principles it had laid down elsewhere for the proper interpretation of the Malawi constitution in the courts.[2] A Malawi court, it said, must first recognise the special nature and character of the constitution before interpreting any of its provisions. It is an amalgam of the Parliamentary and presidential systems of government, and care must be taken in interpreting it so that a balance between these systems is achieved. It must also be recognised that the constitution gives greater prominence to the traditions, usages and conventions which are a common feature of the Parliamentary system more than those of a presidential system. It must further be appreciated that the constitution is a single document. Every part of it must be considered as far as it is relevant to get to the true meaning and intent of the constitution. "The constitution must be considered as a whole to ensure that its provisions do not destroy but sustain each other."[3] In line with these principles the Court considered section 80(2) together with sections 80, 77, and 6 of the constitution, and section 96(5) of the PPEA. It came to the conclusion that the word "electorate" was intended to refer to those who actually voted in the elections. Section 80(2) of the constitution intended to provide for the election of the President by a majority of those actually voting in particular elections, as found by the High Court, not by "fifty per cent plus one" of registered voters as canvassed by the appellants. Authorities from other jurisdictions also suggested that provisions putting in place different, special mechanisms are normally more specific.

The second issue for the Supreme Court was the failure of the High Court to ascertain the intention of the framers of the constitution from other sources, such as Law Commission and Parliamentary records. A report of the Law Commission had apparently discussed these ambiguities in the law. In November 1998, an attempt to amend the constitution to address the issue was also frustrated by the opposition in the National Assembly, possibly with an eye on the 1999 elections and the litigation that ensued. The Supreme Court held that statements made in Parliament on that occasion did not provide an agreed meaning of section 80(2). They were mere opinions of those who made them. The report of the Law Commission also reflected the opinion of the Commission. That some members of the Commission were among the framers of the constitution did lend further credence to the opinion. The framers of the constitution may have confused what they intended to do with the effect of the language which was in fact employed. The Court felt that it had the advantage,

---

1. MSCA, Civil Appeal No. 20 of 2000, before Banda, CJ, and Unyolo, Mtegha, Tambala and Msosa JJA. Banda CJ delivered the judgement of the Court.
2. *Fred Nseula v Attorney General and the Malawi Congress Party,* MSCA, Civil Appeal No.32 of 1997.
3. Page 19 of the transcript.

which members of the Law Commission, Parliament, the Electoral Commission or the constitutional Consultative Conference did not have. It had received submissions from very competent Counsel and considered authorities from different jurisdictions. It was better placed to discover the true meaning of section 80(2).

This case may be notorious in some political circles for providing the legal seal of approval to Muluzi's re-election after a poll severely mismanaged by the Electoral Commission. The case may give the impression that the Judiciary, yet again, mediated in favour of a government it prefers, and continues to act like the MCP's nemesis, exacting retribution for the ills and excesses of Banda's rule.[1] The problem for the MCP and its indefatigable leaders is that the judicial reasoning in this case is technically sound and legally defensible, in the light of the language employed in the haplessly constructed constitutional provisions. Some legal experts may also argue that this case has advanced the country's jurisprudence by articulating more clearly the manner in which the courts must approach Malawi's troubled constitution. We must turn to other political cases arising after the 1994 elections for evidence, if any, of partiality in the treatment of political actors in the courts.

Post-Election Disputes

Strangers in the Gallery

The first of the notable political cases in which the pattern of results in the 1994 Parliamentary poll was the underlying *causa* was *Dr Mapopa Chipeta v Attorney General*.[2] Soon after the 30th session of the National Assembly commenced after the elections, the High Court was invited to determine whether Cabinet Ministers who were not elected to the Chamber were "strangers within the precincts of the Assembly", who may enter and remain within the precincts by admittance of the Speaker, and sit in the "Strangers' Gallery", not with their Cabinet colleagues on the "front bench" of the Government's side of the Members' Gallery. At issue were the Standing Orders made under the 1966 constitution, which excluded nominated Ministers from the definition of "strangers within the precincts of the Assembly"; and section 96(1) of the new constitution, which described the functions and duties of members of Cabinet as requiring availability in Parliament "for purposes of answering any queries or participating in any debate pertaining to the content and policies of the Government".

In the High Court, Chimasula Phiri (then Acting Judge) held that section 96(1) did not confer rights on Cabinet Ministers who were not elected to the Assembly to enter or remain within its precincts as of right. The Standing Order excluding such Ministers from the definition of "strangers" was subsidiary legislation. As it was never published in the Government Gazette, it had no legislative effect. In any event

---

1. See Chakuamba's letter, "The Law and You", in *Malawi News*, 18-24 December, 1999, also circulated to all Heads of Diplomatic Missions, Heads of the various religious organisations, The Law Society, and all NGOs. Chakuamba's bitter complaint, which bordered on defamation and contempt for some members of the bench, was triggered by the ruling in *Attorney General, Malawi Electoral Commission and The United Democratic Front v Chakuamba, Kalua and Nkhumbwe*, MSCA, Civil Appeal No 20 of 1999. The Supreme Court granted the respondents restricted rights to discover and inspect ballot boxes, ballot papers and other materials used in the 1999 Presidential elections, which they suspected would yield concrete evidence of malpractice and irregularities. The restrictions were seen as pre-empting further challenges to the results of the poll. The possibilities of mounting a successful challenge from what may have been discovered are receding with the passage of time.
2. Civil Cause No. 1504 of 1994

it was inconsistent with the new constitution. It ceased to have effect when the new constitution entered into force.

The Supreme Court disagreed.[1] The issue, in its assessment, was not whether Ministers not elected to the Assembly were Members thereof. They clearly were not. The issue was whether they were entitled to sit in the Chamber in order to carry out their duties effectively. The question as to who should sit in the Chamber during its deliberations was a matter of Parliamentary privilege. It was generally not for the courts to inquire into the existence of privilege, or the internal proceedings of the House, except to ensure that the House did not exceed its privilege. If the Assembly in its wisdom, as manifested by the Standing Orders, decided that Cabinet Ministers were not strangers, courts have no jurisdiction to intervene. The Court also held that Standing Orders were not subsidiary legislation. There was no requirement for their publication. The Supreme Court further concluded that a constructive interpretation of section 96(1) suggested that members of Cabinet not elected to Chamber must be present in the Chamber at all times in order to carry out their constitutional duties effectively. They would not do so if they were present only by the Speaker's invitation and admittance.

The Supreme Court probably should have agreed with the trial court judge on the inconsistency of the particular Standing Orders with the new constitutional imperatives. The suggestion that a large aspect of Parliamentary privilege should not be subject to interrogation in the courts is also difficult to reconcile with the doctrine of supremacy of the constitution and the access to justice provisions. These are minor queries, however. This was an irritating case for the Judiciary, involving no fundamental legal problem that could not be resolved by Parliament. The case was mostly about political posturing or point scoring in the reconfigured National Assembly. This incidentally became unnecessary when leading members of the opposition party, AFORD, including the plaintiff and lead counsel in the case, were appointed to Cabinet by the time the case was finally disposed of in 1995.

Crossing the Floor

The third of the trilogy of notable political cases after the 1994 elections may be considered second. This is *Fred Nseula v The Attorney General and the Malawi Congress Party*.[2] Nseula, UDF Member of Parliament for the Mwanza North Constituency, was alleged to have joined the MCP after he was relieved of his position as Deputy Minister of Finance in 1995. On or about 25 November, 1995, a motion was raised in the National Assembly and debated, at the end of which the Speaker decided that Nseula had "crossed the floor". To use the more appropriate language in section 65(1) of the constitution, Nseula had "voluntarily ceased" to be a member of the UDF and "joined another political party represented in the National Assembly", the MCP.

Nseula, maintaining that he had "resigned" from the UDF but had not joined the MCP, subsequently appealed to the courts. The MCP joined the action with leave of court because of the evidence it possessed on the matter. Mwaungulu J. criticised the manner in which the Speaker allowed the debate in the National Assembly and arrived at a decision. He was of the view that the debate could not generate appropriate, fair evidence for disposal of the matter. In any event, although there was sufficient ev-

---

1. MSCA, Civil Appeal No. 33 of 1994, Banda CJ presiding.
2. MSCA, Civil Appeal No 32 of 1997, being High Court Civil Cause No. 63 of 1996.

idence that Nseula had joined the MCP, the matter was "otiose". Nseula's seat in the National Assembly fell vacant by operation of law when he was appointed to Cabinet as Deputy Minister of Finance.

The Court arrived at this astounding conclusion from its reading of mainly three provisions in the constitution. Section 88(3) in part states that the President and members of the Cabinet "shall not hold *any other public office*" (my emphasis) and "shall not perform remunerative work outside the duties of their office". Section 51(2)(e) provides that, unless so permitted by the constitution, no person shall qualify for election or nomination as a Member of Parliament who "holds, or acts in any public office or appointment". Section 63 (1)(e) also states that the seat of a member of the National Assembly shall fall vacant "if any circumstances arise that, if he or she were not a member of the National Assembly", would cause the disqualification of that person for election under the constitution or any Act of Parliament.

Nseula's counsel filed a notice of intention to appeal, which his principal subsequently attempted to repudiate. The Attorney General also intimated his intention to challenge, not the outcome, but the grounds advanced by the trial court. Counsel for the MCP, on the other hand, for understandable political reasons, strenuously attempted to have the notice of appeal struck off, and withdrew from the case in a huff when the courts resisted his efforts. This earned him severe rebuke from the Supreme Court. The decision of the High Court also came in for unprecedented, heavy criticism. The Supreme Court held that it was palpably wrong for the trial judge to decide on a matter not raised by the parties in their pleadings. He could have expressed his opinion, but he should not have made it the definitive basis for his decision. The Court also felt that criticism of the Speaker's handling of the matter in the National Assembly was unfair and unwarranted. It is not required or expected that the Speaker should act like a judicial officer before making a declaration under section 65(1) of the constitution. There was sufficient evidence in Parliament, and subsequently in the courts, on which to base a declaration that Nseula had "crossed the floor".

On the substantive constitutional issue now manufactured for determination, the Supreme Court[1] held that it would be "a contortion of construction" to read into section 88(3) an indication that the President and members of Cabinet shall be public officers. Looking at the constitution as a whole, and various provisions in which the words "public office" appear, the Court held that the words must be interpreted in the strict sense of "public office in the civil service", not "any public office of whatever description". Examples of public officers indicated in the constitution include civil servants like the Attorney General, Secretary to the President and Cabinet, and the Inspector–General of Police. The Court held that President, Cabinet Ministers and Members of Parliament must be regarded as holders of "political offices", not "public offices".

A narrow, literal reading of section 88(3) suggests that the trial court's interpretation of the provision was not a complete contortion. Section 63(1)(e) was also overlooked by the Supreme Court in its heavy criticism of the view that it is the Parliamentary seat that must fall vacant if a Member of Parliament is appointed to another public office. The Court suggested that it was the second appointment that would be null and void. But the Supreme Court cannot be queried for censuring the trial court for the decision on a matter not pleaded and therefore not properly argued before it. The Supreme Court's interpretation of "public office" is also prefer-

---

1. Banda CJ delivered the judgement of the Court. He sat with Mtegha, and Kalaile, JJA.

able. It is consistent with the approach and principles the Court has been espousing for the interpretation of the troublesome Malawi constitution. It is also consistent with what the framers of the constitution may have intended. Political parties did not seriously contest the appointment of members of Cabinet from members of the National Assembly when key features of the new constitutional order were under discussion between 1993 and 1994. It was disingenuous for a counsel for the MCP to attempt to pre-empt the appeal, so that a questionable High Court decision should remain the authority on the matter. This may have reflected poorly on the case and concerns of his client.

Reconstruction of the Press Trust

A fitting case on which to conclude this discussion is the Press Trust Reconstruction case.[1] The Press Trust was created, and the deed registered under the Trustees Incorporation Act,[2] in February/March 1982. Banda, "freely and voluntarily and in consideration of his love and affection for and dedication to the Malawi Nation and in furtherance of his desire to encourage, assist, promote and advance the well-being and welfare of the Malawi Nation", granted and conveyed to the trustees, all his shareholding in Press Holdings Limited.[3] The initial trustees notably included Banda himself, the person holding office as Minister of Finance, as ex officio, the then Secretary to the President and Cabinet, and a senior figure in the MCP. Banda held 99 per cent of the shareholding in press Holdings Ltd. A senior member of the MCP always held the remaining share as a nominee. Press Holdings Ltd was the parent company for numerous Press subsidiaries, operating or trading in almost all the important sectors of the Malawi economy. Through overt Government support and patronage, the Press Group had grown to dominate the Malawi economy from humble origins as a company set up to print newspapers for the MCP.

On 6 November, 1995, the Minister of Finance circulated to members of Parliament the Press Trust Reconstruction Bill. Its main thrust was to restructure the mechanism for the management of the Trust, ostensibly to maximise the realisation of the objects of the Trust for the benefit for the entire Malawi nation. It was also not a secret that the MCP was the only political party in the transformed political landscape deriving financial support from the Trust. Strict regulation of disbursements from the Trust, in accordance with the objectives, would conceivably have reduced the financial viability of the main opposition party. On 7 November, 1995, the Minister moved a motion in the National Assembly to dispense with Standing Order 114(1), which required publication of Bills in the Government Gazette, and passage of a period of not less than 21 days between the first publication and the first reading in the National Assembly. Standing Order 114(4) permitted a Minister to move such a motion if "in his opinion" a Bill was "so urgent or of such nature" as not to permit compliance with the publication requirements. MCP members of Parliament, not unexpectedly, sternly opposed this development. They walked out the Chamber in protest when the motion was debated and carried. After a tea break, all but one of the MCP members stayed away. The Bill was read and processed on the same day, and subsequently received presidential assent as the Press Trust Re-

---

1. *The Malawi Congress Party, L.J. Chimango, MP and H.G. Ntaba, MP v The Attorney General and The Speaker of the National Assembly*, High Court, Civil Cause No. 2074 of 1995.
2. Cap. 5:03 of the Laws of Malawi.
3. Clauses III and XI (4) of the Press Trust Deed.

construction Act, 1995.[1] The lone MCP member attempted to draw the Speaker' attention to the absence of a quorum in the Chamber, but the Speaker allowed the proceedings to continue.

The MCP and two of its senior members with seats in the National Assembly resorted to the High Court. The main constitutional questions were whether section 96(2) of the constitution was violated, and whether the Assembly was quorate in terms of sections 50(1) and (2) of the constitution and Standing Orders 26 and 27. Section 96(2) of the constitution states that the Cabinet in the performance of its duties and functions "shall make legislative proposals available in time in order to permit sufficient canvassing of expert and public opinion". Section 50(1) states that the quorum of the National Assembly "shall be formed by the presence at the beginning of any sitting of at least two thirds of the members entitled to vote", excluding the Speaker. Section 50(2) provides that the Speaker "shall adjourn the Chamber" if it is brought to his attention and he ascertains that there are less than the number of members prescribed in Standing Orders for continuing with the business of the Chamber. Standing Order 26 stated that a quorum of the Assembly "shall consist of two-thirds of all the members of the Assembly besides the person presiding". Standing Order 27 provided for the adjournment of the Chamber "if at any time the business of the Assembly had commenced, or when the Assembly is in Committee and a vote is required to be taken", the attention of the speaker is called to the absence of a quorum. The other constitutional issue raised by the case was whether the Act effected arbitrary deprivation or expropriation of property contrary to sections 28(2) and 44(4) of the constitution. This was linked to possible infringement of rights to non-discrimination and equal treatment under the law in section 20 of the constitution.

In a lengthy, meandering judgement, punctuated by copious references to and citations from authorities from different jurisdictions, Mwaungulu J. found for the plaintiffs on all the constitutional issues. He found that the Minister of Finance did not comply with section 96(2), and this rendered the Press Trust Reconstruction Act invalid and unconstitutional. He also found that the Assembly was not quorate. Although section 50(1) suggested that a quorum for the Chamber must be determined at the commencement of the sitting, he interpreted section 50(2) and the standing orders as requiring the presence of two thirds of the members at all times for legitimate business to be transacted. The Speaker, furthermore, violated the constitution and the Standing Orders by failing to adjourn the House when the absence of the required number of members was drawn to his attention. The fact that the Chamber was rendered inquorate by a deliberate act of the plaintiffs was a political, not constitutional issue. With a touch of political innocence tinged with naivety on the role of the Judiciary in these matters, the Judge said:

> It might really be painful when the government, like in this case, is in the minority in the House that the majority will hold Parliament in a ransom. It is equally sad for the country to say that the laws of the land represent the will of the nation when really an insignificant number of the nation's representatives have passed the legislation. That situation, however, is a political stalement (sic) which is not solved legally. It is solved by politicians, not the law. The courts cannot prescribe to the voter to vote in such a way that the Government has a majority. Statesmanship should leave politicians to enter into coalitions to solve political stalements (sic). The law cannot be that the number, however small, of the governing party should form the quorum. This is implicit in the submission that government will be held in ransom. The duty of the court is not to create a constitution. The duty of the court is to interpret it. On the constitution as it is now the quorum for the National Assembly shall be two-thirds at the beginning and two-thirds during

---

1. Act No 16 of 1995.

proceedings. Any other view requires changing the constitution. Courts cannot do that. Parliamentarians can with requisite majority.[1]

Mwaungulu J. also held that the Press Trust Reconstruction effected an arbitrary deprivation of property contrary to section 28 of the constitution, but probably not expropriation in terms of section 44(4). In the less convincing parts of the judgement, he found that there was arbitrary deprivation partly because stakeholders like Banda and the MCP were not consulted or given an opportunity to be heard in the framing of the legislation, and partly because individual property of one person or institution was targeted. This was also discrimination contrary to the constitutional rights of the deprived person. He also found that the government had no right at common law or under statute law to interfere with private property arranged under a charitable trust.

The Supreme Court disagreed with and reversed Mwaungulu's judgement on all the main legal issues.[2] On section 96(2) of the constitution, the Court observed that it was addressed to Cabinet, not the Legislature. An Act passed by the Legislature following relevant Parliamentary procedures should not be declared invalid on account of Cabinet's failure to consult on the proposals and to seek public or expert opinion. This would not be compatible with the separate status, functions and powers of the Legislature and the Executive underlined by the constitution.

On the quorum for the National Assembly, the Supreme Court held that section 50(1) clearly required the presence of two thirds of the members at the commencement of each sitting. The Assembly was quorate at the commencement of the sitting at which the Act was passed. If Standing Order 26 required the presence of two thirds of the members at all times, it was inconsistent with the constitution and invalid to the extent of that inconsistency. The Court acknowledged that the Speaker failed to adjourn the Assembly as required by section 50(2) of the constitution and Standing Order 27. But it suggested that the Speaker's attention was called prematurely. It should have been called when a vote was required. The Court suggested that failure to comply with Standing Order 27 was also a matter of Parliamentary procedure, which courts should not regulate unless rights protected by the constitution are adversely affected. The Court surprisingly held that "by acting in breach of SO 27, the Speaker of the House did not infringe on any constitutional right which is justiciable before the Courts. The remedy for such breach can only be sought and obtained from the National Assembly itself."[3]

Possibly for the future guidance of the more exuberant judges in the High Court, the Supreme Court also held that rules laid by the constitution in respect of the Legislature fall into three broad categories. First, there are rules that go to the capacity of the Legislature to act. If the National Assembly were to act in breach of a capacity rule, it would not be acting *qua* the National Assembly, and such acts would *ipso facto* be invalid. Section 50(1) of the constitution provided an example of such a rule in respect of a quorum at the commencement of a sitting. Other rules regulating the

---

1. Pages 33–34 of the typed transcript of the judgement.
2. *Attorney general v Malawi Congress Party, L.J. Chimango, and H.G. Ntaba*, MSCA, Civil Appeal No. 22 of 1996, before Unyolo, Mtegha and Kalaile, JJA. Unlike Mwaungulu, J in the High Court, all these are senior judicial figures with first hand, personal experiences of the treatment of the legal profession during Banda's era. Mtegha, JA, who delivered the judgement of the Court, served as Clerk of Parliament before his elevation to the Bench. Unyolo, JA was for some time senior magistrate and the only professional sitting with lay judges in the Traditional Court that handled some of the infamous political trials of the Banda era. Kalaile JA was Solicitor General before his redeployment to the Public Service Commission. He was appointed to chair the Electoral Commission in 1999, after the abrupt resignation of the much-criticised chairperson, Hanjahanja J, on grounds of ill health!
3. Page 24 of the typed transcript of the judgement.

National Assembly, secondly, are rules of procedure only. Breach of these rules does not deprive the National Assembly of its identity and capacity to act. Examples of procedural rules in this category include section 50(2) and section 96(2). The third category comprises rules that limit the content and substance of the laws that the National Assembly may make, such as Chapter IV on Human Rights. Laws infringing human rights will to that extent be invalid. This classification meant that even if section 50(2) of the constitution had been violated, the result would not be to render the Press Trust Reconstruction Act invalid.

The Supreme Court also noted that the High Court was mistaken its categorisation of the Press Trust as a private and a charitable trust. It was not a charitable trust. The objects it espoused were not "wholly and exclusively" charitable as required for a charitable trust at common law. It was not a private trust either. It was a public trust, for public objects that were partly but not exclusively charitable. Charitable trusts at common law are exempt from the operation of the rule against perpetuities. Public Trusts are not. Without reference to the relevant law, Mtegha, J.A. claimed that this rule was abolished by statute in Malawi.[1] The Press Trust was therefore a valid public trust. As a public trust, its reconstruction was a legitimate concern of the government of the day, representing the Malawi nation as beneficiaries.

The Supreme Court disagreed that the Act effected arbitrary deprivation of property. It was not impressed by the argument that stakeholders had no opportunity to comment on the Bill, in so far as it applied to the plaintiffs who deliberately walked out of the Chamber. The Supreme Court held that "to act arbitrarily is to act without reasonable cause". There was reasonable cause for the Act. Its purposes and effects were "solely to serve and protect the interests of the people of Malawi",[2] and to promote their welfare and development. These were reasonable objectives that also met the requirements in sections 12(1), 13 and 14 of the constitution. Since the Act served the purposes of a public utility, the Court also felt that if it effected expropriation of property, this would have been in accordance with the derogations in section 44 of the constitution. The right to property in the constitution is "derogable". The regulation through the Act of "such an important economic giant" as the Press Group was in the assessment of the Court reasonable and necessary in an open democratic society. The importance of the Press Trust to the Malawi economy and its unique character were also such that it was not discriminatory for the Act to deal with it alone, more so as the Act did not alter the original nature of the Trust.

The Court further held that trustees affected by the reconstruction of the management of the trust did not have the type of property rights protected under section 28 or 44 of the constitution. Related to this was *locus standi* of the plaintiffs, an issue entirely overlooked by the High Court. The Supreme Court held that the MCP, as the opposition party in the National Assembly, and the other two respondents as elected members of the Assembly, had the standing to litigate on issues related to the passage of the Act in the Chamber. But they had no standing or sufficient interest on the issues related to deprivation or expropriation of property. Banda, as the original trustee, presumably would have had the standing on this issue, and the outcome of the case would have been slightly different had he been a party.

1. Page 30 of the transcript. This must be an error. Many lawyers in Malawi do not know of such a statute.
2. Pages 34–35 of the transcript.

The Doctrine of Necessity

The judgement of the Supreme Court in the Press Trust case was handed down when opposition parties were boycotting the National Assembly for another reason. When the AFORD terminated its coalition with the UDF government, four of its members in the Assembly chose to remain in Cabinet. The AFORD, now in coalition with the MCP, accused the ruling party of attempting to increase its voting power in Chamber by undemocratic means. After the repeal of section 64 of the constitution in 1995, their constituencies could not recall the four Ministers. Section 65 on "crossing the floor" was also not applicable because the Ministers had not "voluntarily ceased" to be members of the AFORD. The opposition parties attempted to compel President Muluzi to sack them by boycotting the Assembly.[1]

The Supreme Court in the Press Trust case reflected on the application of the constitutional law doctrine of necessity to both boycotts. The Court noted the original application of the doctrine to legitimise acts or measures taken by insurrectionary governments in effective control of State, as long as they are necessary and reasonably required for the normal State operations, do not impair the rights of citizens, and do not run contrary to the policy of a lawful ruler. From the authorities and jurisprudence canvassed, the Supreme Court held that the doctrine can and has been used to uphold laws enacted by a lawful government in contravention of express constitutional provisions, in extraordinary circumstances rendering compliance with constitutional procedures impossible.[2] The Court held that it was not necessary to apply the doctrine to the Press Trust Reconstruction Act. It passed muster under the Malawi constitution. But the Court warned that it could invoke the doctrine to legitimise any other piece of legislation passed while the opposition parties maintained their boycott of the Assembly. In stark contrast to the essence of what Mwaungulu, J. said in the High Court, Mtegha, J.A. observed:

> In our view, an imperative and inevitable necessity or exceptional circumstance now exists in Malawi. It is clear to us that Parliament will not be able to pass and approve the March Budget, with the result that no public funds will be available to support essential services, such as the Armed Forces, the Police Force, Health Services just to mention a few. In addition there is no other remedy to redress the situation since the next General Elections are due to be held in 1999. Section 67 prescribes a fixed term of life for the National assembly for five years.
>
> We also believe that the decision which we have arrived at is proportionate to the situation that has arisen and is of a temporary character, limited to the duration of these exceptional circumstances; in other words, until the Opposition Parties call off their boycott of the National Assembly.[3]

The advanced invocation of the doctrine of necessity ambushed opposition politicians, and provided the clearest indication that the Supreme Court would not permit a constitutional coup. It would not allow the opposition to subvert a government it probably prefered, under the guise of enforcing the constitution. Of all the cases re-

---

1. The second boycott of Parliament was the subject of litigation and was narrated by the High Court in *Chakuamba v Ching'oma*, Miscellaneous Civil Cause No 99 of 1996. Ching'oma claimed that he was deprived of his right to be represented in Parliament by his Member of Parliament, Chakuamba, who was leading the boycott. He sought an order to compel his Member of Parliament to attend the current sitting of Parliament without delay. The High Court vacated the order initially granted to Ching'oma on the ground that his constitutional rights had not been infringed, and he had no justifiable claim. The Court opined that to compel Chakuamba to attend Parliament might indeed infringe rights to conscience, belief and choice secured by section 33 of the constitution.
2. The Court referred to and relied mostly on the following commonwealth authorities: *Special Reference No. 1 of 1955*, (Pakistan), P.L.R. 1956 W.P. 598; *Attorney General of the Republic v Mustafa Ibrahim* (1964) Cyprus Law Reports 195; *Madzimambuto v Laderner-Burke*, (Southern Rhodesia), 1969 A.C. 645 (Privy Council); and *Re Manitoba Language Rights*, (Canada), (1985) S.C.R., 758–767.
3. Page 49 of the transcript of the judgement.

viewed in this study, this is the one that yields some indication of the political preferences of the higher Judiciary. This is not to suggest that the Supreme Court fabricated the law or contorted the constitution in a severe manner. This case fits the pattern emerging from all the other cases considered in the chapter. The Supreme Court, on balance, tendered a technically sound judgement, justified partly by the hapless language of the constitution, and partly by perceived lack of merit in the case for the opposition.

The Supreme Court can be legally vindicated for the sensitive, careful assessment of conditions for the application of the doctrine of necessity; on its reading of section 96(2) of the constitution; on the *locus standi* of the plaintiffs, and on the nature of the Trust at common law. Although it did not take full and proper cognisance of government motives, its conclusions on arbitrary deprivation or expropriation of property and on non-discrimination or equal treatment under the law are defensible. So too is the interpretation of section 50(1) and Standing Order 26. The Court was palpably wrong on the rule against perpetuities. Its justification for the Speaker's violation of section 50(2) and Standing Order 27 is not convincing. The suggestion that Parliamentary procedures should not generally be subject to scrutiny in the courts is contrary to the letter and spirit of the constitution. It smacks of unyielding fondness for the doctrine of Parliamentary sovereignty, assimilated by many on the bench during their law school days.

Conclusion

History may repeat itself in contemporary Malawian politics. Not so long after a political transformation to which the legal profession contributed immensely, the body politic is disenchanted with the mediating role of the Judiciary in political disputes. Allegations of bias, manipulation or contortion of the law spew from actors on both sides of the political divide, and there are echoes from the ruling UDF party of Banda's vicious tirades against the Judiciary. The stereotype—untested, of course—is that the older, more experienced judges, now sitting as Justices of Appeal in the Supreme Court of Appeal, are inclined to manipulate the law in favour of a government with which they sympathise, and which some of them may have helped to install even, more so in disputes involving the party that so tormented them in the dark days of one-party dictatorship. Some of the younger Puisne Judges, now sitting in the High Court, on the other hand, would have had no unpleasant experiences under Banda's rule. They are likely to be anti-establishment and more robust, exuberant even, in their assertion of the supremacy of the constitution over acts of the Executive or the National Assembly. In the perception of politicians in the ruling party, they are likely to favour the opposition. What does the record suggest when assessed from a technical, legal perspective?

A straightforward count of the ultimate winners or losers in the cases referred to the Judiciary for mediation after the 1994 and 1999 Parliamentary and presidential Elections does provide some corroboration of the perception that judges, like all other Malawians, have their political preferences, and would not be disinclined to rule in favour of those preferences. But the evidence falls far short of supporting allegations or accusations of bias, manipulation or fabrication of the law to suit political preferences. All the major cases reviewed in this chapter involved construction of haplessly or ineptly crafted constitutional provisions, capable of yielding genuinely differing legal interpretations and conclusions. Some of the cases also involved issues that probably required a political as opposed to a legal solution, and involved litigants who were not always meritorious, keen to exploit legal ambiguities for political ends. The overall conclusion of this study is that the Supreme Court, in particular, has been adept at finding acceptable legal solutions to some of these disputes. Probably due to the manner in which most of the judges were schooled in law, and partly due to the foibles of the constitution, decisions have tended to turn on narrow technical issues, and to avoid philosophising about the new political and constitutional order. The decisions have generally been sound in law, even if technically wrong or disagreeable in parts. It may be more than a happy coincidence that a preferred result was arrived at in each case analysed, but the cases analysed here do not yield sufficient evidence with which to justify a return to the dark days of political denunciation, vilification or persecution of the Judiciary or sections of it.

4. Hate Speech in the New Malawi

Edrinnie Kayambazinthu and Fulata Moyo

Introduction

From the pluralism of periodic electoral contests to respect for human rights, "democracy" is a multifaceted concept that has come to mean different things in Africa. Despite a number of authoritarian African countries undergoing a transition from one-party rule to multipartyism, it has become clear that "the current struggles and transitions to democracy have been dazzling and messy, their results contradictory and unpredictable, yielding both successes and defeats, concessions to the future and compromises with the past, heroism and tragedy, hope and pessimism" (Zeleza, 1997: 11). The euphoria that greeted the transition period is being qualified by the new leaders' desire to go against the fundamentals of democracy they fought for by clinging to power using various strategies, some of which may lead to changing the new democratic constitutions.

This chapter examines the phenomenon of hate speech in Malawi's "new political dispensation" as a basis for discussing the conflicting realities between the rhetoric of democracy and actual practices; and how far Malawi has consolidated its democracy. The period under review extends from the referendum in 1993 to the aftermath of the second democratic elections in 1999, analysing samples of hate speeches of various political players (the state president, regional and district governors) during this period, focusing mainly on the ruling United Democratic Front (UDF) during the 1999 election campaign. The chapter is divided into three sections. Section One reviews literature on the ongoing debate on hate speech and how to curtail it, language use and the culture of violence. Section Two provides a contextual background to Malawi's culture of intolerance, and Section Three presents data on hate speech and the linguistic strategies used. We argue that language changes manifest social changes, and that even under the so-called new political dispensation the violence emanating from hate speech has not abated in Malawi. Our main argument is that the new democratic constitution does not make sufficient provisions against hate speech and the violence and intolerance that it fosters.

Defining Hate Speech

We conceptualise "hate speech" within the definitions given by Neisser (1994) and Brekle (1989). Hate speech encompassses "all communications (whether verbal, written, symbolic) that insult a racial, ethnic and political group, whether by suggesting that they are inferior in some respect or by indicating that they are despised or not welcome for any other reasons" (Neisser, 1994:337). This definition includes not only a virulent personal epithet hurled at a particular individual in a threatening manner, but also a political speech or tract addressed to the general public advocating new policies or a particular electoral result. In relation to this, "political violence" refers to actions carried out not only between rulers but also between their individual supporters, with the intention of injuring the other party by means of physical violence or psychological pressure or aggression (Brekle, 1989). War is waged on others by means of words. Proponents of particular parties or policies also seek to adversely affect the conditions of other people's lives, to obtain power over them, to rob them of human dignity or, in the extreme case, of their physical existence, using, among other means, words, statements and texts (Brekle, 1989:81). Yet, as Wodak (1989) states, the language which *constitutes* hate speech only gains power in the hands of the powerful.

Neisser (1994:338) looks at hate speech from two perspectives. The first is the ethical or intrinsic perspective, which condemns unjustified harm to others, whether or not that harm has pragmatic consequences for the life of the community. One way of understanding the harm caused by hate speech is by comparing it to that caused by other insults such as nasty comments, deprecating a person's or a group's intellect, beauty, athletic ability, technical skill, height, weight or any other characteristic that is valued in a society.

The second one is the utilisation perspective which focuses on consequences of hate speech without making any prior judgements as to the moral property of hate speech. A history of violent repression will make a racial slur into a threat of physical violence when addressed to a member of the repressed community. Apart from the fear generated by the threat of violence, racial slurs typically impose the injury of stigma and exclusion. Even when people are not literally placed in fear of physical violence by a racial invective, they will feel devalued, stigmatised, degraded, unwelcome and excluded (Neisser, 1994:339). Neisser further argues that apart from causing danger of physical assault, hate speech risks a violent reaction—revenge, self-help, or personal remedy. The destabilising societal effects of physical retaliation and the use of physical force to solve disputes are common (Neisser, 1994:341).

While this chapter's major focus is on hate speech, our viewpoint is different from Neisser's, because racial hatred is not a glaring feature in Malawi as it is in South Africa. However, his contextualisation provides a sound base for discussing hate speech in the Malawian situation from an ethnic, gender and political perspective. This chapter also grapples with the complex question posed by many scholars working on hate speech: should hate speech be banned? The question is complex because it is intricately bound with the idea of freedom of speech as a basic human right. This question however also begs another question: What limits should be imposed on freedom of expression, considering the way politicians are able to utilise the same freedom of expression to abuse other people's rights? To answer the above questions, we now contextualise hate speech within the constitutional provisions of a select number of countries, subscribing to the view that "a constitution is a statement of society's basic values—such as fairness, equality, and respect for individual dignity—and is intended to have symbolic as well as practical effect, therefore, moral judgement would seem more in order in a constitution than in a commercial code" (Neisser, 1994: 354).

Malawian Constitutional Provisions on Freedom of Expression and Hate Speech

According to Neisser, equality is generally given priority over free expression, suggesting that equality is a pre-condition to the exercise of free speech, a view plainly consistent with regulation of hate speech (Neisser, 1994:353). The Malawian constitution provides a number of rights pertaining to political participation, that is, right to freedom of association, freedom of conscience, religion, belief and thought and academic freedom; freedom of opinion and freedom of expression.

Article 32(1) provides that "every person shall have the right to freedom of association, which shall include the freedom to form associations". Article 32(2) states that "no person may be compelled to belong to an association". On freedom of conscience, article 33 says "every person has the right to freedom of conscience, religion, belief and thought, and to academic freedom". Article 34 provides that "every person has the right to freedom of opinion, including the right to hold opinions without interference to hold, receive and impart opinions". Article 35 states that every person shall have the right to freedom of expression. Further to this, article 45(1) says that:

> No derogation from rights contained in this Chapter shall be permissible save to the extent provided for by this section and no such derogation shall be made unless there has been a declaration of a state of emergency within the meaning of this section.

Section 3(a) of the same article states that "derogation shall only be permissible during a state of emergency—with respect to freedom of expression, freedom of information, freedom of movement, freedom of assembly and rights under section 19(6) (a) and section 42(2) (b)". Thus whilst there are provisions on freedom of expression, there is no provision on hate speech. This can be contrasted with the South African provisions.

South Africa, with all its history of apartheid and eventual freedom, provides an example of the effects of hate speech and provision of its resolution in the constitution. Under section 16(2), freedom of expression does not extend to hate propaganda as an expression which constitutes an incitement, particularly to racial hatred (Johannessen, 1997). This hate speech is classified into three categories: 1) propaganda for war; 2) incitement to imminent violence; and 3) advocacy of hatred that is based on race, ethnicity, gender or religion, and that constitutes incitement to cause harm. The South African constitution has a hate speech clause that a) does not give room for unreasonable or unjustified restrictions on freedom of expression; and b) targets only the kinds of racial expressions intended (Johannessen, 1997:136).

According to Johannessen (1997:142), Article 20 of The International Covenant on Civil and Political Rights (ICCPR) has influenced the drafting of Section 16(2) in South Africa. ICCPR obliges states to enact legislation which prohibits "advocacy of national, racial or religious hatred that constitutes incitement to discrimination, hostility or violence", as well as any propaganda for war. However, the adoption of Article 20 was controversial in that many countries expressed concern about its effect on freedom of expression (Johannessen, 1997: 142). However, the hate speech clause would send a "powerful message" that this type of behaviour would not be tolerated in a democratic society where equality and human dignity are fundamental (Johannessen 1997: 156).

The freedom of expression clause of The European Convention on Human Rights (ECHR) also has its own limitations attached to it. Article 10(2) provides that "the exercise of these freedoms (freedom of expression) since it carries with it duties and responsibilities, may be subject to such formalities, conditions, restrictions, or penalties as are prescribed by law and are necessary in a democratic society, in the interest of national security, territorial integrity or public safety . . . for the protection of the reputation or rights of others " (cited in Johannessen, 1997:156).

The Canadian experience exemplifies that it is possible for a country with a constitutional order similar to that in South Africa to limit racially offensive speech by a considered use of the general limitation clause. The Indian example, on the other hand, shows that a balance has been attempted between freedom of speech and the containment of its abuse by legally acceptable means. This was accomplished by including in the chapter on Fundamental Rights (India's bill of rights) a clause (article 19(1) (a)) which stated simply that "all citizens shall have the freedom of speech and expression". This right was then qualified by a subsequent clause which provides that "nothing in sub-clause (a) above shall prevent the state from making any law in so far as such law imposes reasonable restrictions on the exercise of the right conferred to in the sub-clause in the interest of *inter alia* the security of the State, public order, defamation or incitement to an offence" (cited in Johannessen, 1997:148).

> The linkage between hate speech and harm in the constitution of South Africa is the recognition that racial, ethnic and other forms of polarisation which characterise South African society are enough to make the causal relationship between hate speech and resulting harm more than a speculative prospect. (Kanyongolo, 1999: 127)

In this context, speech does not exist in a "free market of ideas", because the history of racial and ethno-regional polarisation has distorted that market by weighting the bargaining power in favour of individuals who have particular racial and ethno-regional identities. To preserve the "free market" in those circumstances entrenches the pre-existing inequalities. Kanyongolo further argues that the provision on freedom of association is loose, in that "the right has no limitations and thus, individuals hold and exercise it regardless of their respective communal identities" (1999:127). Consequently, the relevant constitutional provision simply guarantees that every person has the right to freedom of association without the duties and responsibilities.

Although the Malawian constitution guarantees freedom of expression, respect for legal and ethical responsibilities is flouted. Ethical issues centre on value judgements concerning the degree of rightness and wrongness, goodness and badness in human conduct. Societal expectations of politicians' ethical and moral standards hinge on similar parameters. That is, public speakers are responsible to their listeners for what they say in terms of truth, facts and accuracy of information given. It therefore becomes unethical to utter lies or statements which cannot be substantiated. Legal responsibilities include refraining from any communication that may be defined to present a danger such as inciting people to riot. Included in legal responsibilities is also refraining from using obscene language and language that defames the character of another person by making statements that convey an unjust, unfavourable impression without solid evidence (Verderber, 1989). Consequently, the lack of limitations on these issues in the Malawian constitution is worrisome, given Malawi's history of ethnic and political polarisation. To understand the importance of limitations to the freedoms enshrined in the Malawi constitution, one needs to understand the history of Malawi's ethnic and regional tensions and the current political dynamics.

Contextual Background to Malawi's Culture of Intolerance

Malawi is divided into three regions: Northern, Central and Southern Regions. The regional divisions have also given rise to political polarisation and ethnic divisions that were ambivalently suppressed and promoted by Kamuzu Banda (Vail and White, 1989; Chirwa, 1998a) but that came to the fore during the 1994 and 1999 general elections when parties were voted for on ethnic and regional lines. A number of publications have stressed the closed society that Malawi was under Banda. Scholars have also looked at Banda's period with little favour, if not disdain, in human rights terms. One only needs to read Jack Mapanje's collection of poetry, entitled *Of Chameleons and Gods* (1981), written at the height of Banda's rule, and other banned publications that came out during this period to understand the excessive abuse of power and suppression of free speech (see also Mapanje's Afterword in this volume).

In order to protest but also to protect themselves from unwarranted arrests, poets such as Mapanje, Steve Chimombo and others used poetry as a medium of expression and communication (Chimombo, 1999). Poems and plays could be brief and safely obscure. The use of allusion within the Malawian context of oral literature and its caricatures became a way of driving the message home (van Alstyne, 1993). Whilst some writers such as Mapanje were bold, others were cryptic, such as Chimombo in his play *Wachiona Ndani* (see Moto, 2000). Mapanje's work demonstrated "the ambiguities of aesthetic in the jungle of post-independence African politics" (Vail and White, 1991: 280). Cryptic or bold, the literary works were critical of the denial of human rights in Malawi, the exploitation of the poor masses, and the denial of constructive criticism of the head of state. For example, Mapanje contrasted the oral praise poems which traditionally told chiefs what their subjects thought of them with the new praise poems during Banda's era, "which lack(ed) an element of constructive criticism of either the leadership or the society. The criticism was necessary in the original song because it was one way of helping the chief or traditional leader to improve. It was also a way of knowing what the people think about the leadership" (Mapanje, quoted in Vail and White, 1991:286).

The fact that this was a dark period in the history of Malawi is evidenced by a proliferation of newspapers, pamphlets and works of fiction shortly before and after Banda lost power (Chimombo and Chimombo, 1996; Phiri and Ross, 1998). The underlying themes in all these publications were the lack of freedom of expression and the press, nepotism, ethnic intolerance, brutality and other general human rights abuses. Kamwendo (1999a and 2000) has discussed the inflammatory language used by the MCP-led government that incited violence and the lessons to be learnt from such actions in order for Malawi to sustain the young democracy.

During both colonial and postcolonial periods, tribalism and regionalism have been central to the history of Malawi. Whereas the northern part of Malawi is linguistically predominantly Tumbuka, it is one of the most diverse ethnically with about eight ethnic identities, all able to draw upon different languages. Chitumbuka became the northern regional language and a political rallying point for people with diverse ethnicities during the colonial period (Vail and White, 1989; see also Kamwendo's chapter in this volume). The treatment of the North as one block has had its political ramifications as regards employment, schooling and political party leanings as people pigeonhole each other by the areas they come from. That is, the Alliance for Democracy (AFORD) Party is seen as a Northerners' party, the Malawi Congress Party (MCP) a Central Region party, while the United Democratic Front (UDF) is a Southerners' party. Central Region is linguistically more homogeneous than the other regions, with Chichewa (Chinyanja) commanding overwhelming importance. In the Southern Region, three ethnic identities—Chewa (Nyanja), Yao and Lomwe—have interacted for a long time and Chinyanja is the *lingua franca*. The ethnic and political dynamics of these divisions has been well expounded by Vail and White (1989), who have provided a historical perspective on political polarisation along ethnic and regional lines. This also became very clear during the 1994 general elections when people voted along regional lines rather than on national issues. The extent to which the undeniable regionalism in Malawian politics builds on distinct ethnic identities is, however, a moot point (see Kaspin, 1995; Englund, 1996a). More research is needed to show how politicians' hate speeches fuel intolerance and manipulate ethnic and regional differences for leaders' selfish gains.

The fact that there has been tribalism in the political history of Malawi is apparent in Banda's project of "ethnic cleansing" of the civil service in the late 1980s. Whilst he preached unity, he also divided the nation through hate speeches. He sent all teachers from the North to teach in their region of origin in 1989. The mass removal of top Tumbuka civil servants from the National Statistical Office, government ministries and parastatals in an attempt to cleanse the system of nepotism created further tribalism. During the Cabinet Crisis of 1964 most of the so-called rebels were either Northerners or Southerners of Yao origin. Their relatives lost their jobs and some were severely beaten and detained without trial.

Both religion and politics have played a crucial role in the creation of regionalism and tribalism. The Church of Central Africa, Presbyterian (CCAP) has upheld this regionalism as its administrative boundaries echo the political boundaries. A clergyman from Livingstonia Synod, which is in Northern Malawi, cannot be automatically accepted as a minister in Nkhoma Synod (Central Region) or Blantyre Synod (Southern Region). These differences are, however, mitigated by the provision of a central unifying administrative body, the General Synod.

The above observations necessitate a hate speech clause in the constitution if Malawi wants to consolidate democracy and distance itself from the past. This is made all the more urgent by the fact that some of the above practices can also be seen under the so-called new political dispensation. When Muluzi took over in 1994, Malawians were under the euphoria of *zinthu zasintha* (things have changed). Theoretically, the "new" Malawi ensured that all the necessary institutions of democracy were in place. In contrast to Banda's era, Malawians were promised a culture of tolerance, preservation of human dignity and respect for the rule of law. However, the politics of tolerance has been difficult to practise, the war of words culminating in violent acts between rival parties when politicians have conducted their rallies. It has been noted by Kamwendo (1999a and 2000) that the thirty years of dictatorship in Malawi were characterised by hate language against those who opposed the MCP. Our contention is that many in the "new" Malawi have experienced both physical and psychological violence perpetrated by both the MCP and UDF camps. We present evidence that the culture of intolerance in Malawi is growing and that no real transformation has taken place to uproot this evil. There has been violence in the form of physical fights between rival parties, not to mention the burning of each other's vehicles or houses because of intolerance and the desire for power. Hate speech has played a crucial role in inciting this violence.

Barely five years after the referendum for multiparty democracy, the Censorship Board of Malawi observed the escalating hatred and violence emanating from verbal abuse and hate speeches. The Board intervened with a press release circulated to all media houses. *The Weekly News* of 9–12 July, 1999, reported that

> the Censorship Board says it has noted with concern the proliferation of indecent, obscene, offensive and harmful publications, music, songs, language and other public performances within the Malawian society. ... Chief Censoring Officer, Geofrey Kanyinji says as custodians of public morality, the Board wishes to condemn such acts in the strongest terms and appeals to everyone to refrain from promoting obscenity, indecency, hatred and violence among morally upright and peace-loving Malawians.
>
> The Censorship Board also appeals particularly to all entertainers, artists, cartoonists, drama groups, songwriters and singers, bands, electronic, print media and indeed all Malawians to

promote a culture of peace, tolerance, love, reconciliation and forgiveness. Hate songs, violent songs, hate speeches, hate talk, hate articles in papers, hate interviews on radio or television do not promote peace and love and therefore should not be condoned or promoted by any peace-loving Malawian, adds the release.

Malawi as a God-fearing nation should not be subjected deliberately by entertainers, artists, broadcasters, print media and song writers to songs, interviews, articles or images which promote hate, tribalism, ridicule, violence, vengeance and sadism, it adds.

At this sensitive time of our beloved mother Malawi, we urge artists to sing songs of love and reconciliation, peace and forgiveness, drama groups to depict plays whose heroes are people engaged in peace and reconciliation, reporters and media to condemn violence and interview real heroes who have contributed to making peace, or those with constructive views on how Malawi can forge ahead in peace and reconciliation, development and prosperity, eradicate disease, ignorance and poverty.

Do not glorify troublemakers, violence or foul mouthed speakers. Ignore such people or condemn their actions. Unbalanced interviews also promote hatred, the Chief Censoring Officer says.

He also advises entertainers, artists, drama groups, songwriters and singers, print and electronic media, to promote peace, tolerance, love, reconciliation and forgiveness, and to condemn the evils of hate, tribalism, regionalism and vengeance. Let's build Malawi on a culture of peace, love, tolerance and forgiveness the release says.

Like the Censorship Board, Chimombo (1999:215) also noted the disturbing rise in hate speech leading to violence—evidence that speech can, and often does, provoke action. Political hate speeches are intended to bring down the opponents and weaken it. The Censorship Board, while failing to specify politicians as central conduits of hate speech, pointed both to Malawians' abuse of freedom of expression and to their lack of public responsibility.

The democratic era has also brought to the surface a new significance of regionalism in Malawi. There is every reason to fear that this regionalism will perpetuate the tribalism created in Banda's Malawi, building on ethnicity as "an ideology according to which a given people are able to assert their identity, interest and loyalty on the basis of kinship, a common language, a shared history and world view usually in contradiction to other similarly defined groups" (Chirwa, 1998a:53). Regionalism, on the other hand, refers to the sentiment of loyalty a given people have toward the administrative sub-territory from which they come, and the discriminatory behaviour towards those coming from other parts of the country to which it usually gives rise (Chirwa, 1998a:53–54). Neither ethnicity nor regionalism develops in a vacuum. They flourish within specific socio-economic and political conditions, nourished by the practices adopted by a government. In 2000, for example, a female civil servant was recommended to the post of Chief Executive of Zomba District Assembly after a successful interview. She was officially offered the job. However, because she came from the Central Region, it is alleged that a cabinet minister and political adviser to the state president who comes from Zomba blocked her appointment and replaced her with a man hailing from Zomba, her junior who had failed the interviews. President Muluzi has also on a number of occasions shown favouritism by stating publicly that only those areas that vote for his UDF candidate will see development. The democratic momentum of the referendum period is not sustained in Malawi, and regionalism and ethnicity are currently the focus of renewed political importance.

Evidence of Hate Speech in Political Discourse

In analysing the linguistic means to spread hatred in the interest of power, speech acts by the authorities in power (statement, question, command, promise, threat, etc.) are important, because they enforce their interests. Of importance to this chapter is the intention of an utterance. Some speech acts are associated with special supporting conventions that enforce one's power and serve one's interests such as insult and slander, condemnation, and so forth (Brekle, 1989). The use of words—put together into appropriate texts and propagated through the media—is a powerful means of exerting influence in order to advance political causes. It is generally recognised that the feelings evoked, be they feelings of fear or timidity, the will to win or the impulse to destroy, depend on the words used. And these feelings are of course evoked by particular groups in positions of power with particular interests.

Malawi is not unique in the use of violent language and propaganda. According to Brekle (1989), the methods and ingredients of the war-time British propaganda against Germany can be reduced to eight basic features: stereotypes, negative name calling, selection and suppression of facts often with palliative terms, reports of cruelty, slogans, one-sided reporting, unmistakably negative characterisation of the enemy and the so-called bandwagon effect. We use these basic features as a framework for analysing some of the elements noted in Malawian politicians' speeches.

Examples of abusive language during the MCP and UDF eras are listed in Table 3.[1] Their meanings should be understood within the Malawian social context where political songs, phrases, metaphors and imageries contain allusions that only those privy to their meaning can unravel (van Alstyne, 1993: 18). The allusions are meant to relay insulting and demeaning messages to their political rivals.

Politicians use a number of metaphors and a variety of other forms of indirect meaning, including innuendo and circumlocution, as a means of cushioning the dangers inherent in political discourse and helping politicians protect their jobs, parties and governments (Obeng, 1997). It is important to understand the role of allusion and the skill of the general public in interpreting the non-literal meanings of political communication. Banda referred to his opponents as meat for crocodiles, President Muluzi has constantly referred to the MCP as *chipani chankhanza* (brutal party), a party of doom, or a dying party, decadent and dilapidated. In other words, the MCP will never change, and Malawians should never forget what this party stood for in the past thirty years or so. The imagery of perpetual terror, brutality and destruction, lies and despotism is sustained by UDF functionaries who use words with such negative connotations. The following quotes taken from a speech by Chakakala Chaziya, then Central Region UDF Governor, illustrate these negative connotations:

> Malawi Congress Party has not changed. It is still a killing party. How can the members of this party now declare their party clean? How can they even claim that the people who made MCP a bad, cruel party have now joined the UDF? . . . Some of us who moved from MCP and joined UDF did so because we could not stand the witchcraft and the filth in the MCP. We could not stay. MCP had killed so many people. The evil people still in MCP should not come to UDF because they will defile the UDF party. (Chakakala Chaziya at Bembeke, Dedza District, 17 June, 1997)

---

1. We have used Kamwendo (1999a and 2000) as our source for the MCP era, while the information on the UDF era is based on our own research.

Table 3. Examples of Abusive and Intimidating Language Used during the MCP and UDF Eras

MALAWI CONGRESS PARTY ERA		UNITED DEMOCRATIC PARTY ERA	
Vernacular Word	English	Vernacular Word	English
Bongololo	Millipede	Openga	Mad persons
Anyani	Monkeys	Mafia	Crooks/killers
	Meat for crocodiles	Ninja	Troubleshooter
	Confusionists		Insane
Ankhweri	Baboons	Makatani oyoyoka	Threadbare curtains
Zitsiru	Fools	Chipani chankhanza	Brutal party
Agalu	Dogs	Zitolilo	Useless wind instrument
Ziboliboli	Curious or mentally retarded person		Warlords
(Sena language)			
Kukodzera	To urinate into the Bishop's mouth		Party of doom
maBishop Mkamwa			
Zigawenga	Thugs or rebels	Wina alira	Losers
Tikonza	We will kill	Wina amwa termic	Losing by committing suicide
			Enemies of democracy
			Criminals
		Kumtunda	The most powerful ruler, unsurpassable
		Owinawina	Obvious winner
		Akakowa	Referring to NDA as a powerless party

Thus the image of the MCP as a brutal party should not be forgotten, and reform within the party is not possible. On the same day, Chaziya said:

> For MCP to win the 1999 elections, it means John Twaibu Sangala should come back from the dead, Mr Matenje should rise, Mr Gadama should rise from the dead, then Congress can rule again. People who had worked for the government were being hated to the point of being killed. Police officers were killed for not carrying out their orders. They have now turned away from politics and have gone into ethnic issues. They tell people not to join the UDF party because it's a party for Yaos. ... Do not join the party because you will all be turned into Muslims. Sir, (referring to Muluzi) your UDF party is a party for everyone in Malawi because your vice-president is a Chewa from Ntchisi, a person who eats mice and is an Anglican priest. I am also a Chewa by tribe. ... UDF party is a national party, not a tribal or regional party. ... How come Dr Kamuzu Banda, as Malawi's president, spent most of his ruling time living in the South and yet nobody seemed to complain about him being regional? Banda lived in Blantyre even after his retirement. (The crowd: *ufiti!* Witchcraft!)

In this speech, the Regional Governor evoked ethnic and religious tensions that still beleaguered the "democratic" Malawi. He also referred to the MCP's brutality in the killing of the four ministers (see van Donge, 1998b), and that the MCP should not be considered for re-election. And yet his predecessor in another speech had this to say whilst responding to the numerous criticisms levelled against Muluzi by the opposition about his incompetence to lead the country:

> *Bakili ndi Pulezidenti osamasewera nayo. Alumatu ameneyu. Njoka yopusa ikaluma munthu sachira. Boma ndi Boma, osasewera nalo.* (Bakili is the President, do not fool around with him. He will bite. When a quiet snake bites, it is difficult for the person to be healed. A government is a government, do not play with it!) Kachimbwinda, UDF Central Region Governor, Kayembe Headquarters in Dowa, 30 November, 1994.

This speech was urging the president to act and in a harsh way to the point of death (lack of healing) to those who were criticising him. Kachimbwinda, in a fiery speech and using abusive language, lashed at John Tembo, an MCP strongman since Banda's era, and called him a Mafioso, while he, Kachimbwinda, was a Ninja (a person who fights evil- doers), who would deal with crooks like Tembo. The use of personal names was provocative and demeaning. Kachimbwinda's speech was unfair to a person who had no platform to answer back on the state-controlled radio. Although the language was creative in terms of evil vs. goodness, moral vs. immoral, it also provoked images of violence of the underworld (Mafia).

Selection and suppression of facts

The selection and suppression of facts entail the presentation of half-truths which might end up being no truth at all, merely aimed at marring the image of the opposition. The print media has also played a crucial role in this war of words. *The Mirror* of 17 December 1998 reported that people in the Northern Region who out of "blind emotion" felt that Chakufwa Chihana was "the Messiah" to free them from the shackles of poverty and degradation, had now realised that the man is "totally incapable of any meaningful thing and in their mass they (the people) are moving to the ruling United Democratic Front (UDF) which for the first term in government has shown its seriousness in developing the region" (see also Article 19, 2000:62). This, in the light of how people voted, cannot be substantiated (see Patel, 2000).

The report by Article 19 (2000:48) on the Malawian media during the 1999 electoral campaigns shows that the ruling UDF government embarked on spreading misinformation. When the Electoral Commission wanted to break up the electoral alliance between the AFORD and the MCP, the Voter Action Plan of the UDF reported on the non-existent Northern Region Solidarity Movement, which "vehemently rejected (sic) the dubious electoral alliance and questioned (sic) Chakufwa's mental sanity and called the readers' attention to the fact that MCP is just bent on using and exploiting Gwanda and through him the entire Northern Region" (*Weekly Time*, 10 February, 1999). Chihana is said to have pawned his party (*wapinyoletsa chipani*), a man who is power- hungry and prepared to stoop so low as to sell the AFORD and betray the Northerners who had entrusted him with the party. This misinformation questions and insults Chihana's intelligence, sanity, merit and authority and waters the seeds of regionalism and intolerance.

Two other unsubstantiated but damaging claims by the government were used to scare people and make the citizen feel that the opposition was bent on destabilising the nation and should not be trusted. For example, it was reported that women in the ruling ZANU-PF party in Zimbabwe were going to smuggle arms into Malawi to help the MCP and John Tembo seize political power under the pretext that Malawi is in danger of becoming an Islamic Nation (The *Weekly News*, 27 January, 1999). The *Weekly News* of 2–4 February 1999 stated that Tembo had sent his henchmen to see Afonso Dhlakama, the leader of the Mozambican ex-guerrilla movement RENAMO, to work out a strategy on destabilising Malawi. It would involve the deployment of the Malawi Young Pioneer cadres from their Mozambique hideout to unleash a reign of terror through armed robbery and outright terrorist attacks on government installations and civilians. The opposition was reportedly plotting to kill Muluzi. The issues gained wide coverage through the national radio and Television Malawi (TVM). The state president even commented on the coup plot without investigating the truth of the matter. When the falsity of the story was discovered, the integrity, moral and legal responsibility of the president in power and the journalist who wrote the story could well have been questioned, but no one was disciplined on the issue.

Rhetorical evocations

Political discourses become especially inflammatory when they are expressed in a language that evokes a personified threat: an enemy, deviant, criminal, or wastrel. It is through metaphor, metonymy and syntax that linguistic references evoke mythic cognitive structures in people's minds (Edelman, 1977: 13). Edelman further argues that public language takes many political forms. Exhortation to patriotism and support for the leader and his/her regime are obvious forms. Other forms include, firstly, terms classifying people (individually or in group) according to the level of their merit, competence or authority. These forms justify status levels but purport to be based on personal qualities, such as intelligence, skills, moral traits or health. Secondly, there are terms that implicitly define an in-group whose interests conflict with those of other groups, for example issues of loyalty, references to the reliability or hostile stance of individuals (Edelman, 1977:110). Such terms permeate the everyday language of the political parties. Their employment by any group, together with the provocative behaviour they encourage, also elicits their counter-use. Indeed, as argued by Edelman (1977:115), in tense times, political leaders make statements that shock thinking people; threats to deploy terrorism and kill the opposition/ruling leaders, and rhetoric exalting violence. Such language typically consists of short incomplete sentences and confounds reasons and conclusions to produce categorical statements. It also repeats idiomatic phrases and relies upon sympathetic circularity among adherents of the movement to induce support for the social structure that the politicians favour.

Sornig (1989, citing Bork, 1970: 9) states that words can, in fact, be used as instruments of power and deception, but it is never the words themselves that should be dubbed evil and poisonous. The responsibility for any damage that might be done by using certain means of expression still lies with the users, those who, not being able to alter reality, try interpretative strategies to change its reception and recognition by their interlocutors. The imagery of the opposition as enemies of democracy, deviants, criminals, warlords and good-for-nothing people is clear from the misinformation that was transmitted by politicians during the 1999 election campaign.[1]

The use of pro-UDF slogans also illustrates these general observations. UDF—*boma* (UDF—government), Bakili—*Kumtunda* (Bakili—the highest in the land), *owinawina* (obvious, perpetual winner), *opanda nkhanza* (not cruel, alluding to the difference between "kind" Muluzi and "cruel" Banda), *oyenda m'maliro* (a person who attends funerals unlike Banda who did not do so), *wachitukuko* (a propagator of development)—these are some of the most common slogans used at UDF rallies and at virtually any mass meeting where the state president is present.

One-sided reporting done by the pro-government Malawi Broadcasting Corporation (MBC) covered only the UDF campaigns. The opposition had been denied access to both MBC and TVM. None of their meetings was aired, the opposition receiving publicity only when its member of parliament crossed the floor to the UDF.

---

1. As these reflections indicate, the political discourses in Malawi are not unique to that country. Holly aptly remarks:
   > politicians are not reputed to be personifications of credibility. The image of the politician who doesn't instil confidence has a long tradition. Aristotle's tyrant seizes power by defaming the nobles and stays in power merely by playing the part of a good king. Macchiavelli's 'principle', the prototype of the modern bad politicians, has no scruples about being hypocritical. There were times when the word *politic* and its related words in European languages seemed to be synonymous with *feigning* or *dissembling* (1989: 115).
   The Chinyanja word for politics—*ndale*—also carries connotations of cunning (see also Englund, 2000: 600). As we argued in the beginning of this chapter, however, Malawi's political history makes the general features of political discourse particularly inflammatory if they are not restrained.

The campaign became a time for castigating the opposition in favour of the UDF. This allowed for plenty of misinformation about the opposition parties through the radio and TVM, while some pro-UDF newspapers were specifically set up to undermine the campaign of the opposition (see Article 19, 2000:96).

The division within the MCP was well documented as being a party "wrecked by a power struggle. . . The MCP is fighting . . . to derail the general elections and take over power by hook or by crook as the party loses support on a daily basis to the UDF, currently riding on an enviable wave of party popularity". Article 19 (2000: 96–97) states that thirteen out of 24 issues of *This Is Malawi*, a government periodical, were expressly party-political—all favouring the UDF and antagonistic to the opposition parties, especially the MCP. The titles included the unsubstantiated story of the MYP-MCP-RENAMO plan to overthrow the UDF government and the split in the MCP over the MCP-AFORD Alliance. Titles such as "The Dying MCP Resorts to Lies" outlined the work of the MCP-paid lobbyist (Martin Minis) in London. The title "Hell Hath No Fury Like a Scorned Woman" was a derisive article about John Tembo's position in the Alliance where he was the second Vice President.

Admittedly, "it was not clear how a magazine that goes out of its way to publicise the fact that Malawi is politically unstable and that a coup plot is being planned when there is no evidence provided actually benefits tourism and foreign investment or improves the country's image abroad. Such party political reporting does an injustice to the nation as a whole" (Article 19, 2000:97). That this is happening during a democratic era is intriguing. One-sided reporting creates animosity and frustration in the opposition parties. It also denies the citizens the right to hear them and make their own judgement. For example, in 2000, it was reported that Chihana said he was going to unleash a Mau Mau (guerrilla) kind of war on Malawi. Objective criticism on the issue was difficult to obtain, because the nation did not hear him in the mass media as they do with the hate speeches uttered by the ruling party.

President Muluzi on his inauguration day in 1999 stated in Chinyanja that:

> If others are not happy with this day then they really have a problem. I will not allow anybody because they have lost an election to start civil strife in this country. I have heard that some have threatened to go into the bush! Honestly, just let them try it. I will blow them up, try it and see. You will see aeroplanes without wings (missiles) come against you. We want peace in Malawi.

In early 2000, the Centre for Advice, Research and Education on Rights (CARER), a non-governmental organisation headed by Vera Chirwa, a widely respected former politician who had been imprisoned by Banda's regime, issued a press release denouncing the practice of women dancing at political rallies. Chirwa, exercising her freedom of opinion, argued that women's dancing did not respect the dignity of women and, if not checked, would lead to the creation of another dictatorship. In response, this is what the state president said:

> Since time immemorial, where I come from in Machinga, people used to dance *litiwo*. . . If a person danced very well, raising his/her leg nicely, he/she was appreciated or rewarded for it (*kufupidwa*).
>
> On the issue of dancing, for us the black people, singing is our tradition. So, I wonder when people ask, why is Bakili rewarding dancers? As for me the little that God gives me I share with the poor of Malawi. (The crowd: cheering)
>
> If you are having problems with that, that is your own problem. (*Ndi mavuto awo*, that is their own problem).
>
> In this country of Malawi, human rights, yes, very much, I am one of the champions on democracy issues, alright?
>
> For Malawi to have NGOs, there were no NGOs during the MCP era. Were there any NGOs during the Congress Party era? (The crowd: They were not there!, *kunalibe*!, cheering.)

If there are any NGOs, they are here because of Bakili Muluzi and the UDF party and democracy in Malawi.

So, do you think somebody can teach me about human rights? Who are you? No, no.

If you have joined another party, just join your party. Some people have an agenda of wanting to make women in this country stop dancing. (The crowd: We will not be discouraged, we will not be discouraged! The prisoner, go back to the prison!) After all my government is a political government. It is a UDF government.

And yet how are the women going to go to parliament? I thought they go through a party. Whether it is Ambuye Amunandife Mkumba, or Kamlepo Kalua's party, but they must belong to a party. Who are you trying to fool? Ladies and gentlemen, do not just copy Western ideas. In this country, democracy yes, human rights yes, we respect women in Malawi.

Yet if we are to restrict them so that they do not sing because of a certain individual (the crowd: It won't happen!, *sizitheka!*, cheering), who has received money and s/he wants to advertise in the newspaper, you will be finished!

Let me just say that they are saying that I should not give you money for dancing for me. Do you agree with them? I do not use government money to give you, not even a Tambala. (The crowd: Jealous!)

Everything that I give to you is my own money and not government money. I am a Godfearing person. I listen to His counsel and laws, so that the little that I have, I have to share with the poor. So, some of you, if you are the agents of some other things, that is your own problem. These women will continue to sing. (The crowd: cheering).

Singing is our part of our culture. Giving each other money in recognition of a good dancer is also our culture. These things you learn from England, that is your own affair…Do not be fooled by other people in the name of human rights. Do not bring unnecessary things in this country. After all who did s/he consult? How can somebody just think about this on her/his own? (The crowd: S/he is mad, S/he smoked marijuana, *chamba*!) (Speech delivered at the Handover of Rab's Snowwhite Win A House and Launching of Mandazi Ready Mix Flour, 26 February, 2000.)

President Muluzi's speech should be understood within the context that during the 1993–94 campaign he had denounced the dancing of women for Banda as an oppressive practice that his party would abolish if voted to power. However, when he was reminded about this campaign promise, he denounced Chirwa as someone who had political ambitions. The most disturbing features of this hate speech were the unchecked violent interjections from the UDF women at the rally who kept on castigating and deriding Chirwa as a prisoner (*mkaidi*), urging Muluzi to send her back to where she belonged (prison). Chirwa and her late husband Orton Chirwa were prisoners of conscience for 12 years under Banda's regime. Chirwa did not deserve such a violent response for expressing her views on issues activists had fought against during the Banda era. The speech contravened the freedom of expression. It is increasingly becoming the president's habit to condone the epithets for the opposition expressed by his female supporters, including *amisala* (mad people), *afiti* (witches), *odwala m'mutu amenewo* (they are psychics), and that the president should tell them so, *Bwana, auze! Auze! Auze!* (Sir, tell them!, tell them!, tell them!).

Despite calls from the Censorship Board, hate speech has continued. On 19 June, 2000, President Muluzi, addressing the people at Makanjira in Mangochi, said again in Chinyanja, *wina alira lero, ndithu wina amwa mankhwala a makhoswe* (someone is going to cry today, yes, someone is going to take rat poison to commit suicide), *tsiku lake ndi lero* (today is the day), *otsutsa boma ndi openga* (members of the opposition are mad people), *akuti Mau Mau, chiani … asiyeni adzaone ndege za nkhondo zopanda ma injeni* (they are talking about Mau Mau, what is Mau Mau, just watch them, they will see war planes without engines, if they are not careful), *siyine wosewera naye iyayi,* (they cannot play around with me), *sindili ndekha* (I am not alone, I have friends who can assist me). He went further and interfered with MCP politics by selecting a candidate for their planned convention in the name of John Tembo, because "he is the only one who makes worthwhile comments in the

MCP camp". When did John Tembo, a Mafioso, become a Ninja? When did Tembo, a reputedly cruel figure during the Banda regime, become a saint? Ironically, the president, after strongly deriding the opposition, ended his speech on a reconciliatory note urging Malawians to work together in order to develop the country. After such a tirade, the conditions of "working together" could only be unilaterally stipulated by the UDF government.

Evidence on Consequences of Hate Speech and Intolerance in Malawi's Democracy

> Someone born not a long time ago somewhere in Tsabana in his newspaper alleges that Muluzi was removed from his position as Secretary General in the MCP government because of imprisonment. Where and when was Bakili arrested? He has no record of imprisonment. ... We do not like being abusive yet we are told that Civil Liberties will protect such a newspaper. Why and what for? This same newspaper has used very obscene language against Mrs Maimba (an ex-MCP MP in Dedza Distirct turned UDF). The language they have used is so strong that not even me, a member of *gule wamkulu* (a Chewa secret society), can use such language. ... These people will feel the heat up to next year—for we are still in power (Chakakala Chaziya , UDF Governor, 8 July, 1997).

This speech threatens the freedom of expression and at the same time cuts at the core of the functions of civil liberties. It is a very strong speech against the author of a newspaper article, but it also reveals the lack of limitations on freedom of expression. In terms of language and obscenity the paper had gone overboard. Yet instead of calling for registration against such obscenities, the speaker resorts to threats.

As we have already noted, hate speech flourishes in a political climate where the government is reluctant to allow opposition parties to campaign freely and fairly. For example, the *Daily Times* of June 4 1999 reports on violence that erupted between different political party supporters. The article, entitled *Bloody Violence*, states that:

> Hordes of UDF roughnecks Wednesday this week again, unleashed terror when they savagely beat anyone flying opposition party flags in their business premises along the road from Blantyre to Lilongwe during President Bakili Muluzi's whistle drive campaign in preparation for the crucial June 15 polls. The vigilant group which was travelling in a white Pajero vehicle...was sent in advance and severely beat innocent civilians at their homes and business premises wherever they found any opposition Malawi Congress Party posters and flags to ensure the president only met UDF supporters on his way.

Chimombo (1998) traces the interference in the media by the democratically elected government, despite the increasingly democratic rhetoric of the newspapers. The lack of transparency in the new Malawi was also revealed to us by the MBC's reluctance for a long time to grant us access to the recorded speeches of the president and the regional governors. Some "privileged" information was not readily accessible. Although we did eventually gain access to the archives of the MBC, it was not without an intervention from a highly-positioned individual.[1]

From a human rights point of view, the lack of transparency can be seen in the way the government handled the death of James Njoloma, Captain in the Malawi Army. He was wrongly convicted of mutiny and died mysteriously in Zomba prison.

---

1. Other sources for this chapter include the Article 19 Final Report, the oral speeches we have listened to, backed up by newspaper articles in the leading newspapers *The Nation* and *Daily Times*, and press releases by various organisations. The book *Malawi's Second Democratic Elections*, especially the article by Gregory H. Kamwendo (2000), was very helpful.

The government did not allow his relatives to attend his post-mortem nor to view the body. In 2000, there were reports of violence and intimidation in Kasungu district during the by-elections held in two constituencies. The MCP President's car was stoned and his life threatened by UDF Young Democrats in front of the Kasungu Police Station, the police merely watched. The Assistant District Education Officer in Kasungu also received and carried out orders, transferring teachers deemed to be unsympathetic to the ruling party out of the constituencies where by-elections were taking place to schools where they were no danger. Teachers were transferred at night regardless of whether accommodation was available or not, and some of them ended up sleeping in classrooms and the kitchens of fellow members of staff. This was also done regardless of the number of teachers in the schools. As long as they won the seat, the ruling party was oblivious of the disruption this caused to the quality of education of the pupils who lost their teachers (Ngwira, Kayambazinthu and Kamchedzera, 2000).

The violence that has accompanied some by-elections and political meetings has been against the rule of law and the freedom of expression. It has also contradicted what the UDF government had promised. In April 2001, for example, both MBC and TVM announced the death of a UDF sympathiser who died because of the violence which erupted at a meeting conducted by the newly-formed National Democratic Alliance (NDA) in Blantyre during a by-election. Since the formation of the NDA, a number of violent clashes have been reported. The NDA's first meeting at Ndirande was disrupted with live bullets despite the police clearance of the meeting. The mayor of the City of Blantyre, himself a UDF sympathiser, was prosecuted and convicted of ordering the shooting at the rally. The same mayor was implicated in the killing of a UDF supporter in a fracas that ensued between the supporters of the UDF and the NDA in one of the Blantyre constituencies where there was a by-election. In Zomba at Sakata where the NDA was holding its rally a UDF supporter employed to disrupt the NDA meeting was beaten by NDA supporters.

Public Affairs Committee (PAC), a human rights watch-dog, stated the following concerning violence:

> We observe with regret some problems in the cooperation among political parties, especially the ruling party and the opposition. Most of the political statements being made during rallies do not promote the spirit of peaceful campaign because political party leaders are using threats against each other. On the other hand, the incident (sic) of political violence continues to mar the face (sic) of political campaigns. A (sic) most recent example is the death of one political party supporter in the Blantyre East by-election campaign on 8 April 2001. We fear that such ruthless violence will promote divisions in society and threaten the rights of people to freely participate in politics. Our appeal to political leaders is that they should set an example to their followers by condemning violence and adopting more civil methods of campaigning. (PAC Statement on Recent Social and Political Developments, *The Nation,* 10 May, 2001)

These examples typify the predicament faced by the leaders of new democracies. How to provide for freedom of expression and association and still hold on to power amidst powerful opposition parties? During the Banda era, people were victims of exploitation by being forced to give money to him as gifts. Currently, due to abject poverty and the desire not to relinquish power, the government is manipulating people by giving them money to silence them. The same strategy is used to woo women to dance for the president.

The above discussion and many other incidents deepen the fears that the UDF can become the MCP II. It has become common to deny the public and the opposition, through both the television and radio, the right to express their opinion against the government. When the CCAP church issued its pastoral letter in 2001, criticising the government's performance on both political and socio-economic fronts, the Attorney-General strongly criticised the church as being political and not biblical at all and said that they were attacking the president personally. This criticism came out even before the letter was read in the churches. Constructive criticism is being muzzled by the lack of access to the mass media, and by destabilisation through encouraging members of parliament in the opposition to cross the floor, and also by having their public rallies disrupted. Thus their ideas and opinions are not widely heard. The argument of Chimombo and Chimombo (1996) several years ago still holds true —a culture of democracy is yet to take root in Malawi.

Conclusion

This chapter has traced the culture of violence in Malawi through political hate speeches during the postcolonial era. We have shown that violence can be traced from the Banda era and the referendum period, but that even during the new democratic era, hate speech has continued to be a political weapon. Current Malawian leaders appear to want "democracy" and at the same time cling to power at all cost, even when it requires physical and psychological violence. The period of "consolidating democracy" has been even more violent than the transition period. We have focused on hate speech as a key strategy used by politicians to perpetrate violence. Malawians are getting accustomed to an official discourse that depicts Malawian opposition leaders as untrustworthy, criminals, warlords, incompetents, and so on, while untrustworthy politicians within the ruling party are endowed with trust through such political discourse as propaganda and slogans. We insist that wrong values, beliefs and perceptions are being transmitted about issues that sometimes do not exist, whilst chronic socio-economic and political problems are trivialised in the political discourse. The politicians' responsibility and obligation of upholding moral and human dignity in a democracy are misdirected and overshadowed by non-issues which fuel violence rather than good governance, the rule of law and economic development. Unless Malawian politicians in the new era understand their moral and ethical responsibilities, Malawi runs the risk of facing more political violence and intolerance. It is important for political parties to guard their language, and to this end the Malawi constitution needs to put reasonable limits to free speech and discipline those who neglect responsibilities in the freedom of expression and association.

5. "Mzimu wa Soldier"

Contemporary Popular Music and Politics in Malawi

Reuben Makayiko Chirambo

Introduction

A simple definition of contemporary popular music would be in the terms suggested by Johannes Fabian: "Expressions carried out by the masses in contrast to both modern elitist and traditional 'tribal' culture" (1997:18). Traditional music in Malawi is, however, associated with or produced by the masses, and it has been adapted and appropriated by politicians for entertainment and as a vehicle for their political pursuits. It has become an instrument for hegemony in the Gramscian sense. And the effect of hegemony on national culture is that

> class division might not appear to be necessarily conflictional. Rather, the élite, through its cultural hegemony, solidifies its rule by establishment of bonds that transcend class. In manufacturing consent, … cultural hegemony eliminates the masses' ability to conceive of the conceptual tools to challenge the structure of the system. Hegemony keeps alternatives from the public's consciousness; revolution, or reaction against the system, is beyond the range of the mass ideology and thus impossible. More simply put, that revolution is not within the masses' range of consciousness keeps revolutionary movements from developing. (Taffet, 1997:92)

For example, when the Malawi Congress Party (MCP) adapted traditional songs and dances for the praise repertoire for Kamuzu Banda (Nurse, 1964),[1] it gave the impression of consent instead of control of the masses who produced the songs. The problem is that such music "tends to be conservative, escapist, or merely vacuous; and in this way it works against the real interests of the people, accepting and reinforcing the values that maintain the status quo" (Barber, 1987:6). In contrast to coercion and repression, the political control of national culture as a means of securing power contributes to stable domination and strengthens the élite's hold on power (Taffet, 1997: 92). It is therefore pursued even by democratic regimes. However, popular music may be different to the extent that it may challenge hegemony by providing outlets for expressing discontent against injustice, domination and exploitation.

Since 1992, popular musicians in Malawi have been trying to challenge political domination and exploitation by the élite. Popular bands and individuals are able to take up the cause for the masses by using popular music as a platform for debate and action against the élite's dominant ideology. I use the concept "dominant ideology" to refer to the élite's idea of the state or condition of the nation which, though often merely reflecting the élite's own condition, is thought to subsume that of the masses too. In the case of Malawi, the élite's description of the state of the nation emphasises self-sufficiency in food, economic viability, the right course for democracy, so-

---

1. Nurse (1964) discusses how traditional songs were transformed into propaganda songs in praise of Kamuzu Banda and the Malawi Congress Party. A similar situation exists now as politicians in all parties in Malawi seek to use traditional songs and dances as part of political activities, particularly during rallies and campaigns.

cial viability as a unified nation, and that ordinary people are happy and satisfied with the way things are. Anything that contradicts this is denied and suppressed—sometimes with violence. Songs and dances are used to praise the situation and cover up the terrible conditions suffered by the masses.

In this chapter, I discuss the lyrics of Lucius Banda as a contemporary popular voice for the masses. I also examine Lucius Banda's contest of the voice of the politicians, challenging the "truth" and "legitimacy" of their stories about the masses. In conclusion, I discuss popular music as an emerging political discourse; as a space for debate and action against the dominant ideology of the élite. Several popular artists have emerged in the "new" Malawi, making significant contributions to the growth and development of popular music in relation to politics since 1992. I single out Lucius Banda and his music for discussion, because, first, Lucius Banda has set the pace for contemporary popular music, not least as a prolific songwriter. Second, the range of political issues he explores is wide. The explicitly political subjects and themes that he explores make him a compelling representative of the role of popular music in politics in Malawi. He has become a major voice for the masses.

Lucius Banda was born in Sosola village, Traditional Authority Msamala in Balaka district in Southern Malawi. He did his primary school at Mponda Parish and entered High Cross Seminary at Ulongwe with the intents of becoming a priest. A major influence in his music career has been Paul Banda, his brother, who founded the Alleluya Band in the 1970s. Paul began to teach Lucius music in the mid-1980s. The Alleluya Band continues to operate under the auspices of the Catholic Church, with a recording studio in Balaka, known as Imbirani Yahweh. This is also the "headquarters" for Lucius Banda's own band, Zembani Music, founded in 1998. Lucius Banda recorded his first album in 1993, *Son of a Poor Man*, which he released in 1994. He has released seven more albums to date, *Down Babylon* (1995), *Cease Fire* (1996), *Take Over* (1997), *Yahwe* (1999), *Unity* (1999), *Jah* (2000), and *How Long* (2001).

The second major influence on Lucius Banda is his mother, who raised him and his siblings almost single-handedly, because the father cared little about them. She died in 1995. Her story is told in the song "Mayi Zembani" (1999). Lucius Banda has dedicated his second album, *Down Babylon* to her and named his band after her. This background, coupled with the Catholic upbringing, which emphasises social and communal justice, is an important factor in making Lucius Banda sensitive to the suffering of the masses. Although most of his songs are about politicians, they are full of images of suffering children and women, victims of politics. He sings about war, corruption, greed, political bigotry, disease and poverty, among other things, as they affect the masses.

Lucius Banda's desire and mission in his career are summed up in this song:

Mzimu wanga udzakondwa poona kuti,	My spirit will be happy to see,
Odwala athandizidwa mwachangu ndi chikondi,	The sick helped with speed and love,
Amndende aweruzidwa asanamangidwe,	Prisoners are tried before being jailed,
Ana, amayi, amasiye zawo alandile.	Orphans, widows receive their inheritance.
Ana amphawi ndi olemera aphunzire zimodzi,	Poor children and rich ones should learn the same,
Ngakhale olemera, akalakwa amangidwe,	Even the rich when wrong should also be jailed,
Olemara ndi akhungu alembedwenso ntchito,	Lame and deaf people should also be employed,
Abale anga osauka, mutawaganizira.	My friends, these poor people, think about them.
Ngati muzafune kunena kanthu,	If you want to say anything,
Mzati ndinayesetsa kumenya,	Say that I tried to fight,
Kumenya nkhondo yabwino,	To fight a good fight,

Ndinali Soldier wa amphawi.	I was a Soldier for the poor.
Abwenzi anga sanali achuma	My friends were not the rich
Anali olema ndi amphawi	They were the lame and the poor
Amndende, olira mchipatala	Those in prison, the crying in hospitals
Ndi amayi amasiye.	And widowed women
Mzimu wa Soldier udzagona	Soldier's spirit will rest.

("Mzimu wa Soldier", Soldier's Spirit, 1999)

This song illustrates what I suggest is an evolving relationship between popular music and politics in Malawi since the dawn of democracy; a relationship that reflects the relationship between those with political power, on the one hand, and the poor masses excluded from positions of power and its privileges, on the other. The song defines the role popular musicians and their music are trying to play in politics in Malawi. This is a role that pits them and the masses against the élite, especially politicians. Lucius Banda says he is not a friend of the rich but is a soldier fighting for poor people. The war he is fighting is one where his songs are a voice against exploitation and oppression by politicians.

His idea of social justice is that poor people are also considered and given the same opportunities to survive as the rich. He is against discrimination in the way services are provided or public resources are distributed. Lucius Banda sees rich people not only as having the privilege of better services in the country but also as being able to afford services abroad. This makes them care less about the services or resources available to the poor. He also speaks specifically for orphans and widows who often lose their little inheritance to the greedy relatives of the deceased. He asks for equal employment opportunities for people with disabilities. He has, in recent years, advocated for the abolition of the death sentence and improvements in prison conditions. He believes innocent people are killed by the death sentence. Lucius Banda travels tirelessly around the country giving concerts in parish halls, stadiums, hotels, and prisons to promote his message.

There are two major political periods in Malawi to which I want to relate Lucius Banda's music. There is, on the one hand, the era of Kamuzu Banda's autocratic rule from 1964 until 1994. Lucius Banda sings about it now, because it was difficult to talk and sing about autocracy while the regime was in power. One risked detention without trial, torture, or even death. The few that dared to speak had to be cryptic to camouflage their criticism.[1] For this reason, the one-party regime thwarted the growth of critical popular music or any subculture fearing they would become a platform for political resistance. Concerning the autocratic era, Lucius Banda sings about the atrocities that characterised it and the change to democracy which he calls "the fall of Babylon". Included in this era is the referendum in 1993, after which the country adopted a constitution allowing multiparty democracy. Then there is the post-Banda era, 1994 to the present. As a democracy, the post-Banda era provides a context for popular music to debate social and political issues without undue censorship. Popular music in this era describes the frustration and disillusionment of the masses who have been given the promises of democracy. Lucius Banda says that the masses live in poverty, political exploitation and oppression in forms that are only superficially different from those of the Banda era. Lucius Banda also comments on election violence and regionalism/ethnicity that threaten democracy and national unity in Malawi.

---

1. One such artist is Wambali Mkandawire, who coded his message in the oral traditions and history of the nation in order to speak about the political conditions under Banda (see Chirambo 2001; see also Mapanje's Afterword in this volume)

The Fall of Babylon: Kamuzu Banda's Era and the Transition to Democracy

Lucius Banda evokes Babylon to allude to the Israelites' experience of captivity in Babylon in the Bible. He uses it to define the oppressive political system in Malawi under Kamuzu Banda and the MCP. His song "Down Babylon" is dedicated "to all families that have lost their loved ones through this system (of Babylon)". In describing Banda's Malawi as Babylon, Lucius Banda views Malawians as the captives of a dictator. The following quotes from his songs comment on some of the atrocities committed by Banda and his party.

Anthu anzeru opempha chilungamo	Wise people asking for justice
Ankangofa mmene zifera ntchetche.	Died as flies do.

("Mabala", Wounds, 1994)

This song is against a man who was called Messiah,
And killed thousands of people whose remains are still being discovered
in the rivers of Malawi today.
A man who killed wives and children for the wrongs of their fathers.
This song is against a certain political party found in Malawi
from the 60s to early 90s.
A party that killed and tortured people,
A party that had power more than God,
A party that could have its way and never be wrong,
A party that was never wrong.

("Down Babylon", 1995)

Pali mtengo wina wake,	There is a tree
Panjira yakuThambani, mbali yakuMwanzaku	On Thambani Road in Mwanza
Umaoneka ngati kamtengo	It looks like an ordinary tree,
Koma ndi mboni yazovuta zija,	But it is witness to those murders.
Mmtengo munalira njelo.	In that tree, angels cried.
Mwazi wamunthu ndi wodabwitsa,	The blood of a human being is strange,
Mkapha munthu, mungabise bwanji,	If you kill a person, no matter how you hide,
Muzayalukabe.	You will be scandalised.

("Mizimu", Their Spirits, 1995)

"Mabala" and "Down Babylon" say that many people died trying to oppose the oppressive system of government. There were others who were detained, tortured and even killed for simply being relations of Banda's supposed "enemies". "Mizimu" was inspired by the report of the inquiry into the murders in Mwanza in 1983. The police appeared to have killed three government ministers (Dick Matenje, Aaron Gadama, and Twaibu Sangala) and a Member of Parliament (David Chiwanga) on instructions from the MCP leadership. The police then staged a road accident to cover up the murders. They pushed the car in which the four politicians were packed down a slope to crash.[1] The tree Lucius Banda refers to is a small tree down the slope against which the vehicle came to stop without crashing. Lucius Banda believes angels were in that tree to witness the murders. While the MCP insisted that it was an accident, Lucius Banda wonders why the children of the deceased were expelled from school. Also, why did the police preside over the burials, thereby preventing the proper performance of funeral rites? If it was an accident, the nation would have

---

1. Details of this are contained in a Commission of Inquiry Report released in 1995. Muluzi established the inquiry in 1994 after he took over power from Banda.

mourned the victims since they were serving ministers. This did not happen. These murders and others, Lucius Banda says, contradicted Kamuzu Banda's claim to be the Messiah. For a Messiah is supposed to save and not kill his people.

Kamuzu Banda allegedly transferred huge sums of money to banks in Britain, leaving people in Malawi to suffer poverty and hunger. Bakili Muluzi's government obtained a temporary freeze on Banda's accounts in Britain in 1995, but could not prove that the money was stolen or belonged to the country. The freeze was lifted. The exact figures involved in the accounts have never been confirmed since the estate was long in dispute between the beneficiaries. Nevertheless, rumours and allegations about the accounts are numerous. This is why Lucius Banda in the next two songs says that Banda and his clique plundered national resources at the expense of poor people.

Panali anthu ena ankangovutika,	There were some people suffering,
Pamene anthu ena ankangokondwera.	While others were enjoying.
Panali anthu ena ogwira ntchito,	There were some people working hard,
Pamene ena ankangodyelera.	While others were just eating.
Malume ndalama kubisa kubanki,	Uncle you hid money in the bank,
Pamene mbumba yanu ikufa ndi njala.	While your people are dying of hunger.

("Mabala", 1994)

This song is against
A man who took over twenty billion Kwacha from poor people
And let it be frozen in major banks of the world.

("Down Babylon", 1995)

The national referendum in 1993 was a major step towards democracy, followed by a new constitution allowing for a multiparty system of government. The referendum was not achieved without further suffering and pain. The fact that Banda was Life President made him and his party reluctant to relinquish their power. The Malawi Young Pioneers (MYP), a paramilitary wing of the MCP, disrupted pro-democracy campaign meetings, while city officials denied them access to places to hold such meetings in the cities. The national radio (MBC) ignored the pro-democracy campaigners and sometimes refused to advertise their meetings. The police arrested and imprisoned pro-democracy activists on spurious charges. For example, Chakufwa Chihana was imprisoned for protesting against Banda's politics and calling for a national referendum. At the grassroots, youth leaguers and party officials intimidated people by misrepresenting multiparty democracy as a free-for-all chaos, tantamount to tribalising and regionalising politics that would end up in civil war. Songs in *Son of a Poor Man* (1994)—"Never give up", "Shame on you", "Negotiate", "Stand up for your rights"—urge everyone not to give up the fight for their freedom, because no oppressor abandons power without a fight. Lucius Banda calls for tolerance and perseverance, particularly when it became apparent that the MCP was trying to push people into violence to enable Kamuzu Banda to cancel the referendum and delay democracy. The MCP and Kamuzu Banda lost the referendum, marking what Lucius Banda calls the end of "thirty years of being told what to do, how to do and when to do" ("Down Babylon"). The fall of Babylon represents, therefore, an end to the struggle against three decades of dictatorship. The referendum victory was, as in the case of the Israelites, an instance of God saving Malawians from bondage, because he could not let his children suffer forever ("Mabala").

Immediately following the MCP's defeat at the referendum, some people wanted its leadership to be punished for the atrocities they had committed in office. Others, however, including Lucius Banda, wanted to forgive and forget in order to move forward with democracy. The past seemed to matter less than the future. They wanted to give unconditional forgiveness as expressed in the song below.

Khululuka iwe mzanga wofedwa,	Forgive, you the bereaved,
Puputa misonzi tiyiwale zonse.	Wipe away your tears, let us forget everything.
Nyali yawala, nkhuku yathawa.	The lamp has won, the cock has fled.
Tisangalale poti mbuye watikumbuka,	Let's rejoice, for our God has remembered us.
Zakulipa diso kwa diso izo siyani.	Don't go for "an eye for an eye".
Zikanatero, bwenzi tonse tili akhungu.	If that was the case, we'd all be blind.
Kukhuluka ndiye ndakhululuka,	Forgive, I've forgiven,
Koma mabala ndiye akupweteka.	But the scars are painful.

("Mabala", 1994)

The lamp was the symbol for pro-democracy campaigners in the referendum, whereas the black cock was the symbol for the MCP and the one-party cause. The MCP's defeat was presented as a fleeing cock, running away from the light. This song was released in 1994, immediately after the referendum, when there was excitement that democracy was finally a reality. Yet when some details of the past began to emerge, such as the Mwanza murders, some people began to withdraw their unconditional forgiveness. They realised that reconciliation and forgiveness needed someone to confess to the atrocities or at least to acknowledge what had happened, how, and where. When the graphic details of how the four politicians were killed in Mwanza were revealed, many began to feel that the MCP needed to apologise for the murders and other atrocities. Unfortunately, when the government decided to press criminal charges against the MCP leadership, it eliminated the possibilities for confessions and apologies. The matter had to be decided by the courts. Kamuzu Banda, John Tembo and McWilliam Lunguzi were charged with conspiracy to commit murder and destroy evidence. They were acquitted by the High Court, a sentence that was upheld by the Appeals Court, effectively closing the case but not the issue. The inquiry and the trial had at least established the fact that the four were murdered though it did not secure a conviction (see van Donge, 1998b). Hence, Lucius Banda says

Kwa ena nonse nkhaniyi yatha,	For all of you, this issue is over,
Koma ine ndekha ndinene zoona, misozi sizauma.	But for me, let me say the truth, tears won't dry.
Ndikudikira pamene ndizafa,	I will wait till I die,
Ndikawapeze, ndikawafunse.	I should meet them (the victims) and ask them,
Mwina nzakhululuka.	Maybe then I will forgive.

("Mizimu", 1995)

Lucius Banda puts himself in the shoes of the victims' families and says that tears will never dry. And since the truth will never be acknowledged by the perpetrators, he will wait till death when the victims themselves will explain what happened to them, then and only then, may forgiveness be possible. This is the reason why Lucius Banda says, "We will forgive, but not, but never forget/And we believe you'll forgive us for revenging/What you did to us for over 30 years" ("Down Babylon"). This mix-up in emotions is due to the way people came to know details of the past. Politicians in the UDF government have shown no political will to open up the past and let people examine it, pouring out their emotions as in South Africa. Instead, UDF politicians have decided to investigate and prosecute selected incidents. But Lucius Banda, like many others, says knowing the truth is necessary for reconciliation for one has to know what one is forgiving.[1] The victims of Kamuzu Banda's politics are

---

1. Many other people supported the idea (see Article 19 1993; Ross 1998). Victims of Banda's politics are still asking for a full account of what happened to them or their relatives suggesting a Truth and Reconciliation process is still necessary (see also Mapanje's Afterword in this volume)

asking for an account of what they suffered, arguing that, "We will never have justice on the foundations of injustice" (quoted in Tenthani, 2001).

Lucius Banda dwells on the past for reasons that are obviously different from those of the politicians now in power. For Lucius Banda, talking about the past is a way of coming to terms with horrors that have not been fully explained or accounted for. He is trying to explain the little that he knows or has experience of. He relates to it as a victim as well as someone who has had the opportunity to recount such an experience on behalf of others. Also, he thinks revealing the past helps people to appreciate the present democratic dispensation so that no one takes it for granted ("Cease Fire", 1995, "Mukawauze", 1999). The belief is that if people know what happened in the past, they will avoid travelling the same road again.

On the other hand, Muluzi and other leaders of the UDF have used the past largely to distract the attention of the public from their own failures in government. Such failures are blamed on the systems and traditions that the MCP left behind or what they did wrong. Also, to a large extent, members of the UDF government would like to exonerate themselves from the mistakes of the MCP. By insisting on the undemocratic behaviour of the MCP in the past, they are not only laying a claim to democracy, but legitimising themselves as champions of democracy. This is also instrumental to keeping the MCP away from the possibilities of coming back to power. The past atrocities are used to suggest that the MCP will never change. This assures the UDF of remaining in power. When the UDF government prosecuted for the Mwanza murders, for example, they were also trying to fulfil an election campaign promise. The UDF promised that when it came to power it would open up the past and make those responsible for wrongdoing pay for it. However, with most of the members of the inner clique of the UDF having in the past held prominent positions in the MCP, they have observed considerable discretion in choosing the atrocities to examine. They have avoided those that would embarrass themselves. This may explain the decision to use a Commission of Inquiry instead of a Truth Commission for it allows them to select safe cases to deal with.[1]

In the case of the Mwanza murders, Lucius Banda says that apart from opening up old wounds, the exercise provided no healing or justice to the victims' families.

Dziko lapansi likondera opata	This world favours the rich
Iwe ndi ine kwathu nkulira	While you and me, ours is poverty.
Munthu wachuma ngakhale aphe munthu,	A rich man even if he kills a person,
Mboni zake ndi ndalama izo zili mthumba lake	His defence is the money in his pocket.
Kodi amfumu nanga ndigwire ziti?	Chief (President), what should I hold onto now?
Abale mwangonditsutsula zipyela	You have simply re-opened my scars.
Ndinaiwala, mwandikumbutsiranji	I forgot, why have you reminded me of
Anzanga, imfa yabambo wanga?	The death of my father?

("Njira Zawo", *Their Ways*, 1996)

Lucius Banda situates the Mwanza case within the politics of the rich versus the poor in which money gives "justice", so to speak, to the rich and denies it to the poor. He believes that the case was won because it involved rich people and not necessarily because justice was delivered. Clive Stanbrook, QC, hired from Britain, defended the case, while Kamdoni Nyasulu, a Malawian lawyer and Director of Public Prosecutions, prosecuted it.

The government also tried to prosecute Kamuzu Banda and his henchmen for the misuse of public resources on Kamuzu Academy, a private élite grammar school in

---

1. On this and the use of the past in present politics, see van Donge (1998b) and Chirwa (2000)

Kasungu. It also tried to prosecute the MCP for plotting to kill Catholic bishops in 1992, when they issued a pastoral letter that set the campaign for democracy rolling. Both cases disappeared without the courts ever trying them. They were all safe cases in so far as none of the UDF officials could be held culpable. Such selectivity simply shrouds the past in further mystery, giving credence to rumours and speculation that the UDF's own closet is full of skeletons from the past.

Lucius Banda, however, did not simply dwell on the past but moved on to talk about the new reality in a "new political dispensation". He, like many others, has had different experiences than those they had hoped and fought for.

Cease Fire or Take Over: The Post-Banda Disillusionment

The pro-democracy referendum victory and the UDF's triumph in the 1994 elections raised prospects for a quick and decisive break with the past. It was not just the fall of Babylon but the beginning of a new and better era in politics in Malawi; this, at least, was what people were promised. But even if the fall of Babylon as a political system was thought to be complete, it was not dead. The thirty years of Banda's politics of "death and darkness"[1] resurfaced under Muluzi's leadership in different guises. Lucius Banda is particularly concerned with the continued oppression and exploitation of the masses through increasing poverty, corruption, rising crime and the inability of the police to curb it, unemployment, regionalism and nepotism, political violence, to mention but a few. He sees these as threats to democracy; potentially derailing the process of democratisation.

Lucius Banda sees increasing poverty among the masses and the breakdown in public security as direct results of unworkable government policies devised by greedy and vain politicians. He believes the problem to be politicians' lack of seriousness in executing their duties. They are more concerned with their own personal condition than with the people they are supposed to serve. For example, health and education facilities suffer from neglect, because responsible ministers do not personally need the services. They have access to better facilities in private institutions or abroad.

Ndikuthokoza pondipatsa ufulu,	Thank you for giving me freedom
Koma ufulu ndi njala siumakoma.	But freedom with hunger is never sweet.
Kapolo okhuta apotsa mfumu ya njala.	A slave who is full is happier than a hungry master.
Ndili ndi mavuto ambiri	I have many problems
Sindingaimbe zosangalatsa.	I cannot sing of joy.
Ndili ndi usiwa, zovala kudula	I am naked, clothes are expensive.
Ndili ndi njala, zakudya kudula,	I am hungry, food is expensive.
Ana anga akudwala, mankhwala akusowa.	My children are sick, there is no medicine.

("Ufumu wa Mbuye", God's Sovereignty, 1995)

(UDF) making education free for children
But teachers remain unpaid,
You cry to see the standard of education going down, lower and lower for poor people
While sons and daughters of politicians are getting quality education abroad.

---

1. Chakufwa Chihana, leader for the Alliance for Democracy, used the term in April 1992 to describe the MCP after his arrival in Lilongwe from exile in Zambia. He categorised the party as one of death and darkness by outlining the contradictions between the utterances of the party leaders and their conduct

Go to the hospital,
You'll see doctors and nurses drinking coffee,
While poor patients are dying unattended to in corridors.
And the minister responsible says nothing,
Because when he is sick
He will fly to South Africa, Garden Clinic.

("Cease Fire", 1996)

When I am in the streets of Blantyre and Lilongwe
All I get to see are children saying, "Ndithandizeni bwana" (Help me, sir)
When I get home, I sit and wonder,
Poverty alleviation is not for the poor.

I hear the cry of poor people,
Cry for food.
Hunger that was invited,
By adopting the foolish ideologies of the IMF and World Bank.

("Take Over", 1999)

The rising cost of living has pushed poor people into near destitution. The liberalised economy means more people failing to get basic necessities as rich people increase their wealth. Muluzi has responded to the problem by saying that he does not own a grocery and, therefore, he is not responsible for inflation. The UDF government introduced free primary education in 1994. While enrolment has increased, the quality of education has gone down. In addition to the reasons Lucius Banda gives here —such as late payment of teachers' salaries—resources are inadequate, there are few qualified teachers, forcing government to recruit untrained teachers to meet the unprecedented demand for primary and secondary education. Teaching materials and facilities are not adequate. Comparable problems plague the health sector. Hospitals do not have adequate equipment and medicine to provide quality services to the ever-increasing numbers of patients. Neglect by responsible government officials is only one dimension of the problem. As for hunger, Lucius Banda says that people are hungry, because they cannot produce enough food on their own. Partly to blame is the programme adopted by the government in 1995 to remove subsidies on farm inputs such as fertilizer. Very few farmers can afford to buy fertilizer at the market value. Lucius Banda's verdict is that the government, obeying the IMF and World Bank, did not care to consider the effects of the programme on poor people. The poor are the victims of the programme instead of being its beneficiaries. However, while the overall poverty situation for the masses has worsened, politicians are richer than before. The Poverty Alleviation Programme, which the UDF had as the centrepiece of its manifesto, seems to benefit rich people only.

Lucius Banda is worried about corruption in the country, because he says it destroys the economy and undermines justice. For example, Lucius Banda says the rich are able to get away with crimes while poor people are punished because they cannot afford to pay a bribe or hire a lawyer.

Polisi nayo padziko lapansi   The police in this world
Ili paubwenzi ndi zigawenga,   Are in friendship with thugs,
Munthu wamangidwa lero, mawa wabweterako.   One is arrested today, tomorrow free.

Mbanki namo ukati ukakongole,   If you want a loan from the bank,
Kuyamba kuyang'ana nkhope.   They first look at your face.

("Ufumu wa Mbuye")

The Anti-Corruption Bureau inflicted upon poor people,
While ministers and politicians are struggling free from custom duties,

111

With a badge of diplomatic immunity.
While poor people's goods are being over-valued by the undemocratic and slavish customs officers.

Try to take a bus on the M1 tarmac,
You'll be delayed and searched at over six roadblocks.
But when white people, Indians, rich people and politicians,
Are passing with their Mercedes, BMW,
Full of drugs and guns in their boots,
All they receive is a heavy salute from the polite policeman.

("Cease Fire", 1996)

Politicians have given themselves a lot of privileges at the expense of the masses. Ministers, for example, are entitled to bring into the country duty-free goods that they end up selling at huge profits. Yet ordinary people are taxed heavily. Lucius Banda is not necessarily against the tax but views ministers' exemption from it as an addition to their other privileges. While a lot of money is not collected as a result of these exemptions, the little tax collected is spent on a bloated cabinet ("Ufumu wa Mbuye"). His complaints about police roadblocks arise from the fact that between Blantyre and Lilongwe, for example, a distance of about 350 kilometres, there are often up to six police roadblocks. People travelling in buses are forced out with their luggage even when it is raining. They are lined up for their identities and luggage to be checked. But at the same roadblocks, those travelling in their own cars, particularly whites, Asians and politicians, are often simply saluted and waved to drive on. Lucius Banda not only thinks that the police discriminate in favour of the rich but also allow rich people to carry guns and drugs across the country. Police behaviour and corruption in general, he says, destroy people's confidence that the law will protect them. They also destroy the country's economy ("Yahwe", 1999; "Kola Apa Sono", 1999).

Lucius Banda is also concerned with infringements on the freedom of expression through censorship and the monopoly of the public media, particularly the MBC. The MBC has the only national radio stations. Pro-democracy campaign singled out the freedom of expression as one of the rights that people were denied by the MCP. Many hoped that the mass media as a public institution would be opened for professional non-partisan news coverage without unnecessary government control. And indeed during a brief period in 1993 and 1994 the national radio opened up, as did the newspapers. But when the UDF came to power, the public radio station slid back to party and government control where access to dissenting views is denied. The radio and television have become instruments for misinformation, and for undermininng those who oppose the UDF (see also Kayambazinthu and Moyo's chapter in this volume). Below, Lucius Banda takes on the public radio and the newspapers.

The MBC, a biased diary for politicians,
All you hear is His Excellency, The Right Honourable, and Honourable.
So, when shall AIDS make headlines?
When shall the wise and famous people make news for Malawi?
When shall MBC play our music?

("Cease Fire", 1996)

Go to MBC and you will discover the radio,
It is still undemocratic. It is still biased.
It is still a notice-board for politicians.
Why should MBC choose non-political music only,
And claim to be democratic by the end of the day?
Why should reporters abuse their own profession just to entertain politicians?

And the same problem is found in our newspapers.
It has become clear that if you buy the Daily Times,
You'll hear nice stories about MCP.
If you buy Nation,
You're going to hear nice stories about UDF.
When shall we have freedom of expression.

("Take Over", 1999)

Politicians or parties not only dominate the news but also influence the content. Lucius Banda laments the fact that the UDF has maintained the government's grip on the radio, making it a notice-board for the party and the government. The newspapers too are simply toeing the line of the politicians or parties that own them. This political domination of the media pushes everyone and everything else from the media limelight except the politicians. No matter how important the other issues might be to the nation, politicians always have the priority. Karin Barber makes a similar observation about the media and the élite in Africa:

> The numerically tiny élite not only consume a vastly disproportionate share of the national wealth, they also take up all the light. Newspapers, radio, and television offer a magnified image of the class that controls them. Not only does the ruling class make the news, it is the news—(such) as endless verbatim reports of politicians' speeches, accounts of élite weddings, etc (1987: 6).

Against this background, Lucius Banda calls on politicians in "Cease Fire" (1996) to stop exploiting and oppressing people and to give democracy a chance. "Cease Fire" anticipates "Take Over" because he believes "politicians are too obsessed with wealth to be democratic" ("Cease Fire"). He sums up democracy in Malawi thus far: "This nation is still undemocratic/I've not seen democracy/All I've seen is hypocrisy" ("Take Over"). It is not just the masses that are tired of being deceived and exploited; army generals too are tired. Hence "there are too many coups in Africa" ("Cease Fire"). The masses, including the army, are alienated from the government by greedy and corrupt politicians. "Take Over" is a call to get rid of civilian politicians. He says, "Soldiers take over,/Rastas take over,/People take over". The suggestion for take over should be seen in the context of what he says about the army in "Cease Fire". There he claims that in Africa "men in black suits and red neckties (civilian politicians) have failed while savages in camouflages (soldiers) respect economic equality". Although he refers to soldiers as savages, they are viewed in a better light than civilian politicians. "Rastas" is a term he uses for the youth. The youth form the largest group of Lucius Banda's fans. Most of them are unemployed and live in townships under harsh conditions, surviving by vending cheap merchandise along the streets, or as ushers for buses, among other odd jobs. They are a genuinely frustrated group in Malawi. Lucius Banda says life for the masses is hopeless with no future as long as civilian politicians are the same.

What is long life when your brothers and sisters cannot afford a bag of maize,
When 80 per cent of the money is controlled by 10 per cent of the population.
And the masses are left to die of hunger slowly.

What is the meaning of life when corruption is killing the country yet ACB is there
I'd rather die than let my children go through what I've seen.
Because I can see the future of Malawi dying slowly.

("Yahwe", 1999)

In this scenario where it is not possible to find an honest civilian politician, Lucius Banda feels that the country can no longer entrust politicians with power or the resources of the nation. The masses must take over. How this ought to happen is not obvious from Lucius Banda's texts, and I am hesitant to suggest that he is talking of a military coup. Suffice to mention that by the end of 1998, rumours about the 1999 elections included that if the UDF won, the army would take over. Following the elections, two journalists at the *Malawi News* were arrested for quoting people calling on the army to take over during a demonstration against the election results. The case was dropped later. I have no evidence to believe that the army ever contemplated taking over government, either before or in response to Lucius Banda's song. Following the release of "Take Over", prior to the 1999 general elections, it was also rumoured that Lucius Banda intended to form his own political party. He denied this, although he accepted the title of "Soldier", which initially was "President Soldier". Also, during the same period, young people formed the Movement for the Young Generation. It was a political party for young people to be led by young people themselves. While there may be no connection between Lucius Banda's song and the formation of the movement, it is significant that some youths went as far as showing their frustration by forming their own party. Although the party disbanded shortly thereafter, they had at least registered their sense of alienation from the parties in the country and the politicians in power.

On Tribalism/Regionalism, Political Violence and Democracy

Lucius Banda feels that politicians in both government and the opposition deceive the masses, using them as pawns in their politics of blame and intolerance. The UDF and MCP are singled out, because he feels each has "good" reasons to blame the other, particularly in public. MCP politicians never seem to appreciate anything good UDF politicians do in government. UDF politicians, for their part, seem to use every excuse to blame the MCP and the past for current problems in the country. In the process both the UDF and MCP fan hatred and violence between their supporters. Politicians' speeches in parliament and at political rallies are spiteful, and supporters behave towards each other accordingly. The parties have occasionally sponsored thugs to break up rival party meetings and destroy their campaign tools. Examples include violence in the by-election campaigns in Blantyre (Ndirande), Lilongwe and Chiradzulu in 1995 and 1996. More recent was the death of a young market vendor, Duncan Kanjuchi, stabbed to death during campaign violence in Blantyre in 2001. However, none of the leaders has ever been physically involved in these battles. It is ordinary people, particularly the youth, who are set on each other. This is why Lucius Banda says this public hatred may not entirely be true of how the leaders treat each other in private. Despite the abusive language against each other in public, some of them are known to get along as friends and help each other in private. Yet their followers fight as bitter enemies. The warning in the songs below is aimed at the masses, telling them to be wary of this hypocrisy and deceit practised by politicians.

Ndikulangizeni anzanga otsatira zadziko,	Let me advise you who follow things of this world,
Anthuwa ndi magayi, zawo ndi zimodzi.	These people are guys, their ways are the same.
Iwo amakwera benzi, iwe ndi ine kukanganira basi.	They ride a Benz, while you and me fight over a bus.
Tawasiyani, azinenana, ife tigwire ntchito.	Leave them abuse each other, let's work to help ourselves.

("Tigwirane Manja", Let's Hold Hands, 1996)

Dzana ndi dzulo takhalira kuphedwa,
Lero tikhalira kunamizidwa.
Nanga titani poti anthu ndi omwewo,
Angosintha njira zotizunzira.
Ali ndi njira zawo.

Akamalankhula pakamwa chabe,
Amakhala ngati ngachilungano.
Koma mkhale nawo zaka zingapo,
Mudzadziwa anthu awa ndi amodzimodzi,
Angosiyana dzina.
Ali ndi njira zawo.

Ali ngati mizu ya Kachere.

("Njira Zawo")

Yesterday, and that other day, we're being killed,
Today we are cheated.
What can we do since it is the same people.
They've only changed ways of torturing us.
They've their own ways.

When they're talking, it is just words,
They sound as if they're honest.
But live with them for some years,
You'll see it is the same people,
They only differ in names.
They've their own ways.

They're like roots of a Kachere tree.

His suggestion is that poor people should get together to fight their own poverty rather than be used as pawns in a game in which they are not players. The roots of Kachere trees meet and feed together underground, while above the ground the trees stand antagonistic to each other as if in a duel. Politicians are likened to Kachere trees in that they attack each other in public only to dine with each other in private. The masses are deceived into hatred and violence that may never be there between the leaders. These songs are a warning not to trust what politicians say. Instead, people should ignore them and work together to alleviate their own poverty and suffering. Lucius Banda warns, however, that everyone, including politicians, is in the same boat, and should it sink, everyone will perish ("Tigwirane Manja"). In other words, he sees this violence as capable of destroying the country. And in such a scenario there is no winner; all are losers.

Democracy involves periodic and sometimes intensely contested elections. This competition, in the case of Malawi, has sometimes produced bitter rivalry, even degenerating into serious violence. There have been numerous instances of violent clashes between supporters of different parties, a situation I have discussed above. This situation may not have completely disrupted the social and political order so far, but many, including Lucius Banda, are concerned that it will become a culture of elections in Malawi. It is a culture that in the long run threatens the very democracy elections are meant to promote and preserve. Bitter rivalry and violence between political parties, Lucius Banda suggests, reflect and reinforce regional and ethnic/tribal divisions of the country. Regionalism is most obvious in the manner people are elected into political offices and how government and the employment sector hire and deploy staff. It should be noted that regionalism and ethnicity are not new factors in politics in Malawi. They were there even under Banda. Multiparty politics has just brought them to the fore. Banda suppressed them by insisting that no one talk about them, although in practice, he was regionalistic (Vail and White, 1989). The hope was that the UDF government would take the lead in correcting the situation now that the country is a democracy.[1] But since 1994 the country remains divided and seems to be plunging into a crisis.[2]

---

1. Bakili Muluzi has, by all indications, failed to rise above party and regional politics to unify the country. In his campaign for re-election in 1999 in Mzuzu he declared, for example, that he would not provide government support to constituencies that will elect individuals to the National Assembly from opposition parties; this despite calls for him not to use public and national resources to frustrate democracy and divide the country. He has reiterated his position (*The Chronicle*, 28 March, 2001).
2. For the current situation see Chirwa (1998a) and Kaspin (1995).

In "Unity" Lucius Banda calls on all people in Malawi regardless of their region of origin to unite for peace and stability. He deplores regionalism and tribalism in work places and during elections.

Malawi unite, unite for the sake of the economy.
Unite for the sake of peace.
Unite for the sake of children.

Malawians staying in the north, in the centre and in the south,
It is time to forget the past for a brighter future.

Look at the people of the north voting massively for a man they don't even know
as long as they are being told by Chakufwa to do so.
Look at the people of the south voting in useless Members of Parliament as long as they are UDF.

Malawi can never go far economically if our politics continue
being of racism, fascism, nepotism, regionalism, and of course tribalism.

Look at our offices today,
When a General Manager is a Yao, then all the way down to the messenger will be Yao
If the Director is a Tumbuka, all the way down to the cleaner will be a Tumbuka.

("Unity", 1999)

In the run up to the 1999 elections, Lucius Banda summarised Malawi's history as one of abuse, violence, and regionalism from the colonial era through Banda to the present. However, he says that in the case of colonialists we may understand, for after all they were never a part of us. What he cannot understand is why, now when it is Malawians in power, people should continue to harm each other because of regional and ethnic differences. He sees no reason other than greed. As the 1999 general elections approached, his quest for a leader who would rise above regional and party politics to unite the country was intense.

Matipate pobwera timati nzabwino	When multiparty came, we thought it was good,
Tati mwina zisintha kwa anthu tonse.	Saying we'll all benefit.
Lero umphawi wafika pena.	But, poverty has reached different proportions.
Welensky anatizunza,	Welensky tortured us,
Koma ndi mzungu tinkamvetsa.	But he was a white man, we understand.
Lero ndiye tokha-tokha,	But today, it is ourselves
Kupwetekana anthu amodzi.	Killing each other yet we're the same people.
Koma ndiye tisankhe ndani	Who shall we choose?
Yomwe azatiyanjanitse?	Who will unite us?
Ambuye mulamule ndinu,	God, choose for us,
Dziko lino latikanika.	We've failed to rule this country.

("Tisankhe Ndani"—Whom Should We Choose, 1999)

The Nkhoma Synod of the CCAP implicitly suggested, in a pastoral letter in early 1999, that a person of a faith other than Christianity should not be voted into the high office of president. Nkhoma Synod oversees the CCAP churches in the Central Region and has a large following. Although it did not specifically refer to Muslims, it could be deduced that it meant that Muluzi should not be re-elected. Apart from coming from the Southern Region, Muluzi is a Muslim and was contesting for a second term. The remarks threatened to ignite a Christian versus Muslim struggle over the elections, a potentially explosive situation. In the song below Lucius Banda condemns regionalism and religion in politics as things that will destroy the country and which should therefore be avoided.

Zakuti uyu wachoka kumpoto zisiike,	*That one comes from the north, must stop.*
Zakuti uyu wachoka kumwera zisiike,	*That one comes from the south, must stop.*
Zakuti uyu ndi mLomwe, ndi mChewa zichepe,	*That one is a Lomwe, a Chewa, must stop.*

Tonse ndi aMalawi. Likakhala dziko ndi lathu.	We're all Malawians. If it is the country, it is for us all.
Tisataye nthawi kukumbana mitundu.	We should not waste time digging up tribes.
Zoti ndi msilamu achoke pa udindo,	That he is a Muslim, must be removed, won't help us.
Mavuto athu ndi umphawi, si mpingo.	Our problem is poverty, not religion.

("Zisiike"—These Should Stop, 1999)

Lucius Banda saw none of the parties or leaders as capable of uniting the regionally divided country. This is the context for his proposal in "Yahwe" (1999) that the incumbent President Muluzi be re-elected to form a government of national unity with John Tembo (MCP vice president) and Chihana (president of AFORD) as vice presidents. The choice of Tembo is probably motivated by his coming from the Central Region, while the MCP president, Chakuamba, comes from the South. Chihana comes from the North. Despite the weaknesses of each of the three leaders, he thinks they could form a government of national unity. He believes that the country can no longer entrust the welfare of the nation to one party. While many read this song as an endorsement of Muluzi as a presidential candidate, I suggest that it should be read within the context of a discourse searching for viable alternatives to the political paralysis. Lucius Banda says that virtually all politicians, including Muluzi, have failed to rise above party and regional politics. In this scenario he is proposing a government of national unity.

The songs below refer specifically to the violence that took place after the 1999 elections. Supporters of the UDF, especially in the North, clashed with MCP-AFORD alliance supporters, some of whom were beaten or sent out of the region. Most of the Southerners, suspected of voting for the UDF, were either working on tobacco estates as tenants or vending in the markets in urban centres in the North. Lucius Banda's response to the situation was swift.

Timachokera mzigawo zosiyanasiyana, *Timasapota zipani zosiyanasiyana,* *Koma dziko ndi limodzi.*	We come from different regions, We support different parties, But the country is one.
Chisankho chapita, koma pali zambiri zoti tikonze	The election is over, but there are many things to correct.
Poyambilira, tilunzanitse Malawi, *likhale dziko limodzi,* *Kadziko kathu nkakang'ono,* *sikangagawike patatu.*	First, let's unite Malawi, it should be one country. Our country is too small to divide into three.
Ochoka ku Karonga, *Ochoka ku Mangochi,* *Ochoka ku Lilongwe* *Kwao ndi konkuno.*	Those who come from Karonga (representing the North), Those who come from Mangochi (representing the South), Those who come from Lilongwe (representing the Centre), This is their home.
Masapota a Congress, *Masapota a UDF,* *Masapota a AFORD,* *Masapota a Independent* *Kwao ndi konkuno.*	Supporters of Congress (MCP), Supporters of UDF, Supporters of AFORD, Supporters of Independents, This is their home.
A Malawi, tipewe zankhanza, *Zivute zitani, tikanitsitse za nkhondo.* *Nkhondo imaphweka ili cha kutali,* *Ikamabwera, mavuto inu.*	Malawians, let us avoid violence, No matter what, let's avoid war. War is simple while far, But when it is here, it is problems.

("Kwathu ndi Kuno", Our Home is Here, 1999)

Lucius Banda believes that violence threatens the unity of the country and democracy. But even worse, violence raises the prospect of war between the regions. Lucius Banda says that at all costs Malawians should avoid courting war. The example of some countries in Africa and elsewhere suffering the consequences of civil war should show Malawians its dangers. Malawi hosted Mozambican refugees for more than a decade when there was a civil war in Mozambique. Now Malawi hosts refugees fleeing war in Somalia, Rwanda and The Democratic Republic of Congo. Lucius Banda thinks that Malawians should learn from the situation of refugees living within their country instead of risking becoming refugees themselves. There are people who have been talking of a federal model and dividing the country into three independent states as a solution to regional division. Lucius Banda thinks the country is too small for such a division.

Conclusion: Malawian Contemporary Popular Music as Political Discourse

According to King Dunway, "music may be said to be political when its lyrics or melody evoke or reflect a political judgement by the listener" (1987: 37). And Lucius Banda's songs I have referred to in this chapter not only speak about politics, but also call for and evoke a political judgment or response from the audience. The subjects, themes, and references are explicitly political. Lucius Banda's political subjects include the president, his cabinet and members of parliament, political parties and their supporters. He also sings about the abuse of public institutions such as the police, the Anti-Corruption Bureau (ACB), the national radio (MBC). The sources of his themes are the everyday events, most of which have a political dimension. He relies on his own experience and the masses he sings for.

His music can be described as political action for being confrontational, deliberative and pragmatic, as Mark Mattern suggests for a different kind of popular music:

> Confrontational action is typically cast in the language and practices of resistance, opposition, and struggle; ... Deliberative action occurs when (people) use popular music to debate their identity and commitments, as a communicative arena in which debate and discussion occurs; ...The pragmatic action is when people use popular music to promote awareness of shared interests and to organize for collaborative efforts to solve them. (1998: 32–36)

Lucius Banda may be described as confrontational when he opposes government policies and practices that he deems unfair and harmful to poor people. His calls on soldiers to take over, calling politicians liars, and so on, are confrontational stances, expressed in a language of resistance. As pragmatic action, Lucius Banda's music tries to promote awareness in the audience, particularly the masses, of the shared interests they have in preserving the unity of their country and fighting the forces of disunity, for example. Although some may see confrontation as an extreme mode of action, in a democracy it is useful for "enlisting support for a political agenda, ...for publicizing a political issue, for drawing citizens into active participation in public life, (and) for galvanizing action for specific action on specific issues" (Mattern, 1998:33). They are legitimate goals and reasonable means, which democratic societies provide for and uphold.

As an arena for political debate Lucius Banda's music engages with the elected political officials on the question of who represents the masses—who, in other words, has the trust of the people to speak for them. He also asks who speaks the truth and is honest. He does not necessarily question the politicians for being elected to represent the people, but he does claim that they no longer have the trust and confidence of the people who elected them. Instead, he suggests, most politicians are out of touch with their people or simply do not care about them once elected. For these reasons, he questions the authenticity and legitimacy of their voice as speaking for the masses. Put differently, politicians have lost the mandate to represent and speak for the people since most of them do not know the condition of the people they claim to represent. What they say about the masses is a misrepresentation of the reality, if not outright lies.

As for himself, he claims to speak for and represent the masses, whose condition he not only knows but also shares. As noted above, Lucius Banda claims to be a friend of and a soldier for the masses fighting against greedy politicians ("Mzimu wa Soldier"). His friendship is based on the fact that he speaks of the true condition of the people and loves them too. Even more, he says that he is sent by the masses to speak for them. "You" in the song below refers to politicians who, he says, hate to hear the truth. Since they hate the truth, it is improbable that they can speak honestly of the condition of the masses.

Anthu osauka ndi omwe andituma	Poor people have sent me,
Nanga inu bwanji kudana nchilungamo.	Why do you hate the truth.
Anthu amasiye ndi omwe andituma.	Orphans send me.

("Amandituma"—They Send Me, 1995)

Anderson Jones, discussing popular music in China, observes that it functions as "an arena in which many different voices have attempted to speak for 'the people' to gain the power to construct authoritative definitions of the social and legitimate interpretations of social needs" (1992:3). This is what Lucius Banda is setting up in his music. He brings in the voice of the politicians or challenges them to a dialogue with him on the question of truth and honesty. He is quite definitive about the social needs and problems of ordinary people in Malawi. But most importantly, he believes that his interpretation is correct and valid. His music for this reason is a communicative arena where debate about the politics of Malawi takes place. Popular music is also "an alternative social and cultural space where the dramatization of the political and moral crisis prevalent (in society) is possible" (Szemere, 1996:21). Since hegemony has appropriated traditional music, popular music is possibly the only avenue left for the masses where they can speak out, formulate strategies to improve or act upon their condition.

In "Take Over" (1999), after listing all that he thinks is wrong in what politicians do, Lucius Banda ends with a statement in Muluzi's own voice, "Bwinotu bwino/Osamangonamiza anthu" (Be careful, don't just cheat people). This is a statement that Muluzi often makes when refuting his critics, particularly the opposition whom he accuses of cheating people in the villages. This statement serves to help listeners to judge for themselves who is telling the truth—the president or Lucius Banda. He does the same in "Mukawauze" (1999) when he says, "Ngati ndikunama, muchitchule chonamacho" (If I am lying, show me the lie). He challenges politicians to point out what are lies in what he says in his songs.

Lucius Banda feels, to a large extent, that politicians are enemies of popular musicians and the people. When he says, "I am a warrior fighting for peace/I am a warrior fighting for freedom/I am warrior fighting for my rights" ("Warrior", 1994), he is not just talking about his own fight but as a soldier, a warrior, and a fighter for the masses ("Mzimu wa Soldier"). He takes his musical career as a struggle with forces of oppression and exploitation, against an army of greedy and corrupt politi-

119

cians. Lucius Banda also feels that if politicians claim that he has no right to accuse them of failing the people, his answer is that as a citizen who votes he has the right to speak out against things and people that infringe on his rights ("Amandituma").

The response from politicians to Lucius Banda's music has been cautious. The UDF has had the most to fear from his music, because it resonates with the opposition message, but the party has been measured in the way it has responded thus far. The democratic setting has deprived the UDF of the apparatus that the MCP had in the past to suppress such dissenting voices. The UDF may not detain or openly harass musicians who have become authoritative and distinctive as dissenting voices. This, however, is not to deny or ignore reports of UDF-sponsored thugs. Several people have openly been attacked and beaten by individuals or groups that are believed to be sponsored by the UDF.[1] Lucius Banda himself has often feared for his life suggesting that he may be imprisoned or even killed ("Take Over", "Yahwe"). Neither of these has happened. The most the UDF government has done is to keep his most critical songs off the public radio, a fact he complains about in "Cease Fire" and "Take Over".

As the 1999 elections approached, the UDF adopted patronage as a way of dealing with Lucius Banda. For example, in 1998 Muluzi included Lucius Banda in his entourage when he visited Rome and Libya. Since then the UDF has hired him to sing at some of their major political rallies across the country. Lucius Banda has also acknowledged support from Muluzi in his albums *Yahwe* and *Unity,* which may refer to financial help. My reading of this situation is that the party is using Lucius Banda, firstly, to attract young people to their meetings. The youth are the most difficult to get to political meetings, especially when they have heard the slogans again and again. A live band adds an exciting dimension to attract the youth. Secondly, and possibly most importantly, the party is luring him to tone down the heavy criticism that has characterised his music. It is obviously difficult to be very critical of a patron. At the political rallies where he has played his songs, Lucius Banda has been extremely selective as to which songs he sings. For this reason some of his fans feel he has betrayed the fight, while he denies any compromise in his position. That is why in "Zikomo Aphunzitsi" (1999) (Thank You Teachers), in which he acknowledges his brother Paul Banda as his mentor, he desires to continue to be seen as belonging to the masses. He says that even if he is famous and rich, he would like to be seen as a friend of the masses.

Despite the patronage by the UDF, Lucius Banda has, in my view, generally remained engaged with the critical discourse that he started with. He continues to interrogate the dominant ideology by speaking for the poor and challenging politicians to help alleviate their condition. In other words, he still speaks against exploitation and oppression even in the albums and songs that seem to compromise his stance. Even when he endorsed Muluzi for the presidency, for example, he did so with reservations. "MCP was very bad, but that does not mean UDF is better/UDF has failed us, but that does not mean MCP will manage us/UDF and MCP are children of the same father, the old MCP/This is why we see no change" ("Yahwe"). Muluzi and the UDF have failed to help the country move forward because of corruption, greed

---

1. UDF Young Democrats and members of National Intelligence Bureau (NIB) are believed to be behind attacks on opposition supporters and responsible for disrupting their meetings. For example, members of the National Democratic Alliance (NDA) of Brown Mpinganjira, a former UDF stalwart, have been beaten on several occasions. Sheikhs of the Muslim community and Christian ministers have also been attacked for speaking out against violence and corruption and opposing Muluzi's bid to change the constitution to allow him a third term. Journalists who write about the deteriorating political situation have become targets of attack by UDF thugs forcing some to go into hiding for fear of their lives.

and regionalism. Hence his suggestion is to have all the parties work together in a government of national unity. One other way to read Lucius Banda's message is, as Beverly Best suggests, to "recognize the contradictory nature of popular products, in that they can be the site of both hegemonic and counter-hegemonic ideological production depending on the context of their reception or production" (1997: 19).

The music of Lucius Banda is spontaneous, arising out of and to the immediacy of a situation. However, it also goes beyond mere response. As Barber explains popular art furthers the interests of the masses "by opening their eyes to their objective situation in society" (1987: 6). Music helps the people to see that their condition is deprived because they are exploited and even oppressed. In other words, "popular art does not merely reflect an already-constituted consciousness, (but) in times of rapid social change ... will play a crucial role in formulating new ways of looking at things" (Barber, 1987:4). It does so by providing the masses with opportunities to compare their experiences with those of the élite. Lucius Banda describes the plight of the masses against a background of plenty among the rich in order to raise awareness in the masses of the state of their exploitation and oppression.

Individual popular artists like Lucius Banda are spokespersons, arbiters of public opinion and intermediaries for the grievances of the people. Kofie Agowi explains, for example, how Highlife music in Ghana was able to unite the oppressed population and "undermine the prestige and power of the rulers" (1989:195) by attacking values on which the élite operated; values that reflected the rulers' priorities and concerns but not the masses' condition. Before the 1966 coup d'etat, Agowi says, "popular music had given enough evidence of people's dissatisfaction with government" (1989:195). This is what Lucius Banda tries to do in his music in Malawi. His music is a barometer of the people's feelings even as it expands their consciousness. And several musicians, such as Billy Kaunda and Mlaka Maliro, have joined the discourse.

As a site of counter-hegemonic cultural production, music is capable of being an agent of organised resistance against many forms of oppression. In the case of Malawi and the music of Lucius Banda, there is resistance against political exploitation and oppression, being lied to and abused. Lucius Banda travels across the country, singing not just in order to entertain but to sensitise and mobilise the masses; an endeavour that many other musicians are also pursuing. This is what the UDF politicians fear about Lucius Banda and his music and explains their patronage of him. But all the same, popular music in Malawi should be recognised as having a place and role in democratic politics. It does not just define the rights and condition of the masses, but is preserving democracy itself. It counter-balances traditional music that politicians have appropriated for hegemonic purposes. Popular music is a site for political discourse and potential action against oppression and exploitation by the élite. It is a role it is poised to play as long as democracy prevails.

A Note on Sources

The following audiotapes were used for songs referred to in this chapter.

Banda, Lucius. *Son of a Poor Man*, recorded in Balaka, Malawi, IY Production, 1994.
—, *Down Babylon*, recorded in Balaka, Malawi, IY Production, 1995.
—, *Cease Fire*, recorded in Balaka, Malawi, IY Production, 1995.
—, *Take Over*, manufactured by Audio Digital, Lilongwe, Malawi, 1998.
—, *Yahwe*, recorded at IY Studio, Balaka, Malawi, 1999.
—, *Unity*, recorded at IY Studio, Balaka, Malawi, 1999.

All translations are by Reuben Makayiko Chirambo. Analysis of Lucius Banda's songs is also based on Chirambo's interviews with him in 1998.

6. Are Malawi's Local Clergy Civil Society Activists?

The Limiting Impact of Creed, Context and Class[1]

Peter VonDoepp

Introduction

In the early 1990s numerous observers of African politics celebrated the potential for civil society organisations to play transformative roles in African states. Guided by liberal democratic theory and emboldened by actual democratic movements and reform processes in Africa, the call went out for greater scholarly effort to assess and analyse civil society organisations. Nowhere was such attention viewed as more important than in those countries where dictators had fallen and novel challenges of democratic deepening and consolidation had emerged. For while civil society organisations had been integral to the undermining of authoritarian regimes, they could also play a central part in shaping the survival and quality of new democracies (Landell-Mills, 1992; Harbeson, 1994; Diamond 1994; Hadenius and Uggla, 1996).

As the enthusiasm of the early 1990s has faded, many critical commentaries have emerged that have highlighted the very real problems with overly romanticised notions of civil society. As observers have noted, despite the importance of such organisations in the liberalisation of African polities, in the post-authoritarian context civil society has been either unable or unwilling to contribute substantially to ongoing democratisation processes (Boadi 1996; Kasfir 1998). However, while such commentaries have raised important issues, understandings of critical elements of civil society remain relatively shallow. On one hand, very few scholars have examined the nature of civil society in local, as opposed to national, arenas (cf. Comaroff and Comaroff, 1999). On the other, scholars have not delved sufficiently into the dynamics informing the political role of civil society representatives on the ground.

This issue is especially relevant when considering the political role of churches in Malawi. More than any other civil society organisations, churches played a central part in the removal of the single party regime of Kamuzu Banda. Since that time, moreover, they have remained relatively active in politics, establishing civic education programmes and maintaining a prophetic voice which has challenged the behaviour of sometimes irresponsible political elites. Yet a true understanding of the churches' role in the political system—and their contribution to democratic deepening and consolidation—should involve more than an assessment of their activities in the national political sphere. As organisations, churches have considerable potential to shape not only national politics, but also local-level politics. As such, they can have an important impact on both the quality of democracy as experienced by citi-

1. A revised version of this chapter appears in the *Journal of Commonwealth and Comparative Politics* Vol. 40, No. 2 (July 2002). The author wishes to thank Harri Englund, Kenneth Wald, Goran Hyden, Philip Williams and Kenneth Ross for their help at various stages of this project. Funding for the research leading to this publication was provided by the Research Enablement Program, a grant programme for mission scholarship supported by the Pew Charitable Trust, and administered by the Overseas Ministries Study Center (New Haven, CT); and from the National Science Foundation (USA), Grant no. INT 9511792.

zens at the grassroots, as well as the social and cultural bases for democratic consolidation. Their grassroots role merits serious consideration.

The attention to the church at the local level brings the spotlight specifically to the clergy who represent these organisations at the grassroots. While grassroots clergy are not often considered central political actors, it would be foolish to deny their potential impact on political processes. Indeed, among the actors who represent civil society, clergy are uniquely well-placed to exert positive impacts on local community life. For one thing, activism by clergy can generate improvements in the character of state-local relations. Clerical advocacy for a village borehole or road improvements, for example, can yield important changes in how state actors respond to community needs—leading to the extension of very tangible gains to local communities. Moreover, clergy can play an important part in helping to cultivate higher levels of political awareness and efficacy among local citizens (Levine, 1992; Calhoun-Brown, 1996). Preaching on issues of concern to the community, for instance, can have the effect of validating felt needs and even spur political action by grassroots citizens. Such is a necessary step in the creation of a more responsive democratic system.

These kinds of activities by clergy take on special importance if one considers that one of the major challenges that confronts Malawi's new democracy is a persistent gap between political processes at the level of the state and the concerns of average citizens. For many in Malawi, the current dispensation resembles what Nigerian scholar Claude Ake (1995) described as "the democratisation of disempowerment"—a situation where average citizens obtain few benefits and undertake only minimal roles in the political process. As many Malawians have complained to the author, the politics of predation of the Banda era has been replaced by a politics of neglect under the democratic system. The principal players devote attention to serving their own political and personal needs rather than grassroots concerns. And the average citizen lacks both the channels and skills to help rectify the situation.

The central issue explored in this chapter concerns the character of clergy political activity with respect to these issues. Do clergy serve as civil society activists, helping to bridge the gap between the state and the average citizen at the grassroots? And of greater significance, why or why not? As will be demonstrated, answering these questions offers insight not only into the politics of Malawi's local clergy. It also allows more general commentary on contemporary discussions of civil society and its character in emerging African democracies.

Despite the important role that the clergy might play at the local level, research conducted in 1996 revealed that there were significant limits to their grassroots civil society activism. The majority of clergy interviewed reported that they did not engage or only sporadically engaged in efforts to empower citizens or enhance state responsiveness to community needs. In accounting for this, the chapter argues that the limited clergy activism needs to be understood in the context of three central factors shaping their behaviour: the religious frameworks (or creeds) informing their work, the larger organisational contexts in which they are situated, and their character as members of a distinct class pursuing economic interests.[1] While attention to these factors illuminates the specific constraints on clergy activism, it also helps to reveal how clergy are themselves connected to and embedded in a larger social setting. Influences from that setting undermine their propensity to serve as agents of democratic deepening. This serves as a reminder that the emergent character of civil society

---

1.   This language borrows from Wald (1997: 28–30).

will reflect the dynamics of the larger social setting; often in such a way as to undermine its democratising potential.

The chapter begins with a general theoretical discussion of how these factors operate to shape the political behaviour of clergy. Thereafter, it offers a brief overview of findings from research that highlight the patterns of limited activism by Malawi's local clergy. The two subsequent sections are devoted to analyses of these findings. I conclude with a brief discussion of how the research speaks to both contemporary concerns about the character of Malawi's democracy and larger scholarly discussions about the nature of civil society in Africa.

What Shapes Clergy Activism: Creed, Context, and Class

While there are of course numerous influences on clergy political activity, studies of churches and politics have tended to pinpoint three different types of factors as especially important. The first of these can be labelled "creed"—referring broadly to the kinds of religious ideas and theological frameworks that guide the clergy in their interactions with the faithful and society. As studies have noted, both the extent and type of clergy political activity can be shaped by their subjective understandings of faith and calling. Work on the Catholic Church in Latin America, for instance, has highlighted the decisive impact of liberation theology on how clerics interpreted social problems and understood their role in addressing such problems. Clergy who interpreted their mission in "liberationist" terms tended to show higher levels of activism than others who were solely concerned with promoting salvation and preserving institutional vitality (Levine, 1981:144–170; Mainwaring, 1986:145–181). The importance of such subjective religious variables is also found in studies of American clergy. Studies of clergy during the civil rights and anti-war movements found that "belief variables" and "role orientations" affected clergy involvement in social protest (Nelsen et al., 1973; Tygart, 1977). More recent studies of American Protestant clergy have similarly highlighted the importance of such religious factors. Clergy holding views that see individual conversion to faith and personal piety as paths to salvation tend to be less supportive of political involvement. Those who emphasise social justice as a religious objective have been more active (Guth et al., 1997:162–184).

Research thus indicates that religious frameworks can have an important impact on levels of clergy activism. To the extent that mission orientations or personal theologies direct clergy to take active and prophetic roles in local community affairs, we might expect greater activism. Should religious frameworks emphasise other themes, the likelihood of clergy engaging in political activity on behalf of local concerns diminishes. These are important issues to keep in mind when we seek to understand the limited activism of Malawi's clergy.

The second factor, "context", refers to the organisational setting in which the clergy are embedded. While clergy clearly have a range of opportunities for autonomous activity, it is equally important to recognise that their political behavior is shaped by organisational influences. Two aspects of the organisational context deserve attention. The first is the influence of church leaders. Church authorities can play a key role in either encouraging or discouraging activism by clergy. As research on clergy behaviour during the American civil rights movement details, clergy activism tended to be higher in denominations whose leadership was supportive of civil rights (Ammerman, 1981). The second aspect of the organisational context that deserves attention is the influence of local church members. While local clergy are representatives of larger institutions, they are also associated with church communities at the grassroots. And to varying degrees, clergy are susceptible to influences from that community. Studies of clergy in the United States indicate that the support of the local community can provide an impetus to clergy political activity. Much the same, where local communities frown on active clergy roles in politics, the probability of clergy activism decreases (Guth et al., 1997:158; Friedland, 1998; Winter, 1973).

It is important to recognise that the institutional structure of the church affects which of these two aspects of the organisational context has more influence on clergy behavior. Clearly, hierarchically-organised churches, such as the Catholic Church, make clergy more responsive to the stipulations of church leaders. By contrast, decentralised churches, vesting greater authority with local church members, require clergy to operate with greater sensitivity to the values and needs of the community they serve. Consideration of this institutional factor is quite important in order to understand differences in levels of activism among Catholic and Presbyterian clergy in Malawi.

A final factor that deserves consideration is the class character of the clergy themselves. Many critical perspectives on churches in Africa have emphasised that clergy represent the privileged sector of society, engaging in processes of class formation and reproduction through the use of church resources as well as alliances with political elites. As they have distinct interests in perpetuating the status quo from which they benefit, their efforts to alter relations between powerful and powerless are limited. As Wyatt MacGaffey puts it, "the churches, Catholic and Protestant, inevitably participate in class relations, and their political role is accordingly compromised" (1990:261). Similarly, Jeff Haynes comments that religious elites "seek to achieve a hegemonic ideology that stresses the desirability of stability rather than progressive change" (1996:104; see also Fatton, 1992:77 and Bayart, 1993:189).

While such views do have a deterministic thrust, they bring to attention an important issue. Clergy occupy positions of privilege with access to resources and opportunities far beyond that of the average individual in African societies. And it would be naive to deny that their interests as socio-economic actors exert some influence on their political activities. The critical issue with regards to the Malawian clergy is to discern how the socio-economic interests of clergy operated to limit their efforts to work for the deepening of democracy in their local communities.

Activism by Malawi's Local Clergy: A Brief Look

At the time of research in 1996, Malawi's two-year-old democratic experiment had already begun to reveal significant shortcomings in the extent to which it addressed the needs of local citizens. Owing to their organisational backing and status in local communities, Presbyterian and Catholic clergy were well-positioned to help overcome these shortcomings in the system—either helping to stimulate greater participation on the part of citizens or serving as advocates for their needs. Indeed, many clergy had engaged in activism only a few years previously when churches spearheaded an effort to challenge the authoritarian regime of Kamuzu Banda. And their larger church organisations—both regional and national—remained active in national politics in the democratic era, suggesting some sanction from church leadership for an active political role.

Yet research revealed that the local-level activism of clergy was quite limited. In order to elucidate this I consider, in the first place, the results of interviews conducted with 41 Catholic and Presbyterian clergy in the country.[1] During discussions, clergy were asked about their work in their churches and their interactions in the broader community. The limits to their civil society activism were evident in a number of respects. First, the interviews revealed that the pastoral work of most clergy centred on conventional clerical concerns, and did not include practices designed to address the social and political needs of the faithful.[2] This was especially evident in clergy responses to two questions: "What are the biggest priorities in your pastoral work right now?" and "What are the concerns to which you are devoting attention?". In responding, clergy normally mentioned one to three priorities or concerns. This yielded a total of 95 responses which were then placed into one of nine categories. The table below reviews how often each priority or concern was mentioned.

Table 4. Primary Pastoral Priorities and Concerns

	How often mentioned
Laity	25
Intensification	18
Building Projects	15
Self-sufficiency	13
Charity	9
Youth/Women	8
Contacts	5
HR/J&P	1
Organising	1

Laity:	Lay organisations or training the laity
Intensification:	Intensifying the faith or religious knowledge of the Christians
Building Projects:	Building or improving physical structures
Self-sufficiency:	Promoting parish self-sufficiency
Charity:	Charity, providing education, or development projects (schools, hospitals)
Youth/Women:	Encouraging the role of youth or women in the church
Contacts:	Increasing contacts and visits with the Christians
HR/J&P:	Localising human rights or justice and peace concerns
Organising:	Mobilising and organising citizens for social/developmental ends

As is evident, manifestly political activities were rarely mentioned as priorities or key concerns by the clergy. Indeed, only two clerics indicated that they incorporated such practices into their pastoral work. The first highlighted his efforts to establish justice and peace commissions; the other mentioned efforts to organise groups for development purposes. To be sure, the fact that most clergy focus on conventional concerns is not that surprising. Especially given the demands on their time, a focus on "the basics" makes sense to some degree. Yet it is notable that practices that became the

---

1. Interviews were conducted over a six-month period in 1996 in Central and Southern Malawi. All of the Presbyterian clergy were affiliated with Blantyre Synod; Catholic clergy were affiliated with either the Zomba, Blantyre, or Lilongwe dioceses. To select clergy for interviews, the investigator obtained lists of active ministers and priests from church administrative officers. After removing those inaccessible by road, the investigator randomly selected a modest number of clergy from these lists. When these clergy were visited, so too were other clergy living in reasonable geographic distance from them. In this fashion, the number of clergy interviewed was increased with small sacrifices being made for the randomness of selection. While the final sample of clergy was not biased in terms of age, geographical location, or levels of education, the nature of sampling procedures limits our ability to make concrete generalisable statements about the character of political activities of all the clergy associated with these religious bodies. This said, there is little reason to propose that the descriptive and analytical findings presented here do not bespeak tendencies among the larger body of clergy.
2. The attention to pastoral work follows other research suggesting that pastoral practices and ministry can be a primary means through which clergy intervene to shape local political circumstances. See especially Levine (1992: 217–271).

mainstay of activist clergy in other parts of the world were clearly not high on the agendas of the Malawian clergy interviewed.[1]

A second way that clergy activism appeared limited was in the issues they reported raising during their preaching and spoken interactions in church. The table below presents clergy responses to a question asking them to describe their primary preaching themes. The 41 clergy offered a total of 72 responses. These were then organised into ten categories.

Table 5. Primary Preaching Themes

	How often mentioned
Individual Morality	17
Family Relations/Christian Living	16
Faith/Spirituality	11
Stewardship (care of the church)	6
Doctrine/Instructional	6
Salvation	5
Social Issues: AIDS, crime, youth behavior	3
National Politics: Need for national unity or accountability in public life	3
Local Politics: Local injustices or government neglect of community needs	3
Encouraging participation in public life	2

As we can see, the vast majority of clergy reported that they directed attention to a somewhat standard set of religious and moral concerns. The themes of particular interest are shown in the last two categories of the chart. Here the clergy reported that they either addressed specific problems pertaining to relations with the state or aimed to empower members of their community in public life. An example of the first scenario was provided by one cleric who recounted his preaching about the lack of state responsiveness to citizens:

> I was speaking on the theme of love and asked, "How does the government love its people?" We can ask about those aspects where it is doing well, but also about how it is failing... Even though the wealth in this country is for the people, it seems it is being enjoyed by only a few. When those few people are eating, they are forgetting us here in the village (Interview, 20 June, 1996).

The second is exemplified by clergy who consciously attempted to remove sociocultural impediments to political participation. An example is provided by the comments of this priest.

> Most of the people in these areas still have those fears from Kamuzu. There are very few who will talk. So in church I tell them, "You Christians now have not only the right, but a duty to remind your MP all the time about things in his area. And if he does not listen you should let us know" (Interview, 1 April, 1996).

Yet only a select few clergy indicated that they raised such themes in their routine preaching. Subsequent questions revealed that a slightly larger number addressed such themes on an occasional basis. However, most indicated that they shied away from such topics.

For the third scenario, the interviews revealed that clergy advocacy efforts—raising issues with authorities on behalf of their community—were relatively limited and inconsistent. In order to gauge the extent of this advocacy, the clergy were asked about their contact with local political officials, how they had personally responded

---

1. See Mainwaring (1986:196–199) and Levine (1992: 217–271).

to the problems confronting the people in the area, and how they had responded to any injustices or abuses of power in their area. Out of a total of 41 clergy, 13 (32 per cent) had, on their own initiative, raised a community issue with a local political or government official. Among these 13 cases, however, advocacy efforts varied. As the table below indicates, most of those who engaged in advocacy had done so only on one occasion. Only six had done so twice or more.

Table 6. Clergy Advocacy Efforts

	Number of clergy
No advocacy	28
One act of advocacy	7
Two or more acts	6

In one respect, the overview of these three areas of clergy activity suggests some variance among the clergy in terms of their civil society activism. The more significant pattern, however, indicates relatively limited activism on their part. A relatively modest proportion mentioned that they engaged in high levels of advocacy for community concerns. Only a few mentioned that they articulated political themes in their preaching on a regular basis. Still fewer incorporated empowering or awareness-raising strategies in their pastoral work.

The limits to activism are further borne out when additional findings from the research are considered. For example, despite the fact that some clergy reported local advocacy efforts or preaching on political themes, such self-reports may have overstated the extent of their activism. During two local-level field stays I was in regular contact with two Catholic priests for three months each. Both priests reported to have undertaken advocacy and both also claimed that they did, on occasion, preach about political themes specifically focused on substantive issues at the local level. But in the over twenty sermons observed, such political themes were never addressed. Moreover, their advocacy was neither visible nor reported by parishioners.

Beyond this, although the data indicate some activism by the clergy, this does not necessarily mean that such behaviour was consistent over time. Consider the clergy's responses to the specific question of how they reacted to local injustices or abuses of power of which they were aware. These are represented in the table below.

Table 7. Clergy Responses to Local Injustices

	Number of clergy
Saw none	16
Aware of, did not act	16
Acted of one issue, not others	3
Preached/contacted official	6

Of the 41 interviewed, 25 said that they were aware of a local injustice or abuse of power. However, only six had addressed the issue in their verbal interactions with Christians or by contacting a political official. Three others had acted on one issue, but not on others. 16 had done nothing about the injustices or abuses of power of which they were aware. In short, some clergy who reported local-level activity also provided evidence that their activism was limited in scope and consistency. In this respect, the overall limits to clergy activism become even more apparent.

Before exploring the reasons for the clergy's limited activism, it is necessary to first highlight some of the factors affecting the variances in that activism. Analyses of the data indicate that both organisational contexts and religious frameworks need to be taken seriously in terms of their effects on the political behaviour of the local clergy. This serves as a guide to the more substantial inquiry into the constraints on activism.

Basic statistical analyses were conducted to explore relationships between levels of clergy activism and several variables with the potential to influence such activism. Drawing from the material described above, four measures of clergy activism were used. The first was whether they reported that political topics were among the primary themes of their preaching. That is, did the cleric report engaging in any type of political preaching on a regular basis? The second measure also dealt with clergy preaching, but focused on the extent to which they reported preaching on locally-centred political themes. In this sense, the analysis targeted whether and how frequently clergy raised themes described in the last two categories from Table 5 (either addressing local political issues or encouraging participation among citizens). Based on interview responses to questions about preaching, clergy were scored on the basis of whether they never, occasionally, or regularly brought up such themes. The third measure concerned the extent of clergy advocacy in their communities. Clergy were ranked on a three-level scale, corresponding to their reported level of advocacy as delineated in Table 6 (no advocacy, one act of advocacy, or two or more acts of advocacy). The final measure was a score that indicated the overall level of civil society activism undertaken by the cleric. Based on their self-reports about pastoral work, preaching, and local advocacy, clergy were coded on a four-level scale designating whether they were wholly inactive, minimally active, moderately active, or highly active.

Of the 41 interviewed, 25 said that they were aware of a local injustice or abuse of power. However, only six had addressed the issue in their verbal interactions with Christians or by contacting a political official. Three others had acted on one issue, but not on others. 16 had done nothing about the injustices or abuses of power of which they were aware. In short, some clergy who reported local-level activity also provided evidence that their activism was limited in scope and consistency. In this respect, the overall limits to clergy activism become even more apparent.

Table 8 provides a statistical overview of some of the key findings.

Table 8. Influences on Clergy Activism

		LOCAL LEVEL ACTIVISM		
	Politcs as primary preaching theme	Extent of locally-centered preaching	Local advocacy	Overall activism rank
Catholic vs Presbyterian	-.31**	-.28	-.14	-.32 *
Mission understandings				
Social Issues orientation	-.02	.16	.15	.26 *
Salvation orientation	-.16*	-.15*	-.15	-.20 *
Behavioral orientation	-.28**	-.14	-.12	-.23
Spiritual enrichment	-.01	-.10	-.12	-.07
Pastoral orientation	.15	-.09	-.01	-.06
Educational experience				
Time since ordained	.16	.08	.06	.10
Standard vs foreign	.01	.20	.11	.30 *
Standard vs human rights conference	-.02	.05	.19	.17

* Significant below .1

** Significant at or below .05

Note: Numbers indicate the value of tau, a statistic used to measure the relationship between two ordinal variables. The values indicate the direction and strength of the relationship between the variables.

The key findings from these analyses are threefold. The first concerns differences be-tween Catholic and Presbyterian clergy. As the negative statistics in the top row in-dicate, Presbyterian clergy scored lower on various indices of local-level activism. This is especially true with regard to preaching, but it is also true for advocacy work. The cross tabulations below offer a precise depiction of the differences in these re-gards.

Table 9. Political Preaching by Catholic and Presbyterian Clergy

Political Preaching:	Catholic		Presbyterian		Row total	
Not as Primary Theme	15		19		34	(83%)
As Primary Theme	7		0		7	(17%)
Column Total	22	(54%)	19	(46%)	41	(100%)

Table 10. Advocacy Efforts by Catholic and Presbyterian Clergy

Advocacy	Catholic	Presbyterian	Row total	
None	14	14	28	(68.5%)
Only once	3	4	7	(17%)
Twice or more	5	1	6	(14.5%)

As we will see, these findings are largely explicable by reference, first, to the kinds of organisational contexts in which the clergy are embedded; second, to the fact that, via foreign education, a larger number of Catholic clergy were exposed to unconven-tional religious ideas encouraging socio-political activism.

The second finding from the analyses concerns the importance of the religious frameworks guiding the clergy in their work—specifically their understandings of their mission. This was explored by asking clergy two questions: "How do you see your calling or mission as a minister/priest in the church?" and "What are your goals as a representative of the Church?". While answers varied, most clergy focused on what might be considered relatively conventional or traditional themes. Typical re-sponses placed emphases on pastoral themes such as "to prepare and administer sac-raments to Christians"; or alternatively on the objective of enriching the spiritual life of the community. Many other clergy emphasised their role in uplifting the moral behaviour of people and preparing them for salvation. A select few, however, men-tioned addressing social or community issues as part of their mission. This included specific references to empowering people or addressing community concerns, or raising more general themes of helping people's social development. The following response serves as example:

> I have a duty to take people to God and that involves lots of things: preaching, living as we preach, and visiting the sick. ... But it is our duty to address other areas of man, what problems they are facing, it may be political or anything else (Interview, 20 March, 1996).

In order to gauge the impact of mission understandings on their activism, clergy were ranked according to whether they gave high emphasis, moderate emphasis, or no emphasis to different themes. These themes are listed in Table 8 under "mission understandings". The statistics indicate associational relationships between these different mission understandings and levels of clergy activism. As the second row of the table indicates, clergy who emphasised socially-oriented themes tended to be more active than others. Equally notable, clergy who emphasised that their mission was either to "promote salvation" or "improve the moral behaviour of Christians" tended to be less active. Consistent with the research from the American context, belief variables appear to have a significant impact on clergy political behaviour.

Finally, Table 8 highlights that clergy with foreign educational experiences—disproportionately Catholic clergy—were more disposed to activism than others. Further analysis indicated that foreign education had a significant impact on clergy mission understandings. Those with educational experiences in Europe or the United States tended to have more socially-oriented understandings than those with only standard local education.

Creed, Context and Class as Limiting Factors

The analyses above provide an entry point to a more systematic discussion of the constraints on clergy activism. Returning to the issues raised in the earlier theoretical discussion, the limited clergy activism can be understood with reference to the religious frameworks guiding their activities at the grassroots, the organisational contexts in which they are situated, and their socio-economic interests as members of a distinct class. Beyond highlighting the specific constraints on the clergy activism, attention to these factors illuminates how the character of civil society is itself shaped by influences from the larger social setting. Understanding how the clergy were connected to and shaped by their social context provides insight into why their civil society activism was limited.

Attention to religious frameworks, specifically mission orientations, provides us some understanding of why certain clergy were more active than others. Religious ideas are also part of the reason that many clergy remain relatively inactive. The mission understandings of most Malawian clergy do not direct attention to social and political concerns. In turn, clergy attention to such issues is minimal. How do we account for the relative absence of socially-focused mission understandings among Malawi's clergy? Part of the answer surely has to do with the nature of clergy training. As indicated above, those clergy with foreign educational experiences were clearly the most likely of all clergy to adopt socially-oriented mission understandings. Clergy with exclusively local—that is, Malawian—training experiences were least likely to adopt such orientations. Yet the issue of training only addresses part of the conundrum. For although local institutions of clerical formation may not emphasise such ideas, that does not necessarily explain why local clergy do not independently appropriate or develop theologies calling for activism. Why is it that such socially-oriented theological discourses have limited salience and staying power in the Malawian context?

To understand this we need to recall that religious ideas tend to be shaped by their social context. That is, objective realities and circumstances affect the kinds of religious ideas that take root and resonate in a given setting (among others, see Laitin, 1978). The critical issue with regard to Malawi's clergy is that ideas about justice or empowerment, as often articulated in "progressive" socially-oriented theologies, make little sense given the social and religious problems that ministers and priests observe in their local settings. Consider, for instance, how the nature of sociopolitical division within Malawi shapes the applicability of socially-oriented theologies. The political environment of Malawi is quite unlike the context of the civil rights movement in the United States, the class-ridden environment of Latin America, or apartheid South Africa. In these cases manifest inequity and the visible hand of repression and injustice provided fertile terrain for religious ideas calling for clergy action on behalf of the marginalized and downtrodden. In Malawi's new democracy, while divides between powerful and powerless are of course apparent, manifest socio-political division occurs more along partisan and even ethno-regional lines. Often, such divisions filter down to the local level. In turn, this shapes how clergy interpret and address pressing "political" issues. Rather than being concerned with grassroots empowerment or "justice", the majority of clergy are justifiably concerned with problems of partisan division and the threats to the church imposed by party politics. During my discussions with clergy, many emphasised that it was precisely because of such divisions that they did not raise political issues in church. Witness the comments of this minister:

> The biggest political problem in this country is division; we even see it in the church. There are some Christians who belong to MCP (the opposition party), others to UDF (the governing party). And people don't understand the meaning of democracy. So they may not like the people in power just because they are in a different party from the one they support. And this will cause problems in the future because people will just dismiss and disregard those who are in a different party. (Interview, 4 April, 1996)

Such themes are echoed by a local priest:

> This new political change is hampering relationships even among Christians. There is a lot of misunderstanding, and we are not helped by the members of parliament when they come and make party meetings not constituency meetings.... So I tell them, "Gentlemen, please don't waste your time on politics and parties". (Interview, 15 January, 1996)

Quite clearly, politics is not seen as a solution to local problems, but as the source of community disruption. In a context such as this, it makes sense that many clergy would avoid socially-oriented theologies which call for political activism or efforts to empower Christians in politics. Conventional understandings of faith and calling provide a better guide for how to negotiate the dangerous terrain of divisive local politics. Moreover, where theological change has occurred among the local clergy, the emerging discourses have done little to stimulate activism. Indeed, they might work against it. An instructive example is provided by a self-proclaimed "pentecostal" minister—representative of a highly visible religious movement within protestant, especially Presbyterian, circles in recent years. The minister's own religious background had always been that of mainstream Presbyterianism, though he actively participated in revivals sponsored by pentecostal movements from outside of Malawi. His religiosity reflected as much his appropriation and reworking of pentecostal themes, as it did the training he received prior to ordination. The reference points for his ministry were stark conceptualisations of ultimate designs and his role as a servant of God. In his own words:

> As a servant of God, I have to overcome all difficulties and see that the people will receive salvation ...So my number one priority here is to preach the word of God, especially stressing salvation ... When I preach, my example is to tell them, "You are on a trip. Where are we going to end up? Is it Paradise or *Gehena* (Hell)?". (Interview, 10 May, 1996)

As we might expect, his conscious political involvement was limited or non-existent. Like others in the area, he "knew" that the local MP pocketed poverty alleviation funds designated for the constituency. He, like others, privately condemned the MP and government for corruption and neglect of the area. But his awareness of these issues did not generate a public condemnation. For him, emergent social and political issues were not conceived of in terms of justice or injustice, but as evidence of Satan's designs on earth. Politics—single or multi-party—with its attendant divisiveness, corruptions and duplicities, represented evil. As such, it was consciously avoided in favour of a stress on changing personal behaviour and, in his own words, "looking to heaven".[1]

As Jeff Haynes reminds us, the salience of these kinds of religious discourses can to some extent be accounted for by the "combined effects of social, economic and political disruptions" currently affecting contemporary Africa (1996:229). In terms of this specific case, the theological framework guiding the minister becomes more comprehensible when we account for the difficulties and impossibilities he and many Malawians encounter in their daily lives. AIDS, a fraying social fabric, general declines in living standards, and other hardships provided fertile terrain to inform his religious perspective and approach to ministry. His own comments included references to the world he experienced on a daily basis: "Are we really lifting up the cross? It's high time. When deaths are happening almost every day. One of these days Jesus will come to take his promised people. Are we ready?" Or, alternatively, when he discussed decline in security, "Look around these days, the devil is blinding us and we need to open our eyes".

While this case is not representative of all the clergy who shun activism, it nonetheless indicates that religious views and the social environment operate in a dialectical fashion. Clergy political activities are guided by religious discourses that make sense and resonate in a certain social context. As the above cases suggest, the realities of the social world may be more conducive to religious ideas that provide solace than those that stress justice or human rights (see also Englund, 2000).

In addition to the motives and constraints associated with religious ideas, one needs to consider how organisational contexts affect and constrain clergy activism. This is especially useful in accounting for some of the differences in activism between Catholic and Presbyterian clergy in the sample. The critical issue to recognise is that Presbyterian clergy, owing to the structure of their church, are much more closely connected to their local community. Whereas Catholic priests obtain authority and direction from the ecclesiastical hierarchy, Presbyterian ministers exercise responsibility in conjunction with local congregations—especially the elders who sit on church councils. This places very real limits on the type and extent of political activity they can undertake at the grassroots. Venturing into the political terrain is much more risky for Presbyterian clergy. A suspected bias towards one partisan faction or another could generate challenge and confrontation from members of the local community—disrupting both their clerical authority and the unity of the religious community. As such, it is not that surprising that during interviews Presbyterian clergy were much more likely to emphasise that politics needed to be kept out the church. This is not to suggest that such concerns do not figure in the decisions of Catholic clergy. However, their institutional position insulates them much more from potential challenges by parishioners. An occasional political comment from the pulpit is much more within the realm of possibilities for a Catholic priest.

This attention to the different organisational contexts brings us to the issue of how the socio-economic interests of the clergy can limit their activism. Not only do Presbyterian clergy share authority with local congregations, they also are much more financially dependent on their congregation. This involves not only salary, but also transport, loans, and other benefits. Catholic clergy receive the bulk of their sal-

---

1. For a deeper description of these types of religious discourses and their political relevance in the African context, see Haynes (1996:201–207). A more specific treatment of sociological and political roots of "puritan" religious themes in Malawi is found in van Dijk (1992). It should be added that it is fallacious to overgeneralise or essentialise the political implications of such beliefs. As some have argued, the strict guidelines for social behaviour within the pentecostal discourse may be applied in a prophetic critique of the state (see Marshall, 1995 and Englund, 2000).

ary and support from diocesan headquarters. This position of financial dependence further constrains the Presbyterian clergy's potential for activism. Pure economic considerations require Presbyterian clergy to be much more focused on maintaining amiable relations with powerful local interests who sit on church councils and, by extension, provide their means of survival and relative comfort. Indeed, in some cases, clergy fall into clientelistic relationships with local party leaders, state officials, and estate owners who sit on church councils.[1]

This process can work in very subtle ways. Several clergy located on large sugar or tea estates were privately quite open about the injustices and squalid living conditions which befell workers. Yet in their public discourse they were silent on these issues. Basic needs for survival and comfort meant that personal priorities lay in maintaining amiable ties with the local management of the enterprises who provided a consistent supply of benefits. In one particularly memorable example, a minister recounted numerous concerns which surrounded the conditions of workers on a large sugar estate. Workers lived in hastily constructed mud hovels. Poor sewage systems had led to outbreaks of bloody diarrhea and the deaths of many children. Yet in his contact with the local managers, many of whom were part of his church council, the issue was never raised. Nor had he ever had contact with representatives of the local workers' organisation. He did, however, visit the management to ask for improvements to his own house. Another minister added that he consciously avoided having estate workers on his session (council) because they could not provide the support he needed. A desirable session member had influence and resources. The voice of the marginalised thus failed to obtain an outlet in the church organisation, further limiting the potential for clergy activism on their behalf.

In addition to accounting for the differences between Presbyterian and Catholic clergy, attention to socio-economic interests also helps us to understand the more general pattern of limits among the clergy as a whole. For socio-economic interests shape the politics of the Catholic clergy as well. And the limits in clergy activism become more comprehensible when we consider the clergy as individuals engaged in processes of class formation and consolidation.

That the clergy, especially Catholic priests, occupy a privileged place within Malawi's social structure is quite evident. Educational status and material security provide obvious initial benchmarks that set them apart from most Malawians. Lifestyles and opportunities also distinguish clergy from the average Malawian. In turn, this class character of the clergy has specific implications for their political outlooks and activities. To understand this one needs to have a sense of the pressures that accompany the social position of the clergy. Primary among these are the demands on the clergy to extend the benefits of their own position to kin and family members— many of whom are desperately poor. Many clergy were privately very open about their obligations to provide secondary school fees, iron roofs, credit, and agricultural supplies to expectant relatives.[2] An equally important set of pressures involves needs to consolidate or maintain class status with its attendant benefits. In the con-

1. To some degree this challenges Haynes' viewpoint that rank and file clergy, because they are more closely connected to the grassroots, will be more active in working for democratic change. The evidence presented here suggests that embeddedness in the local context can actually serve to dissuade political activism by clergy (see Haynes 1996: 113).
2. My argument in this respect resembles earlier academic arguments about the sources of corruption and impropriety in African administrations. Both Hyden (1983) and Ekeh (1975) argued that "affective" or "primordial" ties infiltrated the operation of the state, undermining the integrity of bureaucratic and administrative organisations. Here I argue that the same forces intrude upon the integrity of religious organisations.

text of structural adjustment and declining purchasing power, this consolidation is very difficult. Finally, there are pressures to extend and elaborate privilege. For some clergy, desires for material and social advancement are very real.

The extension of these pressures is that economic issues occupy, and can even dominate, the private concerns of many Malawian clergy. In turn, however, these private concerns infiltrate the discourses and practices of the clerical sphere. For instance, within the dioceses of the Catholic Church, debates over distributional issues predominate, often guiding the collective efforts and orientations of the clergy. In the two years following the democratic transition in Malawi, clergy in three dioceses issued written challenges to bishops about nepotism and favoritism in the distribution of various opportunities and resources within the church. In the current era then, the agenda for social action competes not only with more traditional or conventional Catholic priorities (church-building, intensifying the faith, etc) but also with the economic concerns of the clergy. That a discourse on socially-oriented ministries is not more salient among local clergy is more comprehensible in this light. The primary debates in the church are about who gets what, not about the church's role in addressing social issues.

Moreover, the economic concerns of the clergy lead some to engage in private business ventures—often facilitated by clerical access to resources (transport, credit) designated for other ends. In some cases these ventures become paramount, leaving minimal time to devote to even conventional pastoral work. Even assuming that there was some inclination to work for community issues, such efforts would likely fall by the wayside. Indeed, attention to business ventures limits the capacity of certain clergy to have a sense of the central issues in their communities. One Presbyterian minister whom I visited spent four out of six work days running a timber business far removed from his congregation. Another Catholic priest devoted the bulk of his energies to his small livestock and poultry businesses, the proceeds of which went to support his own habits and pay for the school fees of relatives.

This line of argument is not intended to suggest that many clergy are disingenuous in their role as servants of the church or the larger body of faithful. Yet, at the very least, it needs to be recognised that when it comes to addressing issues other than salvation, sacraments, or church administration, the social concerns of the faithful obtain a relatively negligible status when compared to "this worldly" concerns of the clergy themselves. Many local clergy are simply focused on their own projects—be they private businesses, efforts to get "outside" for education, or moving up the administrative hierarchy. As such, the likelihood that they will question their own role in addressing social problems is minimal.

Conclusion: Malawi's Clergy, Civil Society and the Social Context

Clergy are among the most numerous of civil society representatives on the ground in emerging African democracies. Owing to their elevated status in local communities and their attachment to large and often powerful religious organisations, they carry considerable potential to play roles as micro-level agents of political change. Indeed, as I have indicated, their activism might contribute significantly to the deepening of democracy, both in Malawi and in other contexts.

Despite this potential, the research here indicates that many Malawian clergy are quite disinclined to engage in extensive grassroots civil society activism. The descriptive overview from the interviews offers initial insights into this behavioural trend.

More importantly, the statistical and interpretive analyses further indicate that there are very persistent constraints and obstacles to the clergy embracing more active and vocal political roles in grassroots communities. These include the kinds of religious ideas that inform their work and their relationships to other actors who might frown on such activism. This should clearly temper any overly romanticised notions that the clergy will be the champions of grassroots civil society.

These insights carry significance for two audiences. In the first place, they speak directly to those who are concerned with the unfolding character of political life in Malawi. One of the important features of post-authoritarian politics has been the continued voice and activism of national and regional church organisations in public life. In this respect, both the Catholic and Presbyterian churches have worked to enhance the stability of the new democracy and the quality of public political discourse. The activities of the pan-civic Public Affairs Committee serve as one example —issuing public statements on national political affairs, providing civic education, and assisting with election procedures. Church leaders have also directly intervened in politics to help mollify political tensions engendered by disagreements between the primary political players. The clearest instance was Catholic Bishop Felix Mkhori's efforts in 1997 to end the MCP and AFORD boycott of Parliament (Ott, 2000). In the tense political climate following the 1999 elections, Catholic bishops (and other church leaders) also issued public statements decrying the behaviour of both the government and opposition. Moreover, the Catholic Church has certainly not abandoned its prophetic voice and willingness to criticise the government. Since 1996 pastoral letters have called on the UDF government to deal with the growing problem of corruption at the level of the state. Other comments in letters have challenged more specific government actions, such as the 1998 ban on government advertising in opposition papers. Perhaps the most poignant statement from the Church was an October 2000 letter by the Catholic Commission for Justice and Peace. The pretext for the statement was a report by the Parliamentary Public Accounts Committee revealing that 125 million kwacha had been lost due to fraud and misuse of government funds. In pointed language the statement came just short of accusing the government of a "cover-up" and claimed that inaction on the issue threatened to undermine the people's trust in the government. Beyond this, the statement condemned a number of abuses of political authority by the ruling party. Specific comments denounced practices such as giving state resources disproportionately to party supporters, dismissing civil servants viewed as disloyal by the ruling party, and ignoring the violent actions of ruling party thugs seeking to harass the opposition. Clearly then the churches remain important voices and players in national politics.

The research on the clergy suggests two issues with respect to these larger patterns of church activism in politics. First, the research indicates that activism by larger church organisations may not necessarily be duplicated at local levels. Despite the patterns of church political involvement at the national level, local clergy are fairly disinclined to work for more basic changes in political relations at the grassroots. Highly visible interventions by church leaders should not lead one to overstate the extent of church activism in politics. As we have seen, at the grassroots, churches may very well be agents of the status quo, rather than advocates for change in state-local power relations. Second, the research may explain why more local level issues do not find their way into the public statements of church leaders. As research from other contexts reminds us, rank and file clergy can play an important role in setting the tone of political interventions by larger ecclesiastical institutions. Indeed, activism by local clergy can serve as an important impetus to activism by church leaders (Levine and Wilde, 1977, Mainwaring, 1986). Importantly, events in Malawi corroborate these insights. One of the more notable instances where the Catholic Bishops have raised an issue pertaining to specific local level injustices was in their Pastoral Letter of March 1998 when they condemned the working conditions of tobacco estate workers in Central Malawi. What is important to recognise is that attention to this issue by the Bishops was the result of the efforts by expatriate Catholic clergy in Nkhotakota to raise public awareness about the problems confronting tobacco tenants in their area (Englund, 2000:588–589). For over seven years prior to the Bishop's statement, local level priests had been working to organise local tenants, serving as advocates for their concerns, and, importantly, bringing news of their situation to the Catholic hierarchy.[1] It was their efforts that allowed this *local* issue to become *national* via the comments of the Bishops.

Yet, as this chapter describes, such local level activism is fairly "atypical" among the larger portion of Malawi's clergy. As such, an important impetus for greater attention to localised issues by church leaders is lost. Without greater activism by local clergy, the prospects of church leaders embracing grassroots concerns diminish. Ecclesiastical interventions into public life may continue, but the character of state-local relations may not be a central focus of those interventions.

In a second respect, the findings speak to those concerned with the character of civil society in new African democracies. Much of the conventional liberal discourse on civil society assumes that the actors and organisations of the civic realm can operate somewhat autonomously of larger social influences. Diamond (1994) and Harbeson (1994), for example, highlight the functions that civil society organisations should play in new democracies, without adequately interrogating the factors that will affect their willingness and capacity to serve these roles. Yet in ignoring the connections to the social setting, this discourse overstates the possibilities for civil society organisations to play transfomative and empowering roles.[2] The research here suggests that representatives of civil society can be embedded in socio-political processes and relations. These in turn can constrain their propensity to engage in activism.

For example, to understand the relative inactivity of some local clergy, we needed to understand their own embeddedness in processes of social class formation. They were consciously engaged in efforts to consolidate and enhance their position within Malawian society. As a result, they remained relatively unconcerned with expanding their efforts to address the social and political concerns of the faithful. Their interests as social and economic actors were the key determinants of their behaviour. Still other clergy reflected connections to society in the religious frameworks that guided their engagements and interventions in their communities. The salience of certain religious ideas among the clergy cannot be understood in isolation from social conditions they experience and political dynamics they witness. While the liberal vision of civil society might hope for socio-political activism by the local clergy, the religious ideas that resonate and make sense in Malawi may in fact lead them in a different direction.

Highlighting these issues serves to remind scholars that greater attention should be devoted to understanding the deeper social conditions that shape the behaviour

---

1. See "Tobacco Tenants Exploited", *Daily Times,* 18 October, 1996; *Saturday Nation,* 3–9 May, 1997.
2. For a related argument, see Kasfir (1998).

and character of the actors and organisations that represent civil society.[1] Mercantile behaviour among the clergy may reflect moral dissonance on their part. But even more so it reflects the problematic economic opportunity structures in Malawian society, as well as the expectations on the clergy by their larger community which depends on them. The "other-worldly" emphases of certain clergy may seem fatalistic. Yet they also bespeak the impossibilities which confront the average citizen in Malawi—especially within the context of the AIDS epidemic and the current push for economic liberalisation. By focusing our attention in this direction, we may obtain some perspective not only on civil society, but also the contradictory and problematic tendencies which lurk beneath the surface of Africa's new democracies.

---

1. This echoes Kasfir's call for efforts to "open up the notion of civil society to gain a wider understanding of particular societies and their relationship to their states" (1998: 7).

7. Ethnic Revival and Language Associations in the New Malawi

The Case of Chitumbuka

Gregory H. Kamwendo

Preamble

Unity and singularity were key values in the authoritarian regime of Kamuzu Banda: one party (Malawi Congress Party); one leader (Life President Kamuzu Banda); one language (Chichewa); and one nation (Malawi).[1] To this end, cultural and language associations, especially those with ethnic flavour, were not encouraged to flourish for fear that they would encourage disunity. In the interest of national unity, the celebration of ethnic identity was vehemently suppressed. Recognising that language is one of the key markers of ethnolinguistic identity, the Banda regime, at the 1968 MCP Convention, began the process of developing and promoting Chichewa at the expense of other indigenous languages. The party convention gave official status to Chichewa and left the other languages without a role to play in the official domains.[2] Until 1968, Chichewa had been widely regarded as merely one of the dialects of Chinyanja—the African *lingua franca* of colonial Malawi and widely used also in Zambia and Mozambique. Yet the Chichewa dialect happened to be spoken in Central Malawi, where Banda claimed to be from.

One result of the advent of multipartyism in Malawi has been the provision of freedom of association, leading to the emergence of a number of voluntary associations. There now exist, for example, associations in which membership is determined by one's district of origin (see Englund, 2001c). These district- and village-oriented associations, operating in urban centres, aim at grouping together people from the same district in order to contribute to the social and economic development of their home areas. Examples of such associations include the Friends of Machinga, the Kasungu District Development Association, and the Nkhata Bay District Development Association. Their stated purpose is to strengthen the link between urban dwellers and their rural relations. However, because these associations are dominated by people of influential capacity in society—such as businessmen, academics, clergy, politicians—their political importance may extend beyond their apparent developmental efforts in particular rural areas. As has been noted for post-authoritarian Africa more generally (see Geschiere and Gugler, 1998), multipartyism must be seen as a context for the emergence of these associations. When the ideologies of political parties provide few pointers as to how they might be different from one another (see Englund's Introduction to this volume), political differences are expressed in other ways. As chapters in this volume have already indicated, ethnic and regional identities have assumed new significance in the political life of Malawi. Multiparty-

---

1. Such values resonated with the postcolonial "nation-building" elsewhere. Compare, for example, Kenneth Kaunda's "One Zambia, One Nation" slogan. In Tanzania, the Tanganyika African National Union (TANU), later called Chama Cha Mapinduzi (CCM), identified Kiswahili as having the potential to unite people of divergent ethnolinguistic origins.
2. English retained its position as the principal official language in the media, education, government, commerce, etc.

ism appears to feed claims to specific ethno-regional identities, and district-oriented associations may, in some cases, become vehicles for political mobilisation.

The focus of this chapter is on language associations, which often present themselves as language promotion and revival groups. The overall goal of these associations is to promote languages which were previously marginalised by the Banda dictatorship. The relationship between the ethnic revival in Malawi and the emergence of language associations must be investigated. Currently, two vibrant language associations exist: the Abenguni Revival Association, which focuses on the severely endangered Chingoni language; and an association for Chitumbuka. Both associations exist in Northern Malawi, a fact whose significance will be discussed below. The specific focus of this chapter is on the second association—the Chitumbuka Language and Culture Association (CLACA).

The Language Situation in the First Republic (1964–1994)

When Malawi attained its independence in 1964, the new political leadership found itself faced with the task of building a strong and united nation against a background of linguistic and cultural pluralism. This situation is summed up by Timpunza-Mvula as follows:

> Most African countries inherited disparate ethnic communities. Ethnic groups were divided by administrative political boundaries, according to the interests of the imperial powers. The various ethnic groups had different languages. African national leaders, in their attempt to forge nations, saw the immediate need to choose a single language which would serve as an appropriate instrument of national unity, ethnic integration and cultural identity (1992:37).

In line with the above-quoted aspirations, the then ruling party, the MCP, resolved in 1968 to grant the national language status to Chinyanja and simultaneously changed the name of the language to Chichewa. This was the beginning of the process under which the development of Chichewa was going to thwart the development of other indigenous languages. For example, Chitumbuka ceased to be used in education and the mass media. Linguistically and culturally, perhaps even politically, the élite with a Chewa identity came to dominate Malawi, as if other languages and ethnic identities did not exist. The high status of Chichewa was strengthened by, among other factors, the creation of a Department of Chichewa and Linguistics at the University of Malawi; the establishment of the Chichewa Board to monitor and steer the development of Chichewa; the launching of a project to compile a monolingual dictionary of Chichewa; the use of Chichewa as the medium of instruction in junior primary schools throughout Malawi; the existence of Chichewa as a subject of study in primary, secondary and tertiary institutions of learning; and the existence of Chichewa as the only indigenous language accepted in the print and electronic media and in government notices.

Under the Banda regime, therefore, the fortunes of Chitumbuka suffered a serious blow. It was, and is, the *lingua franca* of the Northern Region and the rallying point of identity politics for the linguistically heterogeneous population there, deprived of its official status by the Banda regime, only to reassert itself in political pluralism. Before the political transition, despite the virtual ban on Chitumbuka, the church community continued to use the language for liturgical purposes. The Livingstonia Synod of the Church of Central Africa, Presbyterian (CCAP)[1] and the Catholic Church[2] continued to use the Bible, hymns and other religious texts in Chitumbuka. The fact that the Livingstonia Synod had defied the government's devaluation of Chitumbuka is understandable in an historical perspective. It was the Livingstonia Mission which initiated language development for Chitumbuka.[3] Its pioneer missionaries gave the language its written form, and other developments followed in the areas of the orthography, lexicography and the overall promotion of Chitumbuka as a *lingua franca* for the Northern Region. The Livingstonia Mission won the battle against the colonial government over the choice of Chitumbuka as a medium of instruction in schools in Northern Malawi. In this regard, the Livingstonia Synod has historically been a true developer, promoter and protector of the Chitumbuka language—hence its defiance of the regime's ban on the language in 1968.

Whilst the church was spared, ordinary people who criticised or lamented the ban on Chitumbuka attracted the wrath of the heavy-handed Banda regime. Some critics of the ban were arrested whilst others were harassed in various ways. For example, the wife of Austin C. Mkandawire, a prominent text book writer, was harassed while her husband was studying in the United Kingdom.[4] It is reported that security agents searched her house for banned Chitumbuka books. Keeping a Chitumbuka book at that time could be seen as a rebellion against Banda's quest for national unity. In some extreme cases, Chitumbuka books were set on fire. Despite this harsh treatment, a good number of copies of Chitumbuka books have survived. One of the most celebrated survivals is Mkandawire's translation of Shakespeare's *Julius Caesar*.[5] I was able to find several copies of this translation currently in use at Rumphi Secondary School. The students there found the Chitumbuka translation useful as they prepared for the examinations in English literature—*Julius Caesar* was one of the prescribed texts for the Malawi School Certificate of Education.

During the periods of both the colonial and Banda regimes, dominant stereotypes adversely affected certain ethnic identities, producing negative popular attitudes towards their mother tongues. For example, persons who would identify themselves as Lomwe developed a tendency to shy away from this ethnic identity and were reluctant to speak their language in public. The common stereotype was that the Lomwe were snake-eaters, masters of witchcraft and very wild in their behaviour (Kamwendo, 1999b). Historically, many of their ancestors had fled harsh treatment in Portuguese East Africa (Mozambique), and were also known among their Malawian hosts by the pejorative term "Anguru" (Boeder, 1984; White, 1987). It is not surprising, therefore, that there has been a language shift from Chilomwe to Chichewa, as documented by Kayambazinthu (1989), Matiki (1996) and the Centre for Language Studies (1999).

There were limited opportunities for others than those who identified themselves as Chewa to show pride in indigenous languages. The then sole radio station, the Malawi Broadcasting Corporation (MBC), though officially bilingual in Chichewa and English, tolerated traditional songs in many of the numerous Malawian languages. However, most of the cultural programmes tended to portray "Chewa" per-

---

1. Interview with Rev. M. Banda, Education Secretary, Livingstonia Synod, Mzuzu, 20 February 2001.
2. Interview with Rev. Fr. N. Mgungwe, Mzuzu, 20 February, 2001.
3. Interviews with Rev. M. Banda of Livingstonia Synod, 20 February 2001, and Mr Austin C. Mkandawire, Bolero, 12 March 2001.
4. Interview with Mr Austin C. Mkandawire, Bolero, 12 March 2001.
5. Interview with Mr Gondwe, Headmaster of Rumphi Secondary School, 16 March 2001. The translation has the title *Sobero la Julius Kesare* and it was published in 1967 by the Oxford University Press, Nairobi, on behalf of the Malawi Publications and Literature Bureau.

spectives of life. The radio had two programmes, *Tiphunzitsane Chichewa* (Let's teach each other Chichewa) and *Chichewa cha kumudzi* (Chichewa of the village), whose goal was to promote "good" Chichewa.

Language, Ethnic Identity and History

The observations above indicate the importance of an historical perspective when the ethnolinguistic revival is discussed. Although in Malawi, as in many other African countries, there is a close connection between language and ethnic identity, the relationship is historically variable, moulded by specific political, religious and economic conditions. Superficially, to add the prefix *chi* to an ethnic label is to name the language spoken by the people who claim that particular ethnic identity. Examples would include Chichewa (a language for the Chewa), Chiyao (a language for the Yao), Chisena (a language for the Sena), Chilomwe (a language for the Lomwe), and so forth. Yet we need to guard ourselves against assuming that if one is said to have the ethnic identity x, then that person speaks a language called *chi-x*. A case in point, as already indicated, is the fact that some Malawians are ethnically Lomwe, without being linguistically Lomwe.

Ethnic identities, and the languages associated with them, are, therefore, subject to historical changes—so much so that even the inhabitants of a particular district or region can shift their ethnic identities according to historical conjunctures. For example, in Malawi there is a tendency to refer to everyone from the Northern Region as a Tumbuka; or to regard anyone from that region as a Chitumbuka speaker. There are, indeed, times when a Tonga may accept being identified as a Tumbuka, or when a broader regional identity—"a Northerner" (*wakumpoto*)—overrides ethnic identifications. Although the Northern Region is ethnically and linguistically mixed, Chakufwa Chihana, a Tumbuka from Rumphi district, received nearly 90 per cent of the region's votes in the 1994 presidential elections (see Kaspin, 1995; Appendix in this volume). At least a part of his and the AFORD's success in the Northern Region must be explained by referring to identity politics in which a strong sense of "being a Northerner"—and perhaps even "a Tumbuka"—made people with various ethnic identities and languages support a particular candidate and a particular party. Yet it is crucial to realise that there are also times when people with a Tonga or other non-Tumbuka ethnic identity in Northern Malawi distance themselves from the Tumbuka identity and the Chitumbuka language. When the new government reintroduced Chitumbuka on the national radio in 1994, certain spokespersons for the Tonga asked for the inclusion of Chitonga on the radio despite the fact that there is a very high degree of mutual intelligibility between Chitonga and Chitumbuka. It is conceivable that the very people who had voted in large numbers for a Tumbuka presidential candidate had suddenly decided to go to their own language, and not to Chihana's language.

Ethnic identities can also be created and manipulated, as was the case with missionary and colonial histories of Zimbabwe and Malawi, among many other countries in Africa (see e.g. Ranger, 1989; Chimhundu, 1992). Missionaries, through their efforts to produce vernacular translations of religious texts, also created languages out of mutually intelligible dialects. These mutually intelligible dialects, by virtue of being developed by different missionaries, ended up having different orthographies. This then reinforced the false view that the different dialects were different languages.

As mentioned, the Livingstonia Mission played an important role in making Chitumbuka a *lingua franca* in Northern Malawi. But its religious and educational initiatives had repercussions that provide an historical background to the present-day ethnolinguistic revival in the Northern Region. As Vail and White (1989; see also Vail, 1978) have shown, this region had been conquered by the Ngoni from Southern Africa by the time the impact of the Livingstonia Mission was widely felt, and the Mission's promotion of Chitumbuka was also an intervention into local politics. School texts in Chitumbuka were printed in the 1920s in editions that could be as many as 10,000 copies (Vail and White, 1989:164). The newcomers and their descendants, who may have otherwise identified themselves as Ngoni, acquired Chitumbuka as their first language, consolidating a "Northern" identity among people with different origins—an identity that was to assume more significance under the historical conditions of a postcolonial autocracy.

The Livingstonia Mission had created a small but influential group of intellectuals, who assumed important positions in politics, the civil service and education after independence. The so-called Cabinet Crisis of 1964 led to the removal and exile of well-educated Northerners and Southerners in Banda's government and appeared to deepen his admiration for the "Chewa culture" as the core of the Malawian nation (Vail and White, 1989:179; Baker, 2001). During the 1970s, more Northerners and Southerners were harassed during the "ethnic cleansing" of the civil service and the University of Malawi. Many of them were sent to work in their supposed areas of origin. Such repressive measures could not, however, erase alternative ethnic identities or popular pride in the Chitumbuka language. On the contrary, they merely prepared the ground for another revival of Tumbuka ethnicity and its associated language.

On the one hand, identifying oneself along ethnic lines was a prohibited act during Banda's dictatorship. Everyone was required to identify him- or herself as a Malawian; and not as a Nyanja, Lomwe, Sena or Tonga, for example. On the other hand, Banda often openly identified himself as a Chewa from Kasungu district. The language policy of the Banda regime contributed to a widespread sense of suppressed ethnicity by making languages other than Chichewa invisible and severely marginalised. The reintroduction of multipartyism has opened up people's opportunities to declare their linguistic and ethnic identities. Realising that many languages had for several years been marginalised and despised, some spokespersons felt a strong urge to give these languages new leases of life. It is in this context that an ethnolinguistic revival is currently taking place in some areas. In the light of the historical background presented above, it is not surprising that the Chitumbuka language and the Northern Region seem to be at the forefront of this revival.

The initial reaction of the new government has been permissive. It changed the official name of the national language from Chichewa back to Chinyanja, though so far only in the domain of education. The UDF government has justified its policy of cultural and linguistic liberalisation on the grounds that there can be unity within diversity as long as there is tolerance towards other cultures and languages. This view is also supported by the AFORD, whose manifesto states that an AFORD-led government would promote richness in diversity by fostering the growth of positive elements in the ethnic differences that exist in Malawi, based on a deliberate effort by the majority of Malawians to appreciate alien forms of music, dress, dishes and language. As contended at the beginning of this chapter, however, the ethnic and regional politics fostered by Malawi's current multipartyism makes cultural and linguistic pluralism a sensitive issue. There is a need for empirical research among the new associations in order to assess their motives and contribution to the making of a new Malawi. An association devoted to the promotion of the Chitumbuka language is, as the above discussion makes clear, a particularly interesting case for exploring the nature of Malawi's current pluralism.

The Chitumbuka Language and Culture Association

In 1994, an announcement was made in the Malawian print media about the proposal for the creation of a Chitumbuka Club. According to *The Weekly Mail* of 21 March, 1994, the club would, among other things, aim at "reviving the correct usage of the language, both spoken and written, and promoting and preserving the culture". The press statement went on to mention that "during club sessions members will be conducting debates, folk story telling and cracking proverbs in Chitumbuka. They will also be reviving Chitumbuka traditional dances".[1] The club also planned to have a library, where Chitumbuka art, music and literature would be deposited.

The Chitumbuka club is now known as the Chitumbuka Language and Culture Association (CLACA). The Association holds regular meetings at the Mzuzu Museum, a government building which acts as a temporary secretariat for the association, co-ordinated by A. W. Thole. The Association also uses the Museum's postal address and phone number for its communications.[2] A permanent building for the secretariat has been in the pipeline for quite some time now, but the association's limited financial resources have prevented its construction.

According to Nelson Chilinda, who was the chairman of the CLACA during my fieldwork in 2000 and 2001, the association was formed in 1994 after the UDF government had taken some practical steps towards liberalising language policy and promoting the status of the indigenous languages. The use of Chitumbuka on the national radio soon after the UDF assumed power in 1994 was the most prominent example of attempts towards a new language policy, greatly encouraging the birth of the CLACA. The main concern of the CLACA is to preserve the Chitumbuka language and the culture of the Tumbuka people in order to ensure that the young generations do not lose the language and culture. As such, the association calls attention to the fact that indigenous languages other than Chichewa were marginalised for some thirty years in Malawi, putting their transmission across generations at risk. Note also the close parallel drawn between language and culture, potentially obscuring what was said above about the problems of associating particular languages with particular ethnic groups. In my concluding remarks, I will also address the question of why it is Chitumbuka, which nevertheless continued to be widely used in the Northern Region during the period of the Banda regime, and not some more suppressed language that has become the focus of the most active language association in the country.

More specifically, a leaflet produced by the CLACA lists the objectives of the association as follows: to organise functions which will enhance and promote the advancement and preservation of the Tumbuka language and culture; to revive, teach and promote the Chitumbuka language and culture for the benefit of the young and future generations; to work in collaboration with government and other institutions dealing with the languages and cultures of Malawi such as the Departments of An-

---

1. See also Minutes of the Proposed Association for the Advancement and Preservation of Chitumbuka, Chenda Hotel, Mzuzu, 2 July 1994.
2. Interview with A.W. Thole, Mzuzu Museum, 8 March 2001.

tiquities, Archives, Museums, Ministry of Education, Universities, UNICEF and UNESCO. The draft constitution of the CLACA urges the government of Malawi "to enact a law and policy in the parliament of the national assembly that Chitumbuka language and culture be revived and preserved". The draft constitution provides that membership in the CLACA is open to any interested person of the age of five and over. Membership is not restricted, in other words, to persons who identify themselves as Tumbuka. The active members numbered around 60 during my fieldwork in 2000, many of whom attended meetings at the Mzuzu Museum. Other members live outside the Northern Region, located in major urban centres such as Zomba, Blantyre and Lilongwe. Membership in the CLACA has attracted politicians, but it is important to note that their party political affiliations are variable. For example, the most active politicians in the CLACA are D. Njakwa, a member of parliament for AFORD, Kanyama Chiume, a member of Kamuzu Banda's first cabinet and currently party politically independent, and Robson W. Chirwa, another former cabinet minister in Banda's regime. Other activists in the CLACA include a wide range of professionals, such as both retired and serving teachers, local intellectuals keen to make a contribution as textbook writers, retired broadcasters and members of the clergy.

Despite this somewhat elitist bias in its membership, the overall assessment with regard to the central objective of the CLACA has to be positive. The association has managed to assemble a collection of Chitumbuka texts which were used in schools before the 1968 ban on the language. These texts are now in the custody of the Mzuzu Museum. It is hoped some of these texts will be used when the mother tongue instruction policy becomes operational (see Pfaffe, 2000), subject, of course, to revisions in their orthography, grammar and content.

Realising that Chitumbuka does not have a standard orthography (Kishindo, 1998), members of the CLACA have also taken the initiative to create a new orthography to clarify the situation in which several orthographies are competing. Despite the fact that the CLACA orthography does not conform to the features of a professionally formulated orthography, it is still a very commendable effort undertaken by people who do not have the professional expertise to create or reform an orthography. The orthography is basically a one page leaflet which shows twenty-seven Chitumbuka sounds and the alphabet. What is lacking is a set of informative rules and their justifications. For instance, the leaflet does not offer rules on the sound system and word division. Yet this effort shows how seriously committed the CLACA activists are towards the development of Chitumbuka.

Efforts to reform the Chitumbuka orthography have been supported and taken up by the Centre for Language Studies of the University of Malawi. The Centre has the mandate to review and revise orthographies of Malawian languages (Kamwendo, 1999c). In compliance with this mandate, the Centre carried out a sociolinguistic study in early 2001, the findings of which will assist in the standardisation of Chitumbuka. The report recommends that the orthography "be standardized by a technical committee" (Centre for Language Studies, 2001). The report further recommends that "a special symposium, attracting the major stakeholders of Chitumbuka, be convened to ratify the orthography". Thirdly, the report calls for cross-border co-operation between Malawi and Zambia in order to harmonise the Chitumbuka orthographies.

The CLACA has also lobbied for the return of Chitumbuka to the school curriculum. Under the proposed language policy, mother tongues or dominant languages of an area will be used as media of instruction for standards 1–4 (Kamwendo, 1997).

The CLACA has treated the re-introduction of Chitumbuka in the public media, directed by Muluzi in 1994, as an encouraging sign that the new government is committed to respecting and promoting Malawi's linguistic diversity.[1] In an effort to express its gratitude to the new government's initiative of liberalising the language policy, the CLACA asked for an audience with Muluzi. According to a copy of the CLACA chairman's prepared speech, the CLACA wanted to salute Muluzi as follows: "Soon after assuming your high office, you ordered that Chitumbuka ·be re-introduced on the national radio, MBC, in 1994. This has enhanced the development of Chitumbuka." The meeting, however, never took place. During his presidency, Muluzi has granted numerous audiences to groups and individuals seeking to "thank" him. These visitors have often left the presidential palace with a monetary gift handed to them by the president himself. The publicity which some of these meetings have received in the state-controlled media has underlined the apparently widespread gratitude in Malawi for Muluzi's democratic leadership. Both Muluzi and his visitors, in other words, benefit from such meetings, but it may be a measure of the CLACA's modest political significance that Muluzi did not find time to meet its representatives.

Anticipating the use of Chitumbuka in schools in the near future, some of the CLACA members have produced manuscripts which now await publishers' consideration. For example, Emmanuel Luthuli Chipeta, one of the aspirant textbook writers, has already produced the following manuscripts: *Tumbuka sayings in English; Kuwazga (book 2); Kuwazga (book 4); Jando la kubaga (book 1); Chitumbuka Language and Grammar*. Some of the association's plans are not yet under implementation. They include the launching of a bi-monthly or weekly newspaper in Chitumbuka. There are also plans for a magazine which would act as the guiding organ of Chitumbuka grammar, orthography, Tumbuka moral and cultural practices, social entertainment and other matters pertaining to the language and culture. A journal which will feature research findings on the language is also among the many planned activities.[2]

The CLACA has been able to register some progress in spite of some pressing problems, most of which are due to a lack of financial resources. The association has a very weak financial base, its membership fee of K20 per year and the life membership fee of K100 being too meagre for the secretariat's many needs, such as stationery, telephone calls and transport costs. Currently the association survives on donations from well-wishers. A related problem is that the association remains officially unregistered. The attempt to have the association registered was damaged by a lawyer who misappropriated the funds allocated to the exercise. The registration of the association will also involve the appointment of a board of trustees, whose selection is yet to be finalised.

Concluding Remarks

The observations above do not support the view that the Chitumbuka association has arisen from political expediency in a new pluralist context. It has members whose political aspirations appear to be diverse, and, moreover, some of its leading figures are also active in the Abenguni Revival Association which promotes the language and culture of another ethnicity, Ngoni. By virtue of being active in different

1. Minutes of CLACA meeting held on 18 October 1996.
2. See Chitumbuka Language and Culture Association: Establishment of the Secretariat (Project Proposal).

ethnolinguistic associations, they display remarkable commitment to cultural development. As history has shown, however, such commitments may change rapidly when their historical conditions change. In this regard, it is intriguing to note how resilient the two Northern associations have been, while other language associations have either disappeared or were never formed after the transition to political pluralism. A striking example is the Society for the Preservation of Chiyao. An initiative of academics, it never caught the interest of large numbers of Chiyao speakers, and died after a short time. On the other hand, the other indigenous languages in Malawi have not so far acquired their own associations. As was mentioned, the case of Chilomwe is a particularly pertinent example of a marginalised language which has lost its value even among those whose mother tongue it could be. Other languages, including Chiyao, may be less efficient than Chitumbuka in evoking the need for their "revival" or "preservation" for the simple reason that, during the colonial and postcolonial periods, Chinyanja/Chichewa has made considerable inroads into the language use of Malawians other than Chitumbuka-speakers. It is, therefore, something of a paradox that Chitumbuka should be the focus of the most vibrant language association in Malawi. Of all the indigenous languages apart from Chichewa, it was the one that continued to be spoken and used most widely even during the darkest years of the Banda regime.

The current situation appears less paradoxical, when we recall the history of ethnic politics in Malawi. The activities of the Livingstonia Mission and the persecution of Northerners by the Banda regime consolidated Tumbuka ethnicity and many Northerners' identification with the Chitumbuka language. The history of the Northern Region has also seen more widespread activism in associational life than the other regions—another reason to explain why language associations seem to endure there. What the current political pluralism may create is, in fact, increasing fragmentation of identity politics based on ethnolinguistic markers. The Northern Region, once more, is a case in point. The region, as mentioned, is not ethnically and linguistically homogeneous despite the prominent role of Chitumbuka among its population. For example, the Roman Catholic Church which uses Chitumbuka throughout its diocese, has recently been pressed by Nkhonde spokespersons to have Chinkhonde as one of the languages of the liturgy.[1] The Livingstonia Synod of the CCAP has also received requests from areas such as Nkhata Bay, where there are Chitonga speakers; Chitipa, a linguistically mixed area; and Karonga, another linguistically heterogeneous area; that the church should no longer continue using Chitumbuka in every part of the Northern Region.[2] This, however, does not imply that the requests come from people who do not speak Chitumbuka. These people actually speak Chitumbuka, but they simply want to demonstrate that Chitumbuka is not their mother tongue. It is the mother tongue loyalty which is at work here.

This represents resistance against the dominant position of Chitumbuka, a fact that may become politically more significant than the Chitumbuka association itself. The question is to what extent—and under what historical conditions—the Northern Region continues to be seen as one cultural, linguistic and political unit by the majority of the people who live there. In the 1999 elections, the UDF and MCP already won seats in the region, qualifying the apparently hegemonic position of the AFORD (see Appendix). Yet it is also apparent that the other Northern languages still have a long way to go before they can challenge the status of Chitumbuka. For

---

1. Interview with Rev. Fr. N. Mgungwe, Mzuzu Diocese Cathedral, 20 February 2001.
2. Interview with Rev. M. Banda of Livingstonia Synod, 21 February 2001.

example, the Anglican Church of Northern Malawi, uses Chichewa/Chinyanja as its language, perhaps contributing to the fact that the church has not attracted a large following in the region.[1] In a bid to bring the church closer to the people, plans are underway to have the Eucharistic prayer translated into Chitumbuka.

If we accept that the issue of ethnolinguistic identity has wider ramifications than party political allegiance, what is the significance of language associations to the young democracy in Malawi? First, language associations complement government efforts to raise the status of languages that had been marginalised by the one-party dictatorship. Given that government on its own cannot do everything (because of lack of adequate resources), the language associations come in as non-governmental efforts in the development and promotion of Malawian languages. Secondly, language associations can help in changing negative popular attitudes towards indigenous languages. Positive language attitude and strong language loyalty amongst native speakers are some of the key facilitators of the sustenance of language vitality. Thirdly, language associations can act as a lobby group or as a watch-dog of language rights.

The political side of ethnic and linguistic revival is not, however, easy to dispense with. Given that multiculturalism and multilingualism are a common reality in Malawi, what challenges do they pose to national unity? There is a school of thought which believes in unity being cultivated within linguistic and cultural diversity. Chinsinga for example believes that

> ethnic, cultural and linguistic heterogeneity, properly understood and nurtured, may in fact be the basis for ensuring national unity. After all, the most vibrant and prosperous democracies of the world are highly heterogeneous societies. It is however a sad reality that our own experiences as a nation for the past three or so decades would force us (to) believe that unity in diversity is virtually elusive. It is nonetheless important to note that culturally, ethnically and linguistically homogeneous societies are not immune to divisive forces either. (1999: 19; see also Kishindo, 1993)

The danger with language associations is that politicians may manipulate cultural and linguistic diversity to suit their own particular political motives. This is why some observers are sceptical about the motives of the newly-formed language associations. There is fear in some quarters that these associations may be hijacked by people who want to make political gains. Another fear is that these language associations may strengthen ethnic or cultural loyalties to the extent that national unity may be placed in danger. On paper, language associations are a welcome development in an open society which is both multilingual and multicultural. Fishman (1972) and Nahirny and Fishman (1965) regard such associations as good agents for the maintenance of both culture and language. Language associations may have two contrasting goals or effects. First, they are a welcome development in a young democracy in which respect for human rights, including language rights, is of importance. Democratically, no ethnolinguistic identity should be denied institutions that promote, develop and protect the language and culture associated with it. However, and secondly, the problem sets in when this freedom to form language associations is manipulated for ethnocentric or parochial interests. This fear is relevant to Malawi's current wave of ethnic-inspired politics:

> Along with poverty, ethnicity and regionalism are viewed as being major threats to Malawi's new democracy. By focusing people's attention on local or particularistic loyalties and empha-

---

1. Interview with Rev. Fr. R. Mponda, Anglican Church, Mzuzu, 21 February 2001.

sizing factors which distinguish rather than those which unify, they are a potential threat to unity. (Chirwa, 1998a:52)

As such, there is a need to be aware of the dangers in politicising language associations. Chirwa's remarks are worth giving serious thought:

> Ethnicity and regionalism are more likely to surface in their glaring form under a democratic political dispensation that under an autocratic one. This is because in a democracy, any group of people are free to assert their identity and to lobby for their interests or the interests of the areas from which they come. By creating an enabling environment for particularistic interests of this nature, democracy does give rise to enormous challenges to its own survival as a nationally unifying ideology. (1998a:55)

8. Tikutha[1]

The Political Culture of the HIV/AIDS Epidemic in Malawi

John Lwanda

Buy a newspaper, see that column
What a pity, many people are dying
Coffin workshops are being advertised
Not really because carpenters want money

Carpenters cannot rest, always working in haste
Making coffins one after another
No wonder coffin workshops are everywhere

Billy Kaunda, 1999[2]

During my focus group sessions among primary, secondary and tertiary students in Malawi, there was one persistent question, or rather a statement—surely mosquitoes transmit HIV. The scientific explanation I gave as a medical doctor was received with politeness, but limited conviction. The students postulated variously that scientists knew all about mosquitoes transmitting HIV but kept quiet about it in order to avoid causing panic, or in order to impose abstinence or condoms; that mosquito bites were more frequent than sexual intercourse and more likely transmitters; that mosquito bites could transmit HIV to the innocent; and that those who got fewer bites were less affected by HIV. During a particularly intense focus-group session with third-year university students, the question cropped up again, with the same doubts expressed. In a moment of desperation, rather than inspiration, I posed the question, "Do you think that these scientists would stay in Malawi if this were true?". Since the "scientists" include many Europeans and educated Malawians, the mosquito question is symbolic of issues of a complicated dialogue involving class, race, culture, medicine, science—not to mention how this science, when problematic, is viewed by "transitional and traditional" Malawians (cf. Peltzer, 1986:11). It is these complex inter-connections between "traditional" and "Western" medicine that I try to highlight in order to disclose the particular political culture in which the AIDS/HIV epidemic has come to be embedded in Malawi.

While the origins of HIV/AIDS are still mysterious (Karlen, 1995), the arrival of HIV in Malawi, through the international road trade routes from the eastern and western (Zaire to Kenya) and then eastern and southern (Kenya to South Africa) networks has been more plausibly mapped out, with regular itinerants as the vectors (Orubuloye et al., 1994: 89–95). Orubuloye and the colleagues assumed a Zaire-Uganda entry point for the virus in Africa. While the exact date of HIV's arrival in Malawi cannot be ascertained, the two per cent prevalence rate among ante-natal patients at Queen Elizabeth Hospital in 1985 (Taha et al., 1998) and the work of

---

1. We perish. Cf. the popular song of the same title by Dennis Phiri in which he uses politics, religion and culture in his HIV discourse. My grateful thanks to those who read and commented on earlier drafts of this article: Paul Nugent, Kenneth King, Jack Thompson, Patrick O'Malley and Jack Mapanje. My thanks to Chipo Kanjo for Chiyao translations. The shortcomings, alas, are mine.
2. A popular song by Billy Kaunda, released on the album *Alibe Mau*.

L'Herminez et al., (1992) suggests that HIV may have arrived in Malawi around 1977. Oral Yao, Tumbuka and Chewa discourses agree that HIV/AIDS is "new" to Malawi—*kubwera kwa Edzi* (the arrival of AIDS).

A phenomenological observation of *imfa yothamanga* (increase in unexplained deaths) was noted among young urban Malawians in the early eighties.[1] According to my observations between 1979 and 1984, there was an increase in the number of Malawian students sent for training abroad who died from a number of ailments, including Hepatitis B, a blood borne disease.[2] The first hospital cases of HIV/AIDS in Malawi were described in urban patients in 1985 (Cheesbrough, 1986). Doctors had noted an increased incidence of *Kaposi sarcoma,* a skin cancer, associated with HIV. One early HIV/AIDS case involved a Miss Malawi beauty queen "presumably infected abroad" (Wangel, 1995: 22). These observations were later confirmed by rising HIV positive rates at Blantyre antenatal clinics: 2.0 per cent in 1985; 8.2 per cent in 1987; 18.6 per cent in 1989 (Taha et al., 1998). In rural areas and among traditional practitioners, my informants told me during my fieldwork in 2000, a similar *kuthamanga* of deaths, usually following a "slimming disease" had been noted.[3] Opinions varied as to whether this was a sexually transmitted disease of antiquity, like *tsempho, mdulo, kanyela,* or a new one.

As elsewhere, HIV/AIDS had initially been blamed on foreigners and homosexuals. Kamuzu Banda's stance against "Western youth's immorality and cultural decadence", though not specifically against homosexuality, was well known (Banda, 1993; cf. Forster, 1994). Homosexuality—at least in the "situational variety" in prisons (Mwangulube et al., 1997), boarding schools and labour camps—exists in Malawi. Idioms for homosexual practices, such as *cha matonde* ("like two billy goats"), are found in Chinyanja/Chichewa. The Malawian educated élite joined, however, the pan-African objections to Africa being seen as the "permissive" origin of HIV, with its "wanton sexuality" facilitating the spread of HIV (cf. Caldwell and Caldwell, 1989; Ahlberg, 1994). In the polarised atmosphere of these debates, Malawian elites, led by Banda, resorted to "traditional culture" as an abstraction. In pre-colonial Maravi culture, they were pleased to remind themselves, "adultery was the fault most severely punished" (Stannus, 1910:299). Malawian intellectuals claimed that the "American Invention Depriving Sex" (AIDS) was a manifestation of "American" family planning zeal. Family planning, in its foreign guise, was anathema to both Banda and rural values (MOH, 1994: 2–4).

The Arrival of HIV/AIDS

HIV arrived in Banda's "peaceful state" in an environment that could not accommodate dissent, not even by a disease (see Africa Watch, 1990). Public sexual prudery was at its height, but in practice it was undermined by the MCP itself which, with its sexual exploitation of women (Mkamanga, 2000), contributed to the spread of HIV. There was, therefore, a collective instinctive tendency, inspired—as I discuss later—by the fear of rocking the boat, to downplay the problem. This delayed response to the epidemic was seen in both the "traditional" and "Western" medical spheres. Expatriate practitioners, constrained by the paralysing governance, were

---

1. Note Robert Fumulani's MBC recordings of 1987–1990, making the same point. Compare Katawa singers on the same theme.
2. I worked part-time at the Glasgow Royal Infirmary's STD Clinic for part of this period.
3. Cf. Serwada (1985) and Mhiri (1992).

hesitant to tackle an issue that involved discussions of sex, immorality, traditional culture and government action or inaction. Initially, public health officials sent out signals which failed to face up to the real life as lived, such as cultural attitudes and the cost of condoms—as recently as 1997 only 21 per cent of Malawian women had ever had sex with partners using condoms (Namate and Kornfield, 1997). Condom use rapidly became linked to the deprivation of pleasure, family planning, imposition of Western values and, paradoxically, promiscuity.

Traditional practitioners in Malawi lacked the ability, from their localised bases, to observe the magnitude and extent of the epidemic and to institute effective anti-HIV measures. They could only mount fragmented localised responses. Like their medical counterparts, they required time to understand and influence the epidemic, especially since the initial "slim disease" presentation in Central Africa resonated with witchcraft and sorcery causation. As the young, educated urban and peri-urban potential wage earners succumbed to the epidemic, jealousy and witchcraft were often cited, as the Police Orchestra's *Mwana wanga Koli*[1] illustrated. Both traditional and Western medicine had noted that women became affected and succumbed at unusually young ages. Research data later confirmed that among those aged 15 to 19, 85 per cent of AIDS patients were female, while beyond the age of 30, men predominated (King and King, 1992: 163).

One of the first national reactions was the question of what to call this sexually transmitted disease. In traditional contexts, sexually transmitted diseases had wide-ranging social aspects, such as the diseases *kanyela*, *mdulo* and *tsempho*, thought to be consequences of transgressing sexual norms (see Drake, 1976). For example, a man risked causing his wife *mdulo* if he committed adultery when she was pregnant. The name finally chosen, or rather "imposed from above by the radio",[2] was *Edzi*, an onomatopoeic Chewaising of "AIDS". *Magawagawa*, "something shared" (*kugawa*, to share) had briefly been in vogue, such as on the pages of *Moyo* magazine in 1986; as had *chiwerewere* (promiscuity). Both had the advantage of invoking communicability through promiscuity. Western-trained health workers lost the opportunity to carry traditional healers and their followers at this point. During the subsequent interactions between traditional medicine and Western-trained health promotion workers, it became clear that there was a problem of meaning and communication between the two groups. After *Edzi* had been coined, the HIV virus was translated as *kachirombo ka Edzi*—the little beast that causes AIDS.

While the concept of germs causing infection is now widely recognised locally, the choice of a singular *kachirombo ka Edzi* encouraged the belief, among patients and some traditional doctors, that this tiny beastie could be removed. In terms of local concepts of causality, if one removed the tiny beast, whatever its origin, the disease was likely to go away. Thus Western-trained health prevention practitioners had inadvertently made AIDS a "curable" disease. Some Malawian healers still claim they can cure AIDS. The continued use of *chiwerewere* by some suggests that a section of the population has understood the communicable aspect. However, the choice of the name *Edzi*, in the context of the explanations for its spread, prevention and the government claim that there was no cure for it, led to the impression that this was a "government disease" (*matenda a boma*). This is a concept that still exists—"How could there be no cure or was this a government plot to impose family planning?", one of my informants asked me (cf. Schoffeleers, 1999b; Probst, 1999).

---

1. An MBC recording. In the song the man blamed others for bewitching and killing his educated daughter.
2. "Tinangomva akuti basi Edzi. Ndi m'mene zinali kale lija", (we were merely told [the new disease is called] AIDS. It was like that in those days), one of my informants told me.

Initially, because of its "American origins" and the "American NGOs" promoting condoms, it had been dubbed *matenda a Amerika* (the American disease).

A feature of the HIV/AIDS syndrome itself, the association between shingles and AIDS, also endeared itself to a local causality theory. Shingles, a relative of chicken-pox, occurs, and has occurred since time immemorial, in non-HIV contexts. However, the rapid establishment of the popular association between the heralding shingles, the "slimming phase" and, last, deterioration into death quickly reinforced the sorcery factor since some who got shingles did not die. But there was also a socio-economic dimension. In 1994, the time between the occurrence of shingles and the onset of AIDS in HIV-positive patients varied from a few months to ten years depending on nutritional status and other variables, including HIV seropositivity. In an interesting study, Sr. Gabriel, at Mtengowanthenga Clinic, Lilongwe, found that of all those with shingles, everyone under 13 or over 50 were HIV negative, those between 13 and 50 were all HIV positive. Here, those likely to die would be the recently HIV-positive youth with poor prospects of following the good diet and healthy lifestyle designed to prolong life. Phenomenologically, obesity became a sign of good health, and slimness became indicative of disease. Shingles, with its "hot" blisters, became the harbinger of AIDS and a time to seek medical help. Since Western medicine was only palliative, many resorted to traditional medicine. Shingles resonated with leprosy, and both skin diseases are evocative of "heat". Yet, at this stage in rural areas, despite the "heat" of shingles, the initial HIV "segregationist" discourse prevalent in urban areas was not important, suggesting that taboos about HIV/AIDS were yet to emerge (Liomba et al., 1993). As with leprosy, HIV/AIDS victims received good care.

For much of the early to mid-1980s, Western medical discourse emphasised the lack of exact origin, knowledge of and cure for HIV/AIDS (Malawi AIDS Control Programme Manual 1989). Between 1985 and 1990, there was a strong religious lobby that considered "immorality" and God's resultant "wrath" as the cause of the epidemic (Catholic Church, 1991). A revivalist "born-again" streak, personified by an HIV-positive, self-declared ex-sinner Jambo, demonstrated this "wrath of God" movement (Jambo, 1993). Because missionary hospitals provided almost half of the medical services in Malawi, a significant Christian point of view was placed on the HIV/AIDS debate (Schoffeleers, 1999b).

Some Christian scholars did recognise the "conservative" and formative aspects of what they called African Traditional Religion (ATR): "The AIDS question is the tip of the iceberg that points to something wrong with secular culture, which has belittled ATR and Biblical ethics" (Catholic Church, 1991:51). The discourse conceded that "part of the lawlessness (among the youth) might be the absence of ATR morality" (Catholic Church, 1991:53). Forster (1998:537–545) noted that churches had a great deal of influence in the school syllabus and were influential in pushing the line against condoms. He noted that Muslims were more pragmatic. Furthermore, the idea of "divine punishment" is common in both ATR and Christianity, and it also resonates with the idea of "transgressing taboos"—little had changed. However, in this debate, the issue of how some cultural practices contributed to the spread of HIV, as we see later, was not ignored.

The first concrete indicator of the magnitude of the problem came in 1985, when it was shown by researchers funded by USAID that two per cent of 200 pregnant women were HIV positive (Chiphangwi et al., 1987). This finding, coming against the background of government apathy and inaction, emboldened local and expatriate doctors and donors, culminating in a temporary committee being set up in October 1985 to ensure that blood used for transfusion was safe. This was followed by the establishment of HIV-screening facilities at Queen Elizabeth Hospital in Blantyre in December 1985 and at Lilongwe Central Hospital in February 1986, both funded by GTZ, a German aid agency. The samples tested in Germany provided reliable figures required for further funding to Malawi from the World Health Organisation (WHO) (Wangel, 1995:24).

With this funding, the National AIDS Secretariat was established—with technical assistance from the WHO—under a manager responsible to Hetherwick Ntaba, the then Permanent Secretary in the Ministry of Health (MOH) (Wangel, 1995:25). Ntaba was politically well-connected to both John Tembo and Cecilia Kadzamira, Banda's close aides, and became himself Banda's personal physician. The epidemiologist chosen, the only senior Malawian doctor at the Secretariat, was also close to Ntaba. Consequently, all the initiatives and activities at the Secretariat could be monitored by the Office of the President.

It took two years—until 1987—before the MOH formulated the first national AIDS campaign programme, with a more comprehensive plan following in 1988. There was another year's delay before this formulation led to the establishment of the National AIDS Committee (NAC) in 1989. The NAC appeared encumbered from the start with dominance by Ntaba and his clique. Their involvement inevitably led to a politicisation of decision-making. The exclusion of local staff for political and financial reasons,[1] and the reluctance of locals to provide the input of ideas, led to a donor-led service. Prior to the formation of the NAC, there was little evidence of government initiative and leadership in this area; the Banda regime, with its strict censorship laws and Dress Code, did not encourage open discussion about sex. As a consequence, AIDS research by local researchers was not encouraged either. Expatriate researchers did not, initially, fare any better, not at least until the imperative to provide "statistics for funding" intervened.

A number of factors contributed to government awareness of the unfolding epidemic. The increased number of deaths of young civil servants and politicians between 1985 and 1988, the deaths and state of health of people working at Banda's state houses, the Malawi Army's involvement in Mozambique, the German test results and the WHO impetus, the observation by hospital doctors of the increasing number of HIV-related illness and, in the rural areas, the observation that *kunja kuno kwaopsya* (life is now more dangerous)[2] —these were some of the factors that spread awareness about the epidemic in Malawi. Yet the NAC was not, at first, a vibrant body. Part of the NAC's handicap was the realisation that one of the contributors to the AIDS epidemic was the government itself in its hospitals and clinics. M'Bama (1991) reminded his fellow workers that "unsterilised injection needles can spread HIV/AIDS and a look at how to minimize prescribing injections (was called for)". The donors forced a change of pace by promising funding (Wangel, 1995: 27), forcing the NAC to formulate the 1989–1993 medium term plan for the "prevention and control of AIDS in Malawi".[3] This document was the basis of requests to donors for assistance. There was a realisation at both the state and individual level that the HIV problem could be exploited to secure scarce foreign exchange. At the personal level, the diversion of fridges and video machines meant for HIV work from UNICEF to civil servants and MCP officials between 1988 and 1989 is widely used

1. These donor-funded projects were well-remunerated compared to local salary scales; hence these jobs were usually given to those with the right political connections.
2. Title of a song on the album Tiimbire Yesu by Katawa Singers (1993).
3. Document at the Ministry of Health, Lilongwe.

in Malawi as an example of this cynical use of HIV statistics to obtain donor money. The "seminar culture", prominent then as now in Malawi, made local workers welcome any permitted activity that brought extra income through attendance at donor-funded seminars.[1] At the state level, money meant for AIDS work was sometimes diverted to national coffers to ease foreign exchange shortages (Wangel, 1995).

From 1988, the MCP government used donated national test kits—commandeering an entire shipment in 1991 (Wangel, 1995: 30–32)—to test 2,000 State House staff at a time when there was a shortage of kits in hospitals and when the MCP was minimising the AIDS problem. Despite the fridge scandal and the diversion of test kits, no local employees were fired from the NAC and no important complaints from donors occurred. The testing of the presidential staff was reminiscent of the colonial situation where scarce resources were ring-fenced for Europeans and a few "élite" Africans. When Dr Liomba was appointed in 1989, the incumbent was transferred to the WHO regional headquarters, while in Malawi, Ntaba and the State House preserved their hold on the "HIV industry". The climate of nepotism and fear was to continue for some time. However, Dr Liomba's arrival at the NAC raised the organisation's profile and some media discussion of the HIV in Malawi ensued. His appointment coincided with the slow dawn of political and economic change in the post-Cold War era, with the "reactionary" visits by Pope John Paul and Margaret Thatcher which, despite seemingly supporting Banda's regime, provided grounds for debate and news dissemination out of Malawi. Pope John's visit, for example, was a major stimulus for the cassette industry, later to be important in disseminating HIV-awareness messages.[2] In this early transitional climate such NGOs as Banja la Mtsogolo (BLM), which specialises in family planning services, began to assume a higher profile, and government publications, such as the Ministry of Health publication *Moyo* and *The Malawi Medical Journal* increased their coverage of HIV/AIDS. An exponential increase in research on HIV in Malawi is obvious from 1988–89 onwards (MOH 1991; Centre for Social Research, 1999). However, there was little change to be observed in the popular media between 1989 and 1992.

Meanwhile, the largely donor-initiated monitoring continued to show a rising seropositivity rate at the Queen Elizabeth Central Hospital ante-natal clinics: 8.2 per cent in 1987; 18.6 per cent in 1988; 21.9 per cent in 1990; and 31.6 per cent in 1993. By 1993, some rural areas had a positivity rate of 12 per cent (Chilongozi et al., 1996). Five years after the first cases, surveys in urban and rural areas suggested that people were now generally well aware of the AIDS problem, but lacked specific knowledge of causation. Msapato and his colleagues (1990) found a rate of 96.6 per cent for "general knowledge" of the HIV among school teenagers, but only 67.1 per cent could be graded as "moderately knowledgeable". Kishindo (1990) discovered that 93.1 per cent of the population surveyed had heard of AIDS, yet only 6.8 per cent were able to "identify" the causative virus. Significantly, "prostitution", which is viewed as a "female occupation" in Malawi, was identified as the major "transmitter". This, the earlier female HIV/AIDS presentation and mortality and low female social status compounded the cultural stigmatisation of women. Some traditional practitioners, either instinctively reacting—as all medical people do—to a new disease, possibly influenced by the "slim" pattern, or the widespread "Western" ignorance of the viral cause, either sought to cure the disease by removing

1. See Carr and MacLachlan (1993) for a discussion of the "double demotivation hypothesis" in relation to Malawi
2. The Catholic mission at Balaka supported the establishment of the recording studios and the Alleluya Band.

kachirombo (the virus, "the small beast") or resorted to witchfinding, the formulation of new prohibitions and other "marginal" activities. The more the Western practitioners condemned these traditional approaches, the more biomedicine's own helplessness, at least from rural perspectives, was exposed. In their helplessness both camps seemed to scapegoat culture.

Cultural Practices and Banda's Legacy

In Malawi, the dominant form of spreading HIV is through heterosexual sex. Many cultural forms normal to rural Malawians are considered problematic by Westerners and Westernised Malawians, yet many of them promote good health in the context of rural Malawi (cf. Gwengwe, 1986). Despite the emphasis on discussions of polygamy, monogamy is respected and followed by the majority of rural Malawians. In the early 1990s, only 20 per cent of marriages were polygamous (MOH, 1994). In the past, traditionalists argue, practices such as *lobola* (bridewealth, still common in Northern Malawi) ensured that pre-initiation and premarital sexual practices were few and made men respect women and marriage. Furthermore, initiation ceremonies, practised in various parts of Malawi and known as *chinamwali, jando,* and *nsondo*, among other names, were seen as a form of health promotion. In marriage, beliefs that one could use charms were instrumental to ensuring that partners did not stray. Taboos on illegitimate children were also used to prevent premarital sex. During my youth in the Malindi area of the 1960s in Southern Malawi, a single pregnant girl was told, during the most painful part of labour, that unless she revealed who the father was, labour was likely to be prolonged or the baby would stick in the womb.

Initiation ceremonies have, in written accounts, borne the brunt of criticisms, being blamed for promoting early sex among boys and girls and leading men to have sex with younger girls and early marriages and divorces (e.g. Chiwaya, n.d.). In some initiation ceremonies, a *fisi* (a man tasked with—anonymously—deflowering the virgins) is used. The weak position of women in society, associated with practices that curtail their choices—polygamy, arranged marriages, widow inheritance—compounds the problem. The refusal of men to use condoms (Namate and Kornfield, 1997; Taha et al., n. d.) entails that women are forced into unprotected sexual practices. The associated practice of using vaginal tighteners to heighten male sexual pleasure may cause vaginal injuries which facilitate HIV infection. Such cultural practices as *gwamula* (male students raiding girls' dormitories for forced sex), *chidyerano* (wife sharing or swapping) also privilege men (Kamwendo and Kamowa, 1999; Tembo and Phiri, 1993). The power of men over women extends to the ways in which educated and apparently powerful élite women can be put at risk by the sexual behaviour of their men, who have mistresses, high socio-economic status becoming, paradoxically, a risk factor for HIV infection (Dallabeta et al., 1993). In failing to take note of these, and many other, cultural attitudes, beliefs and social conditions, even when the transmission modes of HIV spread were beginning to unravel, both Banda's and Muluzi's administrations have to shoulder some of the blame. The social conditions of pervasive poverty (Carr, 1994) dictated a reappraisal of the "condoms approach" among both the health workers and government. Banda's refusal to countenance any discussion of family planning until 1982, and then only as child spacing, predated the later distaste for condoms.

Compared to other African countries, the introduction of the condom was delayed. For example, by the end of Banda's rule in 1994, only 43 per cent of the 756 govermental health facilities provided family planning services and only 11 per cent of the 1,169 Mother-and-Child outreach services provided family planning; the reasons cited included inadequate financial material and other resources (Malawi National Family Planning Strategy, 1994–1998). The National Family Planning Strategy was more concerned with the reduction of the "natural population growth rate" than with the reduction of communicable diseases; a major impetus was the high maternal and child morbidity figures. The failure to provide comprehensive antenatal care, care during delivery and the half-hearted and under-resourced attempts to bring traditional birth attendants into the national system did not improve the situation. The post-independence failure to empower and utilise village health committees as "democratic" motivating factors in mobilising rural people in social change (Tembo, 1993) was to inadvertently promote the status of traditional medicine.

There was also the MCP practice of massive rallies, nationwide crop inspection tours, independence celebrations, Youth Week, Mother's Day Celebrations, Kamuzu Day, among other events, all designed to praise the Life President. They involved transporting women from one end of the country to another, their ostensible task being to entertain the Life President with songs and traditional dances. At these venues the women, many away from rural homes for the first time, were sexually exploited by the powerful and relatively sophisticated MCP leaders, accompanied by their forceful youth leaguers (Mkamanga, 2000).[1] Between 1977 and 1985 there were dozens of these national events. The Banda regime can also be faulted for its cynical neglect of duty of care. Even though "20–40 per cent of all in-patients (were) HIV-positive" (Forsythe, 1992), the government was still minimising the problem. As Liomba noted: "It took the government too long to accept that there was an AIDS problem ... The MCP were happy to receive all the money. What Malawi got (were) pre-packaged solutions made abroad" (quoted in Wangel, 1995:26).

Two other major events revealed the negligence by the government. One was the Malawi Army's involvement in Mozambique between 1985 and 1993 to protect the Nacala railway line (Hedges, 1989). The army kept a 500-strong battalion, replaced every six months, in Mozambique. Most soldiers were formally single and aged between 18 and 30. They frequented the sex workers at Liwonde in Malawi and Nampula in Mozambique (Nkosi, 1999). From about 1989, it became obvious that the death rates from HIV/AIDS were comparatively high in the Malawi Army. The pattern of deaths affected not just the soldiers but their wives and girlfriends as well. Yet it took until some army personnel vandalised the *Daily Times* offices, after it had publicised a World Bank report about HIV in the Malawi Army, that the secrecy surrounding one of the major conduits of the epidemic in and out of Malawi could be discussed openly.

Another HIV/AIDS story which brought the medico-cultural and socio-economic strands together was the decision by South Africa, in 1988, to stop recruiting Malawian migrant workers and repatriate those already there at the end of their contracts. TEBA (The Employment Bureau of Africa) had been important to the economic life of Malawi. From the perspective of the South African apartheid regime, it had helped to cultivate Malawi's "friendship" during South Africa's isolation. Many roadside small traders, shopkeepers, tailors, and bar owners were former mi-

---

1. Those who have sketched HIV transmission lines also confirm this pattern of power and state functions facilitating extra-marital and casual sex.

grant workers. Many, too, were regular patrons of these roadside bars and, by virtue of their higher incomes and conspicuous consumption and spending, bought the services of resident prostitutes, making them both vectors and victims of HIV. When testing began in 1985 and 1986, the incidence of HIV positivity was the highest in Malawian workers (Chirwa, 1998b). The South African Chamber of Mines classed Malawi as a high-risk country. By February 1988, the year HIV-testing kits were supplied to 11 district hospitals (WHO/MOH, 1989), the repatriation of Malawian workers began. "Within a period of just 24 months", Chirwa writes, "the number of Malawians employed on South African mines dropped from 13,090 to zero" (1998b:53).

The news, officially suppressed, spread by word of mouth. It corroborated Packard's (1989) argument which saw AIDS, like tuberculosis and other diseases, as facilitated by the poverty, malnutrition and other socio-economic disadvantages related to capitalism. The imperative to hide all adverse news in Banda's Malawi meant that the men were quietly sent to their villages without any attempts at health promotion, putting wives and girlfriends at risk. Towards the end of the 1980s, the number of HIV patients presenting with tuberculosis increased (Kool et al., 1990; Nyangulu, 1990). In colonial and post-colonial Malawi, migrant workers had been an economic tool of the state, tolerated in principle, but an embarrassment in adverse circumstances. In rural areas migrant workers were a major source of income. The treatment of returning Malawians reflected the Banda regime's obsession with presentation and neglect of its subjects' welfare.

There was also a degree of donor collusion with the state apathy. Donors were reluctant in the Cold War era to upset the Malawian government. Family-planning NGOs needed government permission to continue with their restricted research and provision of family-planning services. This collusion extended to turning blind eye to the diversion to the State House of scarce HIV-testing reagents. The WHO regional and local officers were weak and deferred to Banda's "temperament" (O'Malley, 1999; King and King, 2000:34–35). In 1978, the WHO had sponsored a seminar for primary care, where the importance of traditional medicine had been recognised (MOH ,1978:86–92). And yet, at a time when donors were funding all the initiatives and were aware of cultural aspects, no attempt was made to address these wider cultural dimensions of disease and health care.[1] Donors are also accused by some observers of promoting HIV spread by "counselling free choice in a communal culture", leaving people "free to spread HIV" (King and King, 2000: 34).

Despite the palliative health promotion discourse, by 1991 HIV/AIDS was an acknowledged major cause of death in Malawi. When the Malawi Catholic Bishops challenged Banda's government in 1992, they cited health as one of the areas of inequity in the country, calling more attention to the "tragedy of AIDS". This critique of the Banda regime took issue with one of its legitimising constructs; that Malawi was a land of "milk and honey" *(mkaka ndi uchi)*, where people were better fed, dressed, educated and lived, as Banda was fond of declaring, in "houses that did not leak when it rained". This had been a longstanding public health legitimation of his regime. AIDS and its sequel exposed this myth.

At the end of the Banda era, in 1994, the inadequate provision of rural health services continued. This meant that the majority of rural people continued to get STD treatment from traditional practitioners (Helitzer-Allen and Allen 1992), and

---

1. For example, in Uganda more intensive use of the media, educational system and cultural networks were used to fight HIV/AIDS.

the dominant HIV awareness messages were broadcast only on the MBC, the state-owned radio station. These messages emphasised the "condom paradigm", but to a significant extent ignored cultural and socio-economic realities—razors could be shared because of poverty, condoms were unavailable, traditional practitioners had been "free" since 1985, when the epidemic began to be discussed, to formulate and apply their own practices with minimal engagement from the government. The state had displayed indifference to rural areas in the fields of health and education (see Mhone, 1992b; Lwanda, 1996). Ironically—no, tragically—the first substantive AIDS promise from Banda's regime came just before the 1993 referendum.

HIV/AIDS in the "New" Malawi

The second medium term plan, 1993–1998, was interrupted by the change of government when Banda's rule gave way to a multiparty democracy. During the 1993 referendum, various pro-multiparty groups had promised to improve health and education, and all had cited the "scourge of AIDS" as a problem.[1] The Muluzi administration inherited an impoverished country with an infant mortality rate of 134.2; 49 per cent of children under five years suffering from stunted growth; 27 per cent of children underweight; 90 per cent of the population rural; 422 students per classroom; 80 per cent of rural smallholders living on less than US$ 240 (per capita per annum); 41 per cent of rural smallholders surviving on less than half a hectare; a very high dependency ratio, with 106 dependents for every 100 adults of working age, and children often starting to work before the age of 15 (World Bank, 1995).

Despite the promises of the UDF, little has so far been accomplished. Yet the UDF had set the fight against AIDS as a high priority. For a good reason—by 1994, HIV/AIDS-related illnesses were responsible for a third of all admissions to hospitals, while the prevalence rate ranged among pregnant women, by 1995, from 5 per cent in rural Thonje to 33 per cent in urban Blantyre with a median rate of 16 per cent (Kaluwa et al., 1995). When they prepared their manifestos, the main opposition parties, the AFORD and the UDF, were aware of these facts, and at least two medical doctors were involved in the preparation of the UDF manifesto.

On attaining power, the UDF, and later (1994–95) the UDF/AFORD coalition, were accorded a honeymoon period. During this period many deficiencies were blamed on the Banda regime's squandering of resources in the run-up to the elections (Lwanda, 1996). Yet during the first four years of its administration, the Muluzi government did not fare any better than the Banda regime. For most of 1994–95 there was a shortage of reagents for HIV testing and, despite the appointment of another medical doctor to be Minister of Health, no significant initiatives on the HIV/AIDS front ensued. By the time of the AFORD/UDF coalition in September 1994, conditions in hospitals had deteriorated because of the shortages. While emphasising poverty alleviation as a priority, using political rhetoric as well as action in the form of selective disbursement of loans to young entrepreneurs, the UDF did not place a high enough priority on health.[2] In the "new dispensation" Muluzi followed Banda's model and supported the growth of private health care, publicly encouraging clinical officers to establish private clinics since "the government cannot do it all". Apart from one high-profile walk by Muluzi, there were no public statements galvanising

---

1. See, for example, the UDF and AFORD manifestoes.
2. The development policy of the business-led Muluzi administration emphasised small-scale retail business as a major solution to poverty (Lwanda 1996; see also Chinsinga's chapter in this volume).

the public in the fight against HIV/AIDS until after 1997. In an echo of the Banda era of the 1980s, the Muluzi administration spent money on the State House, diplomats and political schemes, thereby neglecting health promotion. As Mburu has noted for Kenya, "The fact that health services are not tangible also significantly lessens their political visibility" (1992:418). Unfortunately, private health systems rarely invest in preventive services, because they thrive by offering "curative" or palliative services.

By 1995, the Secretariat had run into planning and budgeting problems, and by April 1995, the National AIDS Coordinator, apparently unpaid for some months, had resigned to return to a job at the University of Malawi. The apathy, seminar culture and "muddling through" initiated by the MCP, continued under the UDF. The new government missed an opportunity to mobilise the youth through schools and the media as the UDF manifesto had promised. The burden of work on HIV fell on NGOs, mission hospitals and state hospitals with scarce resources. NGOs, now free of the research constraints of the Banda era, increased their research and service provision activities. In 1997, it was estimated that there were 73 international and local organisations dealing with HIV/AIDS (Kakhongwe, 1997). Their major funders were Action-AID, the Malawi government, the British governmental aid agency (ODA), UNDP, UNICEF, USAID and the WHO.

Yet despite his initial inaction on AIDS, Muluzi contributed to a resurgence of the effect of traditional medicine on the HIV debate. He maintained an ambiguous stance on the issue of traditional medicine. His promotion of private Western medical provision was, by extension, assumed to indicate a similar attitude to traditional medicine. Replete with vernacular idioms which made him *kumtunda* (unsurpassable; literally, the one who lives on top of the hill), *tate wa dziko* (father of the nation) and so on, Muluzi embodied some of Banda's ambiguity. Interestingly, much debate ensued from the awards of honorary doctorates to Muluzi, particularly when they became a mandatory form of address. Whether medical or academic doctorate, the same appeal of the *sing'anga* (healer; doctor) was at play, even though the accompanying cultural accoutrements were different or not immediately obvious. Muluzi, in contrast to Banda's authoritarianism, adopted a benign "man of the people" image (cf. Achebe, 1966). At every opportunity Dr Muluzi was seen to "alleviate poverty and suffering" by giving money to the sick and the poor. While this palliative approach initially earned his regime some popularity, the inevitable questions of where the money was coming from and how giving money to patients dying of AIDS would solve Malawi's HIV/AIDS pandemic emerged. His attendances at funerals, many caused by AIDS, led to criticisms about too much "weeping for the dead while the living suffer".[1] But the gestures bought the UDF valuable time. Health—because the rich obtained private and national health care anyway and the rural areas were still dependent on traditional medicine—was not an electoral issue in Malawi.

Paradoxically, the issue of presentation proved to be a problem for Muluzi. As AIDS deaths multiplied towards the end of the 1990s, Muluzi became famous for attending funerals, *pulezidenti wopanda nkhanza, wopita kumaliro* (the kind, caring president who attends funerals). But this gesture also succeeded in exposing the extent of the HIV/AIDS epidemic and the government's lack of substantive activity. Unlike in the Banda era, the public were now exposed by the media to the full extent of the HIV epidemic. The poor state of the hospitals, given the extent of the HIV/

---

1. Compare Ben Michael's song Tilire, tilire (1999) whose lyrics translate, "Let's all cry! Not for the dead, (their turn is gone) but for ourselves!".

AIDS epidemic, could not, as in the Banda era, be disguised by media management. Eventually, as in the political culture of colonial times and during the period of the Banda regime, it was self-interest that roused the Muluzi government from its apathy. Between 1994 and 1998, the UDF lost over twenty of its MPs and senior activists, many, according to the Speaker of Parliament, Sam Mpasu, to HIV/AIDS. The UDF/AFORD elites had initially used scarce government and health insurance money to travel to South Africa for treatment. However, even South African clinics had by 1995 adopted a policy of "HIV-patient repatriation" once the diagnosis had been made, if only because few Malawian patients could afford the anti-retroviral therapy. Between 1996 and 1999, the government was forced to admit that HIV was now a major national problem.

A number of factors other than the self-interest imperative contributed to the change of heart. The freed electronic media had, from 1994 onwards, promoted awareness of HIV/AIDS issues. Many popular musicians had been involved in raising awareness of HIV/AIDS. Socio-economic and human resources surveys by the government and donors had indicated the human resources implications of the HIV/AIDS pandemic on Malawi (Forsythe, 1992). During 1996–98, the Malawi Vision 2020 consultation process had involved all schools and sections of the public, including chiefs, village headmen, industrialists, civil servants and members of the general public. Among the priority areas to emerge from this consultation was the HIV problem. Again there was some pressure from donors; most notably from the EU which provided most of the funding for the public health campaigns, the World Bank, concerned with manpower and population issues (cf. Kalipeni, 1997), and the WHO which was now able to speak forcefully to the Ministry of Health. The visibly debilitated state of both the Army and the Police were important features in changing the president's policy. Finally, the emerging HIV/AIDS statistics for the period 1997-99 were startling. The 1999 Sentinel Survey report, using data from its 19 sites, concluded that the estimated crude national HIV prevalence rate was 8.8 per cent (2.2 per cent among those under 15, 16.4 per cent among the 15–49 age group, and 1.1 per cent for those over 50). Among pregnant women rates varied from 2.9 per cent at Kamboni in Kasungu to 35.5 per cent in Mulanje Mission Hospital. The Policy Analysis Initiative of the Office of the Vice President admitted that "despite the severity of the HIV/AIDS epidemic, the response from the Government and the community is not commensurate with the seriousness of the problem" (Malawi National AIDS Control Programme, 1999:107).

Interestingly, a book compiled between 1995 and 1998, and co-authored by Muluzi and thought to contain a synthesis of his personal manifesto in its epilogue (see Muluzi et al., 1999:187–192), has the following on health:

> Health problems affecting Malawi are poor access to health services, high infant and maternal mortality rates, widespread malnutrition and poor quality services. We need to redress the situation by establishing health centre units, especially in the rural areas. The government is already doing this through MASAF (Malawi Social Action Fund). NGOs also offer health services. Further, the government also believes in providing safe water to Malawians. With the assistance from the private sector and NGOs, the government has sunk boreholes in the rural areas to the benefit of rural Malawians. (Muluzi et al., 1999:187)

The "manifesto" is noteworthy for its exclusion of one of the three most important health issues in Malawi, HIV/AIDS. Yet by 1999, Muluzi had adopted a more proactive role in the fight against HIV/AIDS, his government instituting a number of initiatives. Many involved the dissemination of more HIV/AIDS awareness information on the radio. There was some appeal to self-control, or as Muluzi put it memorably, "Men should learn to dim their (headlights) in the face of temptation!". One of Muluzi's solutions was to "prohibit" and lock up prostitutes. Once again the issue of class arose in the WHO-sponsored innovation to reduce the cost of Combivir, the most used anti-retroviral therapy in Malawi, in the last half of 2000, to K10,000; making it affordable to high-income "economically essential" patients but not the rural poor. The rural areas were still largely untouched by the HIV/AIDS services on offer. For example, family planning services are still NGO-led. Banja la Mtsogolo (BLM), the largest family planning NGO, has the greatest national penetration with its 17 centres, more than those of the government itself. But the fact that it distributed, according to its 1997 Annual Report, only 612,866 condoms in 1996–97, shows how little impact the "condom approach" has made in Malawi.

One event encapsulating the cultural, political and economic aspects of the HIV/AIDS story in Malawi was the *mchape* incident. In 1994, Goodson Chisupe, an elderly villager, claimed to be able to prevent or cure AIDS with a herbal drink whose formula had been given in a dream. People—whose estimated numbers run up to 500,000—flocked to his village in Liwonde to drink *mchape*, an idiom that had long been used for witch-cleansing (see Schoffeleers, 1999b; Probst, 1999). The supplicants included both urban and rural people, well-off and poor, educated and formally uneducated. Chisupe's simple action set in motion a series of events which highlighted the desperation and poverty of the sick in Malawi, exposed the shortcomings of the Western medical establishment, and showed that many among the educated class also still believed in "traditional" remedies.

A long line of witch-finders can be identified in the history of *mchape*: M'bisalira in the 1850s; Kaundula in 1919; Mchape in the 1930s; Ligomeka in the 1940s; Chikanga in the 1950s; Khwakhwa, Antonyo and Dulawaya in the 1960s; Simbazako in the 1970s; Naliere in the 1980s; and Mchape in the 1990s. Crucially, these healers and witch-finders have sought to address new threats by using old wisdoms. Their interventions are reconfigurations of age-old witchfinding traditions of *mwabvi* (ordeals), which sought to establish the legitimacy of new or contested orders. In the holistic ontological and epistemological context between Western medicine, traditional medicine and real life, the *mchapes* were the marginal, if heraldic, practitioners. They could also be seen as testing the position of traditional practitioners, as Chisupe did, within the legal framework of Malawi. During the 1980s, Malawi had at least 50,000 registered traditional practitioners (Msonthi, 1984 and 1986), and, as the analysis of the political culture of disease makes clear, there is no reason to assume that their numbers have decreased. This fact must be compared with the fact that there are fewer than 500 medical doctors in the whole country.

The Medical Practitioners and Dentists Act of 1987 does not prohibit the practice of "any African system of medicine", provided "that nothing in this section shall be construed to authorise the performance by a person practising any African system of therapeutics of any act which is dangerous to life". In 1997, the Vision 2020 Project suggested that traditional herbalists and traditional birth attendants, through their associations, be more involved and integrated into the health care system to improve rural health care. It was an overdue call for an "educated hybridisation" that recognises the limits and possibilities of both cultures. Msukwa (1981:12), after a decade (1971—80) during which the government spent K15 million on health as compared to the K50 million spent on the Capital City project, had made a similar suggestion, as had Msonthi (1982). Between 1964 and 1981, health campaigns had concentrated on eradicating poverty, ignorance and disease, without formulating a transcultural health policy. In the post-Banda era, although some of the issues on both sides of the traditional-Western medical divide have been widely aired, few tangible results have occurred. Maluwa-Banda (2000), for example, showed that secondary students had "adequate knowledge about the basic facts about AIDS, the transmission of HIV and how they can protect themselves from being infected". However, it was evident that among students, correct knowledge about HIV was found to co-exist with "some misconceptions". This work mirrored Forster's (1996; 1998) in the villages around Zomba. During my own fieldwork, I found that at some tertiary education sites "traditional" beliefs influenced attitudes to Western medicine. For example, some second-year university students thought that witchcraft (*ufiti*) was important in disease causality (14.28 per cent of the respondents), the use of magic (*kukhwima*) is protective of disease (57.14 per cent), and the same *kukhwima* is effective (71.42 per cent). Even more, 38 per cent of this élite student cohort had been introduced to a traditional practitioner by their parents. And my work in progress suggests that these attitudes may perpetuate the culture of medical duality.

Conclusion

Mazrui states that culture "provides lenses for perception and cognition, motives for behaviour, a basis for an identity, and modes of communication" (1990:7–8). In the Malawian context and in the case of HIV/AIDS, one would predict that the sites of significant cultural change and effect need to be the localised cores of traditional practices at the village level; for example, initiation rites; residual traditional birth practices, *kukhwima*; socio-cultural activities which involve incestuous or under-age sex; cleansing rites for widows and other practices that may involve sex with HIV-infected people; the multiple use of instruments in scarification. Yet an historical perspective is crucial in order to avoid, as Mazrui may be interpreted to suggest, an essentialist view on culture. In the current predicament, the populace being under attack by both HIV/AIDS and the solutions proposed for it, the power brokers of tradition may consider themselves to be at risk. There may, therefore, be an accelerated process of transmission and manipulation of "tradition".[1]

In the case of women, at such times, cultural values are even more assiduously guarded (see also Ribohn's chapter in this volume). If, in traditional medicine, as I have suggested, change is inspired by new and hostile challenges and occurs after experiments, we can predict that each subject, localised but not confined to a locality, structures its own response. Scholars on Malawi and other African countries have produced a lively debate out of this predicament (see e.g. Kaspin, 1993; Comaroff and Comaroff, 1993; Englund, 1996b; Yamba, 1997; Ciekawy and Geschiere, 1998; and Geschiere, 1996 and 1997). These responses are not merely reactive but also mould the socio-economic realities themselves. When, for example, McAuliffe (1994) suggests that there is no evidence to suggest risk behaviour reduction even after people have recognised HIV, she may be missing the point. Are these people "recognising" the risk in their Western mode or their traditional mode? In the case of the latter, their behaviour will appear risky to the Western observer but logical from whatever is the traditional point of view—and its attendant socio-economic reality—that informs their behaviour. One of the most "modifiable" risk factors for HIV are STDs, but even they are difficult to modify where one of the most powerful

---

1. This is already noticeable when "clan heads" become younger as AIDS and other diseases reduce Malawi's life expectancy, now thought to be about 40 years, as opposed to 46 in the mid-1980s.

forces is sex. Sexual power in its association with dominant heterosexual masculinity, possession of money, political power, key to inheritance—much more is at stake than sex itself.

Effective health promotion measures against HIV will have to tackle localised practices in their own terms. For example, if a *fisi* is to act as a surrogate "husband" to a woman whose own husband is infertile, the intervention may have to be less the banning of the practice than subjecting the man to an AIDS test. The practice would continue at a much reduced risk of HIV transmission. I suggest the same approach for *afisi* who ritually deflower virgin initiates at girls' initiation ceremonies—to the extent that, of course, such a practice is still followed anywhere in Malawi. In their zeal to condemn "tradition", some urbanised middle-class Malawians sometimes create the false impression that such practices are more common than what is the case in reality. Engagement with these practices ought to be, in any case, based on the understanding that while one may not be able to *change* them, one can make them *safe*. An explanation of infective or epidemic dimensions to traditional practitioners is both possible and necessary. But a pre-condition is the understanding that in some of these practices lie gendered, hierarchical power roles and age-old cosmological beliefs that are appropriate for most of rural Malawi.

These cosmologies have mounted responses in the pre-colonial, colonial and postcolonial times of famine and epidemics; during the colonial "subjugation"; and in encounters with Christianity. A response to the HIV epidemic from African traditional medicine is only to be expected. The HIV/AIDS epidemic has now lasted a generation, a period long enough for the brokers of traditional culture to begin to respond. However, some of the "localised" responses emerging, notably the one that advocates sex with virgins or under-age girls as a means of killing the virus, are from a moral viewpoint clearly pathological and need to be dislodged before they become firmly—and locally—embedded. They are an example of the exploitation and corruption of culture by the powerful.

At the same time, socio-economic and cultural considerations must be seen as *political* issues. As my history of the political culture of the epidemic shows, neither the Banda nor the Muluzi administration has accorded HIV/AIDS the priority it deserves. Where action has been taken, both regimes have been motivated by self-interest and short-term considerations. Hours (1986:41–57) described African medicine as "an alibi and a reality". Politicians may use it to disguise their lack of action and prioritisation, but the reality is that 80 per cent of Malawians are, to all intents and purposes, currently only able to benefit marginally from Western medicine. Even élite university students may be torn between theoretical science and the reality of village life and its diabolical mosquitoes.

9. " Human Rights and the Multiparty System Have Swallowed Our Traditions "

Conceiving Women and Culture in the New Malawi

Ulrika Ribohn

Historically, no larger group has suffered greater violations
of its human rights in the name of culture and tradition
than women.
(Nagengast, 1997: 358–359).

Even though human rights are a transnational phenomenon, they are interpreted and understood in local contexts. These interpretations are locally manifested in various ways.[1] Malawians' understandings of human rights and the universal intentions of the United Nations are in many cases dissimilar. "When the salient contrast appears to be between 'the local' and 'the global' it is not culture but the difference between global and local manifestations that becomes the interesting problematic" (Strathern, 1995:154). The salient issues here are the manifestations of transnational agendas represented by official agencies, on the one hand, and local reactions to them, on the other. A key dichotomy revolves around cultural values and human rights in local discourses of human rights, particularly in relation to women's rights.

Deploying official human rights discourses, governmental organisations and representatives of the so-called civil society argue in favour of human rights even if the practical implementation of human rights would conflict with local cultural values. Official arguments have been met by sets of counter-arguments stressing cultural values even when practices based on these values appear to deny certain groups (particularly women) their rights. Cultural practices are gendered in human rights discourses when, for example, official statements identify local cultural practices as threats to women's rights, while the general public identify women as carriers of "traditions". The categories of "women" and "cultural practices" are thus often reified—made abstract and absolute—in current discourses on human rights in Malawi.

The intent of this chapter is to analyse local manifestations of human rights by illustrating how gender, transnationalism, and human rights are intertwined in local human rights discourses. Social changes in the wake of the democratisation process are incorporated into local notions of human rights, and many people apprehend the changes as a threat to "culture". Local reactions against human rights are based on notions of a new "culture", associated with "Western" values. What is interesting is not so much whether human rights and "culture" actually *are* in opposition to each other, but whether such a dichotomy in local human rights discourses has observable consequences. As Henrietta Moore writes: "The particular force of cultural dis-

---

1. When I argue that in Malawi human rights have local manifestations, I do not mean that rights are needs that have been conceptualised into rights, such as is the case in the indigenous rights movement in Australia. Instead, human rights discourses in Malawi are consequences of the belief that the introduction of human rights solves some political and social problems in Malawi.

WOMEN AS KEEPERS OF CULTURE

courses, of course, is that they have material effects, that is they are practically or performatively as well as discursively maintained" (1994:41). One consequence of local human rights discourses in Malawi is that women as a category are placed in opposition to human rights. Both men and women argue that women should maintain "culture". Women's role as keepers of "culture" may be understood through their close connection to community life. A common saying is *azimayi ndi mulungu wa dziko lapansi*, "women are the God of the whole world", which means that women should guide and protect people in the village (Preston, 1995:11).

Dichotomising Human Rights and Culture in Local Official Discourses

After the Banda era, official agencies in Malawi have defined "culture" and "traditions" as threats and obstacles to human rights. Official agencies constitute a force trying to alter practices that according to them are in conflict with the International Bill of Rights. I will here give examples of official agencies' arguments in order to illustrate the dichotomy between human rights and "culture" in relation to women. President Muluzi has stated in one of his speeches:

> Practices such as *gwamula*, *fisi* and others may have been acceptable in the past, but today they clash with the values of freedom and equality which are part of our newly embraced democracy. (*The Monitor*, 10 October, 1995)

Several traditions and cultural practices are identified as causes of violations of women's rights. Khaila (1995), like Muluzi, singled out *gwamula* and *fisi* as "traditions" that encourage rape and sexual violence against women. *Gwamula* is a practice whereby young men break into girls' places of residence at night and have sex without prior arrangement with the girls. The *fisi* (hyena) practice has several variations. The currently much-debated variation stipulates that when a girl has come of age, she must sleep with a man. This man is called *fisi* since he comes at night. This practice is also arranged without the girl's consent to sexual intercourse (Khaila, 1995:6). Another example of attempts to change people's opinions concerning women's rights is Steve Chimombo's poem, *Breaking the Beadstrings*. He writes in the introduction:

> I thought it appropriate to make them (beads and tattoos) part of the women's liberation movement currently sweeping through. They are both the symbols of womanhood and the signs of women's acceptance of their role in society. In the sense of the latter, then, they are a sign of servitude and even acquiescence to male manipulations. It is only by understanding the role these objects play for both males and females, at least in the poem, that women can effect their own liberation physically and mentally. I know that it is not the primary function of art to cure the ills of the society. It can, however, suggest the direction that the society could take or the attitude it could, or should, adopt. (Chimombo, 1995: ix)

Newspaper articles and local research often blame "culture" for gender inequality and violations against women. Some of the newspapers have a gender-page once a week, with themes such as: "Women, Cultural Practices and the Constitution" (*The Daily Monitor*, 18 July, 1995). The article discusses the new constitution's Bill of Women's rights and its differences vis-à-vis customary law. Practices such as *lobola* (bridewealth), arranged marriages, polygamy and wills and inheritance were said to marginalise women. Another article, "As girls', women's rights are abused, violated … the law seems to suggest 'such is life, it is cultural'" *(Daily Times*, 10 August, 1995), discussed how society regarded domestic violence against women as acceptable to the extent that it was perceived as a right. Not only journalists and politicians but also social scientists, NGOs, writers and lawyers argue for a change in women's positions in society. Seminars are organised; research is conducted; information is spread on the radio and in other public settings. In this way people are constantly reminded of the conflict between cultural practices and women's rights.

Dichotomisation between human rights and "traditions" is not a new phenomenon. It was present even during the MCP era. Yet, the tension between human rights standards and "culture" was solved in a different way. While the present authorities want to change cultural practices in order to incorporate women and secure their human rights, the MCP government's attitude was that the "traditions" had to be maintained even if the practices denied women their human rights. The MCP attitude is clearly displayed in their justification for not ratifying the Convention on the Elimination of All Forms of Discrimination against Women until 1991. The MCP stated:

> Owing to the deep-rooted nature of some *traditional customs and practices* of Malawians, the government of the Republic of Malawi shall not, for the time being, consider itself bound by such of the provisions of the convention as require immediate eradication of such *traditional customs and practices*. (quoted in Jensen and Poulsen 1993: 6; my emphasis)

Although both the MCP and UDF governments dichotomised "culture" and human rights, the dichotomisation was used politically in different ways. The former government tried to maintain "culture", while the UDF government's intent was to liberate Malawi from "culture".[1]

Not only has the shift in government altered official perspectives on human rights and "culture". It has also altered perspectives on women's position in politics. In the MCP rhetoric women were seen to be in a dominant position because of their relationship to Kamuzu Banda, the *Nkhoswe* Number One, the ultimate guardian of the matrilineal group of sisters, known as *mbumba*. By turning the MCP Women's League into Kamuzu's *mbumba*, Banda changed a kinship relationship into a political relationship. These women had to praise, dance and sing for him on every public occasion.

During this period, some men complained of being deprived of their wives. The men disliked the fact that they could not express their dissatisfaction with their wives when the latter left them for days. Their aversion to women's position in the MCP could be interpreted in many ways, and interpretations vary on the role women played during the MCP era as Kamuzu's *mbumba* and in Chitukuko Cha Amayi m'Malawi (CCAM).[2] According to my interviews, many educated women—civil servants, lecturers and human rights activists—feel that they did not have any influence on the decision-making process; their participation was based, instead, on force and threat. However, some other women—usually without formal education, living in villages—state that they were happy to see new parts of Malawi, to get away from home, and to meet women from other areas. Many of these women also considered themselves powerful within the party structure. To get away from home also meant getting away from hard labour and their husbands' strict control. Nevertheless, many of these women emphasise that they disliked being forced to participate in rallies or dancing for Kamuzu in the hot sun. Hence some women claim that they played a significant political role; others say that their participation was staged. Whatever was the case, their participation was significant within a politically de-

---

1. "Culture" as something to be protected has, of course, become a convenient reference to Muluzi when he himself has been challenged. See the chapter by Kayambazinthu and Moyo in this volume on Muluzi's apparent defence of women as keepers of Malawian culture.
2. The organisation for the development of women in Malawi, disbanded after the political change.

fined "traditional" framework. They were much less visible as cabinet ministers and members of parliament.

It has been argued that women exploited their position as *mbumba*. Sam Mpasu (1995), a cabinet minister and Speaker of Parliament after the transition, has written about his time in detention during the MCP era. Several of his cellmates were detained because of women who had turned to the MCP government for support against their husbands or lovers. Some men claimed that their wives took advantage of the situation. Many men feared reprisals by the MCP and refrained from accusing their wives of infidelity. They perceived the fact that women had to participate in rallies and other political events as manifestations of men's lack of control over their wives. This sentiment may partly explain a common reaction after the referendum when some men stripped female MCP supporters of their clothes that bore Banda's portrait.

According to two Malawian female researchers, there has been an escalation of violence against women since the introduction of political rights (see Semu and Kadzamira, 1995). They write that the political freedoms have been

> wrongly interpreted by some to mean freedom to engage in any activity without due regard to the human rights of others. In the case of women, this has been a problem in particular due to the nature of politics in the past when women were wrongly seen to be beneficiaries of the system despite their not being part of the decision making system. Violence has thus been wrongly directed at them as a means of settling old scores. (Semu and Kadzamira, 1995: 5)

Another study reports the general view that after the introduction of political freedom, the situation has worsened among women:

> Many ... described the multi-party era as a time of decreasing rights and influence of women. Women participants continued to complain of chronic inequities, and said that men have more economic power than women, that men are the heads of households, that men find wage employment more easily than women and that "women do far more work than men". In addition to these long-standing problems, however, participants said that since the elections women have fewer rights in their relationships with their husbands, their influence over local decision making processes has declined, and "women no longer participate in politics". Most see the decline in importance of local MCP committees, in which women played a prominent role, as the cause of this trend. (Preston, 1995: 9–10)

Whether women actively participated in politics or not during the MCP era, there seems to be a consensus that the situation has worsened for women since the transition to multipartyism. During the MCP era "culture" was often used to defend political decisions. This is no longer the case. The UDF focuses on modernity and change, the antitheses of "tradition". It explicitly describes men and women as equals, defining "culture" as an obstacle to gender equality. Rather than demarcating participation within the traditionalistic framework of Banda's government, Muluzi's government defines participation by using universalistic notions. There has been a shift in official political rhetoric from kinship terminology, such as *Nkhoswe* and *mbumba*, to terms such as gender equality and human rights.

Human Rights and Culture as Opposites in Popular Perspectives

Both men and women in contemporary Malawi express unease about the public discourse that emphasises women's rights. On the basis of my fieldwork in Zomba district, I describe here men's and women's reactions to official discourses on women's rights. Arguments against official political discourses are expressed in a non-universalistic terminology. However, the notion of "culture" is similar in both sets of arguments. Authorities and villagers alike apply the concept of "culture" as a static, reified entity, evenly distributed throughout society but more in evidence in rural areas than in towns. Significantly, both sides in the discursive field use the concepts of "culture" and "traditions" interchangeably.

According to Malawian discourses on "culture", the rural population is believed to be more "traditional" than urban people, and women are believed to be closer to rural life and thus "traditions" than men are. The concept of "culture" is not defined as if it were constantly changing. Instead, "traditional culture" is contrasted with a new "culture". While the political élite argues for a change in "culture", villagers (especially old men) are against such a change. I submit that in political discourses "culture" is turned into something that can be changed, or kept unchanged. In local human rights discourses, gender, "culture" and human rights are intertwined and expressed as closely related. Women's roles in society are rarely discussed without reference to change, "culture" or human rights. For example, Mr Chiona, living in a village outside of Zomba town, claimed that the role of women is to maintain "culture". Mr Chiona pointed to a dilemma, experienced by many others:

> Human rights and the multiparty system have swallowed our traditions, so women should try to bring the traditions back. People have misinterpreted human rights and multipartyism in this country. We are now using a borrowed culture, Western culture. Multipartyism and human rights are good things, but they should coexist with the local culture. I like human rights, multipartyism and traditions. We have lost our culture because of the multiparty system, and this is a misinterpretation of human rights.

There are two opposing opinions among the public in regard to the question whether women's positions in society are changing. One opinion is that women's position in society has changed a great deal, while the other side argues the opposite. Such opinions largely depend on whether present official discourses are perceived as leading to change, or whether the arguments are perceived as empty words. Dr Khapukha, a female lecturer at the University, who regarded herself as a feminist, described it as follows: "Culture evolves faster for men, it is static for women. Women are holding the culture up, men go to school, travel, get new influences, while women stay in the village." She considered the UDF government's arguments to be purely rhetorical, without a foundation or consequences. Her feelings were in stark contrast to the views of Timu, a male lecturer who, however, defined himself as gender-sensitive and liberal. He argued that "culture changes faster for women than for men". He perceived official agencies' arguments as having huge consequences, leading gender relations to a transformational state in which both male and female roles were questioned and re-categorised due to women's new position in society. Naphiri, a female human rights worker, would not be surprised by men's disapproval of the changes. A common notion among many women, especially the more educated and urban ones such as Naphiri herself, was that "men are more positive to traditions because traditions support them".

Discourses construct groups and individuals as particular kinds of subjects with particular characteristics (Moore, 1994:98). Even if men and women are constructed as different subjects, men's actions may be just as "traditional" as women's. Men maintain or change "culture" to the same extent that women do, if we understand and interpret men's actions as "cultural" to the same extent as women's actions. Constructions of masculinities are hence as "cultural" or "traditional" for men as constructions of femininities are for women. In other words, men do not act outside of "culture" while women act within "culture". Attitudes towards cultural change are more dependent on education than on gender. Educated urban people are generally more positive to changes introduced by human rights and democracy than illiterate rural people. Educated women in particular advocate changes while educated men are often more reserved in their appreciation of changes.

The problem, as many Malawians see it, is that "culture" is changing. People find that human rights imply a new set of values. Many people say that changes in political ideologies from Banda's axioms of discipline and obedience to the new slogans of freedom and equal rights have led to a new "culture". According to many, this is a "culture" where criminals can do what they want, where individualistic values are preferred to community values, where women do not show respect to men, and where young people do not listen but rather use drugs, have sex and lack respect for elders (cf. Englund, 2000:583). People feel that the liberalisation of politics and the increased market capitalism have led to a "culture" of selfishness and individualism. This new "culture" stands in opposition to their old "culture" where sharing and helping each other were important dimensions of local value-systems.

The "culture", which most of the villagers I talked to experienced as disappearing, was connected to rural community life. Just as Malawians refer to women when they talk about "culture", they refer to the rural community—the village—in the same way. It is essential to be part of a community, and the village is often perceived as being the community. To be a "real" Malawian is to live in a village. Whenever I described my work as an anthropologist, I was always told to speak to villagers because they had "Malawian culture". This was expressed in various ways. People would say, "Don't talk to him, talk to the woman over there. She is a real villager, she is a real Malawian"; "It is good that you speak to real Malawians and not only with the educated people"; "You have to go out in villages to get to know Malawian culture". These statements indicate that both rural and urban Malawians perceive a gap between urban educated elites and the Malawian "culture". The rural population are "the real Malawians". According to such a logic, "culture" is interpreted as synonymous with rural community life. If "culture" is changed then community life is threatened. This frightens people, because the village is where a person works, lives and has relatives and resources. The village is also a place where people have rights to land and can get help from neighbours and relatives. Informants described the village as a place where they shared ideas and knowledge and understood each other. To be part of a community is essential to one's identity, respect and security. People living in urban areas also identified churches, neighbourhoods and football clubs as communities they belonged to. The work place, however, was described as temporary. Lack of jobs, retrenchment and unemployment seem to have caused a re-emphasis on the importance of the village (see Anders' chapter in this volume).

I would argue that local notions of "culture" not only locate "culture" in the village; they also gender "culture". Women are described as keepers of "traditions", maintaining social relations and institutions in the community. Women's roles as protectors of community and community values are apparent in the term *mbumba*. *Mbumba* has several meanings; it is a matrilineal kinship term; a term used in the political context by the MCP for women in Malawi; and also the Chichewa term for community.

Oral history emphasises the close connection between women and community. In Schoffeleers and Roscoe's (1987) study of oral tales, women are classified as either naturally flawed or virtuous and caring. This dualistic classification of women produces an interesting contrast to the classification of men. According to these stories, men may make wrong decisions but are not described as having fundamentally bad characters. If they make mistakes, it is attributed to their humanness. A man al-

ways receives a second chance; a woman's offence, on the other hand, inevitably leads to a punishment and, in some cases, to death. Returning to the perception of women as keepers of "traditions", it becomes clear why their mistakes are judged more severely than men's. A woman's failure threatens the whole system, because her participation is essential to the continued existence of the community. Her mistakes are unforgivable. These reactions are comparable to perceptions of theft. Just as a thief's actions threaten the community by acting outside of local value-systems, a woman who makes mistakes threatens social relations.

Human rights discourses in Malawi are gendered and closely related to processes that differentiate men and women. Initiations are obvious ways of gendering subjects. During initiation women and men are positioned as subjects in different ways. Girls are taught to become women, boys to become men. Crucial to initiations is the inculcation of respect. At every stage of initiations, novices are taught to show respect to elders and, in the case of girls, to their fathers, their future husbands and the initiators. Showing respect to these categories of people is an essential part of women's obligations and is described as Malawian "culture". Girls are also taught a lesson if they do not show appropriate respect. Rudeness is punished by rolling girls in water and dried maize shells. Women who fail to observe respect, a central aspect of womanhood, are punished. Their lack of respect sometimes justifies wife-beating.

In discussions with Ndeka, who works at a bakery six days a week and is married with one daughter, and Chidazi, a carpenter and restaurant owner with several wives and a large number of children, both observed that they would beat their wives if they were rude. Chidazi gave an example of when it is acceptable to beat the wife:

> A man comes home and sees that a chair is standing the wrong way and not facing the table. He asks his wife, who answers that he should put the chair the correct way himself instead of asking her about it. In such cases he not only has a right to hit her, it is his duty to teach her not to be rude.

In Chidazi's story, rudeness is a reason for beating a woman, not that the chairs are standing the wrong way. Ndeka mentioned other examples, such as his wife not bringing water or food for him. I was surprised to find out that women would give similar answers in discussions on domestic violence. For instance, two women living in a Yao village right outside Zomba town, Tesa who became both a widow and a grandmother at an early age and Mrs Mukumbi who was married to a deaf and mute man, argued in a similar vein. They claimed that their male relatives—that is, their uncles or fathers who lived in the same village—would not normally interfere when they were beaten by their husbands. After all, their relatives would not know why their husbands were beating them. They said that there were circumstances when it was acceptable for a husband to beat his wife, such as when she was rude or unfaithful. On the other hand, excessive or unnecessarily cruel beatings are not acceptable either.

One day when I visited Chidazi, his sister was visiting him too. When I arrived, they were in a heated debate about whether the sister should leave her husband. She had been severely beaten on several occasions, and beatings had caused her two miscarriages. Chidazi wanted her to leave her husband and report him to the police. The sister wanted to stay with her husband, explaining that she had been rude to him. Chidazi claimed that the only reason she wanted to stay was because of the husband's money. The husband was wealthy. Chidazi accused his sister of wanting to maintain her living standard, a standard she would not be able to maintain on her own, while she, on the other hand, emphasised her own rudeness.

Human Dignity and Ulemerero Wa Umunthu

To further explore the categorisation of women as being outside of the human rights concept, it is necessary to consider local notions of human dignity. In Chichewa/Chinyanja, the concept that comes closest to an idea of human dignity is *ulemerero wa umunthu*. There is no exact English translation of the concept; it evokes dignity, worth and honour. My appreciation of this term started with a misunderstanding. I went to a lecturer at Chancellor College in Zomba and asked him for a local translation of human dignity. I did this in order to recognise the word if I heard it, to learn in which settings, if ever, the concept was used. The answer I got was *umunthu*. *Munthu* means "human" or "person" and the prefix "u" makes it abstract. It took several months for me to realise that the concept translates into humanity and not human dignity. Jumbe, my interpreter, defined *umunthu* as "something that goes with dignity, it includes everything a person does, behaviour, it can be both good and bad, you can violate somebody's *umunthu* by displeasing or disappointing that person".

Similar concepts exist in several neighbouring countries and languages. Johannes Fabian argues that in the Democratic Republic of Congo, the concept of *bumuntu* ("what it really means, and takes, to be a human being"; 1998:111) has two lethal enemies: the pursuit of selfish interests by an individual on the one hand, and tribalism and racism on the other. This is similar to Malawian notions of *umunthu*. The South African word *ubuntu* is just as difficult to translate s *umunthu*. The author André Brink writes in his book, "An Act of Terror or the Crayfish Get Used to It":

> Ubuntu, that was what Sipho had called it. That untranslatable word. Missing from Afrikaans and English dictionaries...Ubuntu: sharing, generosity, hospitality, humanity. All of that and much more. Oh, much more. It was ubuntu that prompted you to invite a stranger to spend the night, even when you possessed nothing. That made you shelter at the risk of your own life on the windblown day in Crossroads, two white strangers on the run from the police. (1991:179)[1]

Not everybody approves of the focus on *ubuntu*. Tinyika Sam Maluleke writes:

> For some reason, many people believe that the solution to many of our problems lies in a rediscovery of Ubuntu. Even whites are "prescribing" Ubuntu for typically African problems. However, it is often unclear precisely what this Ubuntu is. How viable is Ubuntu and why is it seldom prescribed for whites? My own feeling is that essentially Ubuntu signifies a type of return to negritude. The basic idea behind proposals for Ubuntu is that the crisis in our nation, which is highlighted by violence and poverty, can only be relieved by the digging out of "values" of our traditions. (www.unisa.ac.za/dept/press/rt/31/samhtml.)

Umunthu is not a political aim or tool in Malawi, as *ubuntu* is in South Africa. *Umunthu* can be seen as a local conceptualisation of Cassese's (1986) notion of humanity, the "quality of man". The concept of *umunthu* in Chichewa and Chinyanja is a wider concept than that of the English concept "human". However, I later realised that *ulemerero wa umunthu* is the closest translation of human dignity. An attempt at literal translation would render it as "worthy of humanness". *Ulemu* means esteem, honour, reverence, respect and dignity, worth and civility. *Ulemerero* is often used in relation to funerals and wealth. *Ulemerero wa umunthu* can be violated by others or be influenced by the person's own actions. Evoking dignity and honour, the concept is closely related to personhood and identity.

---

1. The concept played an important role in South African politics, evoked in the objectives of the Truth and Reconciliation Commission and in the first version of the country's new constitution.

Ulemerero wa umunthu is essential to understanding women's position in society. As Moore (1994) points out, women locate themselves in relation to many femininities, just as men relate to many masculinities. It is crucial to understand how discourses and categories of women and men "participate in the production and reproduction of engendered subjects who use them to generate both representations and self-representations, as part of the process of constructing themselves as persons and agents" (Moore, 1994:51).

Possible femininities women may choose from are difficult to maintain simultaneously, as they are often conflicting. For women, as for anybody else, positioning oneself in accordance with dominant discourses has benefits. In Malawi, dominant discourses are closely connected to showing respect. Most women have fewer arenas to choose from than men do. In Malawi women interact in many settings but most of these arenas are related to village life. According to Moore, questions of identity are intertwined with material benefits and the exercise of power. Malawi, like most other African societies, is hierarchically stratified according to age and gender, men and women alike rejecting the change in relationships between men and women.

I have often asked myself why Malawian women oppose improvement in status. Is it due to the respect that a woman gets from being an honourable woman? A person's dignity is not, after all, only a matter of paying respect upwards. It implies that you treat all people in accordance with the position that they occupy in relation to yourself. If a woman is well behaved and shows respect to those expecting it, she is well respected. In Jessica Ogden's (1996) study of how respect and proper women are "produced" in Kampala, Uganda, the relational aspect is clearly displayed. She uses the Baganda term *empisa,* which is not translatable into an English word but is context-dependent. In everyday situations, the meaning is "conduct", but it also includes being reserved, respectful and sensible. In Kampala as well as in Zomba a woman's behaviour is the foundation for much of the respect she gets in the community. Ogden describes how a woman who is defined as quarrelsome in the neighbourhood is denied help. Her child is visibly malnourished, but because she lacks *empisa*, nobody helps her. A similar situation occurred during my fieldwork in Zomba. Taona had moved from the village where she was born to the village of her uncle. In her village of origin she felt that she was being accused of witchcraft and left. In the village of her uncle, the village court made her physically excluded, because she was perceived to be troublesome. According to most people I talked to, Taona did not behave as if she were a dignified person. She behaved individualistically by neglecting to show respect to her fellow villagers, instead of, as expected, acting as a member of the group.

According to Ogden (1996), it is a woman's responsibility to make sure that respect is practised at home. By teaching children to show respect a woman fulfils her role as the keeper of cultural values in the community. Just as respect at home is the responsibility of women, so is respect in the community. Ogden's discussion is based on research in an urban setting where the neighbourhood is essential for the experience of *empisa*. She writes, "Maintaining good relations with one's neighbours through *empisa* is felt to be one of the keys to urban survival" (Ogden, 1996:180). In rural areas as well, women are expected and encouraged to behave with respect even if they are mistreated. I want to make a similar point. In Malawi the majority of people who argue that women are the keepers of traditions are men. However, women's positions are reinforced by the respect and status they receive from other women if they behave according to local value standards. According to Ogden, a woman's possibility to improve her situation through change depends on her success in demonstrating inner strength and dignity through *empisa*. This is also the case for most women in Malawi.

The close connection between community and women in the local notions of "culture" is important to keep in mind when discussing why women reinforce their positions within value systems that support gender inequality. *Ulemerero wa umunthu* captures central aspects of these categories and discourses. It endorses the traditional perception of women; emphasises community life; and gives meaning to the extended family. Dr Khapukha explained that she felt that a woman should be self-sacrificing:

> I don't think of what I can get out of it, but what others can get out of it. It gives a positive side to the oppression. I stay in a relationship for my children and for my parents' reputation.

Such statements, describing expectations of female behaviour, are common among both educated and illiterate women. In other words, many reject official arguments to change over to a "culture" which is perceived to be individualistic and selfish.

Culture as Power

The popular emphases on "culture" may be interpreted as reactions against political rhetoric and as attempts by men to maintain their position within society. Both of them—a reaction against official discourses and the attempts by men to maintain stable positions—may explain why the category "women" ends up outside of the human rights paradigm. Popular perspectives on gender, notions of "traditions" and poverty are intertwined in ways that render women's rights complex webs of conflicting interests.

The above-mentioned reactions against the government's rhetoric, and against the government's intention of changing cultural practices, may be understood as a power struggle between the populace and the authorities. People react against attempts by the government to define which cultural practices are acceptable. When official agencies state that "culture" is a threat to human rights, they imply that people's "cultural" actions constitute threats to human rights. I would argue that official arguments are interpreted locally as attempts to change "culture" as a top-down initiative. People want to be able to associate their identities with social institutions without being worried that the status attached to such institutions will change. If the institutions change, the status attached to them might change too. A social need for stable institutions is problematic in contemporary Malawi. The need for stable social institutions reinforces the popular rejection of the government's attempts to change "culture".

The tension between the human rights discourses of governmental institutions and their popular understandings may be clarified by focusing on female initiations. Both governmental organisations and members of the general public consider initiation practices and the school system to be conflicting systems of education. Official agencies define certain actions within initiations as violating women's rights. These agencies argue that girls can learn to show respect without having to go through initiations. On the other hand, many of my informants, Afumo Kumalonje, the headman of a Yao village, amongst them, emphasised the need for and the importance of "culture" and "traditions", stressing the role of initiations in teaching "culture". "Culture is good because it teaches the young how to behave towards the old. They learn to show respect." Daddy, another old man and the owner of a bottle store, said that living in Malawi without being initiated is like driving a car without knowing how to read the signs. Even though both girls and boys are initiated, girls' initiations are much more debated. This could be because many of the aspects girls learn or have to go through during initiations are defined as violations of human rights by official agencies.

Chidazi thought that initiations were important and stressed that the knowledge taught was contradictory to what was taught at school. He said that students who study biology do not want to get initiated, because "they think they know how everything works". According to him, school was an institution that worked against "traditional culture". He also argued that many children who never participated in initiations had a different way of behaving towards the old. Naphiri echoed that there was a conflict between initiation and school. Her standpoint was, however, the opposite of Chidazi's. She claimed that girls often believed that they did not need to go to school, because they had learnt everything during initiations. She also emphasised the problem of girls being taken out of school in order to participate in initiations. Naphiri disliked the fact that "traditional" values were given preference to school education. Her point of view was that initiations took away a girl's pride and filled her with shame. According to Naphiri, respect for elders can be taught in the families without participation in the initiations. She stated, "A ceremony does not change anything and it does not make you a better person".

Men's resistance against new standards can also be interpreted as an attempt to maintain local gendered power relations. The interrelatedness between gender, culture and power in human rights discourses might be illustrated through the situation at the University of Malawi. I was told that some female lecturers at the University do not want to speak to Western women because they are then accused of adopting Western values. The women are thus accused of aspiring to be Western rather than equal. Their arguments for a more egalitarian society, where women have the same access to governmental institutions and education and where women have the same economic and social rights as men, are interpreted as Western rather than contributing to gendered power struggles. Consequently the female lecturers chose to avoid Western women in order to bypass such accusations. Men, who say that human rights have come between them and their culture, effectively argue that human rights have come between their own interests and their own positions in society. An acceptance of human rights would imply an acceptance of gender equality. By arguing that human rights and "culture" are in opposition, and at the same time that women are the keepers of "traditions", they exclude women from human rights and gender equality. In other words, men feel they should get human rights while women should maintain "culture" and only get those rights that do not interfere with the existing gender structure.

Concluding Remarks

I have argued that expectations for women to maintain "culture" to a certain extent override their human rights. Local perceptions of women as keepers of "tradition" place women outside of human rights concepts. "Traditions" are the antitheses of the universalistic human rights. The stability that many of my informants explicitly emphasised is understood to be at risk. Women's burden in the villages to maintain "traditions" is thus reinforced. Official statements stressing the importance of changing women's role in society increase the fear of instability and uncertainty. In other words, the emphasis on "traditional culture" and its consequences may be seen as a reaction against transnational policies embraced by the government.

Current tension between particularistic cultural values and universalist human rights has similarities with the process of liberation from the British colonial rule. Leaders of the independence struggle were often members of the urban élite who wanted to modify local cultural values. Yet the project of nationalism did not gain strength until local values were incorporated. Currently, in a similar fashion, some villagers interpret human rights discourses as the urban élite's attempts to redefine Malawian "traditional culture". By positioning human rights in opposition to "traditions", local values are excluded, and a local foundation becomes difficult to build. The emphasis on "culture" is also present in power struggles between Malawian men and women. Women's disadvantaged positions are maintained by arguing against Westernisation and equal rights.

The implementation of human rights becomes a double-edged sword as long as human rights have Western connotations and are introduced in contrast to local cultural values. An incident at the University of Malawi is one more example. Not long before I had arrived in Zomba, four female lecturers[1] conducted an inquiry into sexual harassment at Chancellor College. They wanted to achieve an institution where female students and members of staff could file complaints. At this particular time there were no routines for handling problems of harassment. At the time, these female lecturers intended to continue their inquiry by looking at similar problems in secondary and primary schools. Their research showed that both lecturers and students sexually harassed a large number of female students. Everything from sexual comments to rape were understood as sexual harassment. Research results were broadcast on the radio without clearly defining what the numbers indicated. In the following days, turmoil started at the University. Interestingly, these riots were not in support of the girls who had been harassed. Instead, female students claimed that everybody would think that they had been raped, while male students feared that they would be labelled rapists. Students complained that the research did not show an accurate picture and was methodologically incorrect. Suggestions aimed at improving women's position were ignored. Instead, both female and male students reacted against being identified as the violated or the violator. The focus was moved away from the actual topic. In my view, similar sentiments arise when NGOs or other agencies identify people as the violated or the violators.

Relations between the categories of men and women, and between "women" as a category and political institutions, have been redefined. During the Banda regime the relations were defined in "traditional" terms, stressing "traditional" institutions. The UDF government and official human rights discourses instead define "culture" as violating human rights. People have, however, reacted against attempts to redefine these relations. Whether they are the supposed violators or the violated, they have not subscribed to descriptions that portray their "culture" as a series of violations. In their social relationships, ordinary Malawians continue to pursue elusive dignity and respect through culturally salient notions of what it entails to be a "good man" and a "good woman". The concept of *ulemerero wa umunthu* may enable others to understand better these so-called traditional notions, against the attempts of official human rights agencies to redefine the ways through which people achieve and maintain dignity and respect.

---

1. Isabel Phiri, Linda Semu, Flora Nankhuni and Nyovani Madise. On Phiri's personal tribulations at the University of Malawi, see Phiri (1996).

Afterword

The Orality of Dictatorship: In Defence of My Country

Jack Mapanje

Muluzi should watch out for Tembo.
Hetherwick Ntaba, Treasurer General of the Malawi Congress Party, November 2001.

When Bakili Muluzi was sworn in as the second president of the Republic of Malawi on 21 May 1994, the West did not know how to react. Muluzi and his United Democratic Front (UDF) were largely unknown. The brief announcement of an underground pressure group which appeared as "The Launch of the United Democratic Party" was not common knowledge. The US benefactor who allegedly sent Chakufwa Chihana a limousine in the hope that his political party Alliance for Democracy (AFORD) would sweep the country to democracy had to withdraw the vehicle.

But there was euphoria throughout Malawi. UDF and AFORD supporters could hardly believe that they had jointly beaten Life President Hastings Kamuzu Banda's invincible Malawi Congress Party (MCP) after 33 years of autocratic rule. The numerous daily and weekly papers which had appeared throughout the struggle against the dictator were ecstatic about the new freedom; most commentaries were ebullient to the point of being irresponsible—they criticised anything under the sun without proposing what might take its place.

It was understandable. Banda had not given the people the opportunity to talk and write without the shadow of detention, imprisonment, torture and exile looming over their heads. Now they were free to talk and write about pretty much anything that came to mind. Trade unions mushroomed everywhere; for once teachers, nurses, civil servants, factory workers, even market and street vendors, went on strike about their outstanding causes. No truth and reconciliation commission along the lines of the South African TRC was established in order to resolve the political problems of the past. Muluzi will probably regret this oversight; for he merely put Banda and his permanent mistress Cecilia Kadzamira under house arrest for a short period. Her notoriously crafty uncle John Tembo was also briefly imprisoned for allegedly planning the deaths of popular senior MPs Aaron Gadama, Dick Matenje, David Chiwanga and Twaibu Sangala, during Banda's regime.

Some Malawians at home and in the diaspora, however, were less hysterical. They wrote off Muluzi for being a Muslim and for having been Banda's MCP administrative secretary once; they did not expect him to radically change the legacy of brutality which Banda and his minions had left behind. Did Muluzi have the credentials to control Banda's Lady Macbeth and her extended family? Would Muluzi dismantle the infrastructure of hit squads, agents, spies and informers established primarily by the Banda-Tembo-Kadzamira triumvirate? The counter-campaign was launched by the MCP member and new recruit to the Kadzamiras' inner circle, Kate Kainja, who is said to have made a public, almost cavalier threat: Muluzi's cabinet would be finished one by one, by hook or by crook, until no one of consequence lived! People laughed at her implicit reference to death by witchcraft, noting the tone of sour grapes entailed in her threat. Muluzi confounded his critics; his first term of office was characterised by remarkable tolerance; people almost forgot he was Muslim. He gave Malawians the freedom of speech and association they had not experienced for more than 33 years under Banda.

Of course, nobody knew what freedom and democracy meant. Banda, his inner circle and the entire MCP had taught the country, particularly the politicians, to hate multiparty politics and hunt down political opponents. They had taught the people to treat political and other rebels, dissidents and radicals as outcasts, or as the dregs of society, not as its useful and necessary members that other countries would gladly embrace. Politicians had got used to considering anyone in opposition as an enemy who must be eliminated. Nobody knew how to police democracy either, least of all the police themselves. University academics suddenly had the prospect of having to do the kind of research they had always wanted but were hindered from doing by Banda's Censorship Board. People hoped that historians would now have the chance to reconstruct the history of Malawi which Banda and his cronies had distorted.

But only John Lwanda's (1993) book in 1993 appeared from the diaspora essentially to assess the irrelevance of the dictator to Malawi's 33 years of independence. No historian restored Banda's political rebels to their rightful places in the history of Malawi.[1] Nor did Banda's political opponents who had languished in exile for so long record the story of their suffering when they returned home, if only for the current generation of Malawians to know. It seemed that there was general conspiracy for total silence; it felt as if Banda and his minions had bewitched the entire country into eternal silence about how people suffered; it appeared as if nobody at all had suffered under Banda's regime.

Then the UDF stopped holding its famous political rallies and regular executive meetings where participants addressed one another by their first names and where true democracy first began to establish itself. And the MCP, Malawi's largest opposition political party, began to disintegrate. At their convention the MCP membership, with the support of the courts, voted for Gwanda Chakuamba for the party's presidency. John Tembo was reluctantly elected vice president; the MCP membership wanted to make a break with Banda's past and his closest associates in order to move on. But Tembo, who never believed in democratic elections and had not learned to take second place throughout Banda's regime, refused the vice presidency and invited his cronies to form his own branch of the MCP.

His disagreement with Chakuamba was predictable as Tembo is alleged to have incited Banda's traditional courts to charge Chakuamba for treason for possessing arms that could have been used to assassinate Banda. This led to Chakuamba's 22 years of imprisonment, nicely eliminating him from the contest for Banda's throne, leaving Tembo the sole contender. The second biggest opposition party AFORD began to disintegrate too. President Chakufwa Chihana's advisors were being seduced to join the UDF one by one. Unfortunately, Muluzi's partiality in the various rifts of the opposition political parties began to show; he often openly declared his preference for the Tembo-led section of the MCP.

Muluzi's advisors were frightened by his liaison with Tembo. They feared that Tembo would destroy Muluzi's political image, erode the people's support for him and frustrate the democratic culture UDF was trying to establish. They argued that Muluzi did not need to bolster Tembo's political career which had been cosy under Banda. At any rate, in a democracy the party that forms government does not pub-

---

1. This is going to be rectified soon. The international conference in Zomba in 2000 bore witness to new scholarship on Malawian nationalism and the Banda regime. The papers by, for example, Wiseman Chirwa, Peter Forster, John McCracken, Francis Moto, Kings M. Phiri and Megan Vaughan all presented fresh perspectives on these under-researched issues.

licly support one opposition party against the others. Nor did the ordinary voters forget how Tembo, his nieces and their extended family had placed Malawi under siege but claimed that it was Banda who quarantined the politics of the region.

Sadly, after his apparent support of Tembo's MCP wing, Muluzi began to lose grip of events within the UDF itself. The Malawi Young Pioneers who were secretly controlled by Tembo during Banda's rule had fortunately been subdued, disarmed and disbanded by the Malawi Army's "Operation Bwezani". However, some 2,000 of them had run with their guns into Mozambique where they were thought to have been training with Mozambique's RENAMO dissidents during Banda's reign. Might these pioneers not be the bandits who were destabilising Malawi's banks, streets and homes with armed robberies after the democratic transition? Why were the activities of the UDF's Young Democrats being compared to those of the MCP's Young Pioneers in their intimidation of opposition political parties? Was it the Young Democrats or the old Young Pioneers disguised as Young Democrats who, in July 2001, wanted to beat up an Anglican Church clergyman in Mzuzu for his radical sermon when the entire nation was praying for moral redemption?

By the end of 2001, the UDF rank and file were wondering why they never had another convention to discuss their future policies as governing political parties did all over the world. The very notion of having a convention for the UDF and those "first-name meetings" of the UDF executive were becoming anathema. It was the UDF's turn to disintegrate. Muluzi's key cabinet ministers who tended to get events moving, UDF and AFORD MPs began to die one by one, as Kate Kainja had predicted. Their deaths may have been natural but given the oral culture which the MCP under Banda had created, people remembered Kainja's death threats and wondered where the link lay. James Makhumula—the businessman who, with Patrick Mbewe, effectively financed the UDF's early existence—left the party. Brown Mpinganjira and Cassim Chilumpha, Muluzi's most imaginative cabinet ministers and close advisors, were charged with corruption and sacked.

Then 13 armed policemen broke into the house and the office of university historian Wiseman Chirwa on the pretext that they were looking for documents that were likely to cause a breach of peace. The singer Evison Matafale met what many Malawians believed was a brutal death in the hands of the police, reminiscent of the deaths inflicted by Tembo's Young Pioneers in Banda's days. Despite his mother's vehement protestation about Matafale's ill health, the police abducted him from his home in Blantyre, unnecessarily drove more than 200 miles to Lilongwe where he died in police custody. Many believed that Matafale died essentially because his songs satirised the tendency in current Malawian politics towards nepotism, corruption and patronage. Thousands and thousands of people attended Matafale's funeral. Then the peaceful student demonstration at Chancellor College, which followed the singer's death, turned into riots. One student was shot dead and several injured—the police treatment of the demonstrators was obviously high-handed.

The Memory of Injustice

When Tembo was questioned about the death-threats which the MCP secret convention in 1992 made to the Catholic bishops who protested about Banda's dictatorship and corruption in their Lenten Letter, he was predictably acquitted—another triumph for the oral culture he had helped to create under Banda! The tapes about the event, which are still at large, and were broadcast on the BBC, Radio South Africa and other radio stations at the time, did not provide enough evidence that John Tembo and Wadson Deleza, Banda's most senior MCP members who had convened the secret MCP convention in the first instance, had incited the participants to kill the bishops.

The bombshell dropped recently when MCP Treasurer General Hetherwick Ntaba, who is supposed to be related to Tembo by blood, warned in *Daily Times* of 12 November, 2001: "Muluzi should watch out for Tembo". He alleged that Tembo was threatening Ntaba's life in Ntaba's own constituency; Ntaba, who was seeking Muluzi's protection, reminded Muluzi that people had not forgotten that it was Tembo who tarnished Banda's image by committing atrocities on innocent Malawians in Banda's name. Nothing could stop Tembo doing this again in the name of Muluzi. Every Malawian who is old enough to know what was going on under Banda understood Ntaba's meaning perfectly. It remains to be seen if Muluzi will listen.

Let us suggest why the UDF must take Ntaba more seriously. If the UDF want the multiparty democratic culture they are establishing to continue, Muluzi must allow all opposition political parties to mushroom equally. He must distance himself from the defunct self-styled royal family of the Tembos and the Kadzamiras. If he does not do this, the UDF will not get the necessary votes from the people who know what Tembo and the Kadzamiras did to destroy Malawi's middle class and potential think tank and to frustrate Malawians' various attempts at establishing a free and democratic culture. People who have suffered tend to have long memories of their suffering; and not all die before their torturers and jailers. Let us sketch the facts without fear or favour.

The Orality of Dictatorship

It is a fact grounded in irrefutable oral knowledge, commonly shared by those who knew what was going on under Banda, that for the last 15 years of Banda's life presidency, the country was unofficially ruled by Banda's permanent mistress Cecilia Kadzamira, her uncle John Tembo, her brother Zimani Kadzamira, her sister Mary Kadzamira and their extended family. Banda's security council of police inspector generals, army chiefs and secretaries to the president and cabinet were sidelined and excluded from critical decisions about the country. Those who worked at Banda's palaces and state houses and visited the public houses claimed that Banda was being manipulated at every turn by this extended family. People knew that the Tembo-Kadzamira family were impostors who had not got their lucrative jobs by merit. That is why they were multifariously and derogatorily referred to as "the self-styled royal family", "the inner circle", "the hangers-on", "the higher authorities" or simply "the coterie". The following historical sketch places this view in context.

Dictators are stubborn by nature and inclination, they refuse to learn from the past however horrific it might be, they never hand over power even to those they purport to trust. Life President Hastings Kamuzu Banda was more stubborn than most. Having worked as a general practitioner in the United Kingdom, Banda ran off with Mrs French, the receptionist nurse who worked in his London surgery, to Ghana at the invitation of his friend Kwame Nkrumah, Ghana's first president. When Henry Masauko Chipembere, Kanyama Chiume and other younger nationalists from Nyasaland invited Banda to help his country of birth in the fight against British colonialism, he accepted the invitation with pleasure, abandoned Mrs French in Ghana and returned to Nyasaland. He was offered Cecilia Kadzamira as a companion and receptionist nurse at his Limbe township surgery. When Nyasaland became independent, making Banda its leader, Mrs French was not invited to become the wife of Malawi's first prime minister as she had hoped; instead Banda took Cecilia Kadzamira as his private secretary.

What followed was the story of the Cabinet Crisis and its ramifications, which for 33 years Banda dared anybody to talk about. Essentially it was the story of how the prime minister became president for life, imprisoning, killing or forcing into exile those who had invited him back and raising the status of his receptionist nurse from his private secretary to become the Official Hostess, the so-called Mama. It was the tale of how the permanent mistress launched the promotion of her uncles, sister and brothers and their extended family. For, even after bungling his job as first Malawian Minister of Finance or as Governor of the Reserve Bank of Malawi, Tembo became head of major institutions and commercial organisations that mattered in Malawi, including the chair of the University Council. Mama's brothers were offered lucrative jobs. Zimani Kadzamira was Principal of Chancellor College and awaited the vice chancellorship of the University to come naturally to him even though he had had no major academic publication to show for it. His sister Mary Kadzamira became Banda's private secretary at Sanjika Palace after Cecilia herself had been declared the Mama.

At first Cecilia Kadzamira was satisfied that her extended family played a pivotal role in Banda's politics. As Banda became more senile and his mental faculties began to fail, however, her extended family began to lose their patience with his fragile constitution. Banda was taking too long to declare them heir to his throne. To justify their illegal rule of the country, therefore, they dragged him along with them from one district to another, one crop inspection tour to another, one political rally to another, to show the people that he was alive and still ruling the country, when everyone knew that it was they who controlled the events that affected the people's lives. When Banda began addressing his political rallies and major events with "Mama and I", the country was alarmed. How could he address his permanent companion as if they had been married? Rumours and speculation that they had indeed been secretly married when they visited Germany were rife; none of them were substantiated. At the state house Banda's signature continued to be xeroxed onto the memos which his concubine's extended family wrote on his behalf. Sometimes the president, typical of all despots of the world, neither knew nor understood the true reasons behind the detention orders he was made to sign. Often he indiscriminately imprisoned, sacked or demoted from jobs, exiled and purged from existence his genuine supporters for the security reasons that had been invented for him by Tembo and his extended family.

May 1983. Parliament was dissolved. People heard that Banda had proposed that John Tembo rule the country as he intended to retire from politics. Aaron Gadama, Dick Matenje, David Chiwanga and Twaibu Sangala, the most liberal of his senior MPs, bravely reminded Banda what the Malawi constitution said in the event of the president retiring. Banda was so enraged that he declared that he did not want to see the dissenting MPs when parliament next reassembled. Whereupon Tembo and the inner circle interpreted Banda's angry words—as they had always done—that he meant death to the MPs. Banda's popularity plummeted after the murder of the four popular MPs; his intended hand-over of power to John Tembo never happened. Some people argued that he had not intended to give up power in the first place; no despots have been known to. Others claimed that for once Banda had listened to his security council: Police Inspector General Lunguzi, army chief Khanga,

Young Pioneer chief Mlotha and his Secretary to the President and Cabinet Ngwiri or their predecessors who were still influential.

Banda remained the ultimate architect of the monstrosities that were inflicted on Malawi's supposed dissidents. Invented dissidents continued to be unnecessarily arrested, tied up hand and foot, blind-folded, beaten, shoved into sacks and dropped in the Shire River for the crocodiles. Some were imprisoned, tortured and released having been totally paralysed; others were dumped in secret sulphuric acid baths at select Young Pioneer bases; and yet others were forced into exile by Banda, Tembo and the Kadzamiras. When reports that standards of education in Malawi were worse than during the colonial times reached Banda, allegedly Tembo and the inner circle suggested that the fault was with the teachers from the North who sabotaged the education system in the hope of making Banda's government unpopular in the North. Banda reacted with anger and decreed that teachers were to go back to teach in the region of their birth. There was pandemonium throughout the country's school system; the teachers who had married across regions were particularly concerned, some were forced to separate or permanently break up. Those who protested at the decree filled Malawi's prisons. The culture of ruthlessness, repression, torture, fear, jealousy, rivalry, irresponsibility and lack of accountability, which had pervaded the country for so long, was thus complete.

The Banda-Tembo-Kadzamira triumvirate created a verbal culture which despised the written culture and contested its existence at every turn. Their heinous regime was sustained by selected colonial legislation which they invoked at the appropriate moment; this was fuelled primarily by three major systems of intelligence and many minor ones: the police intelligence, the army intelligence and the Young Pioneer paramilitary intelligence. Each of these intelligence systems worked independently of the others, each claimed to have more direct access to Banda and his coterie than the others. People who were considered rebels were disposed of by any one of them, often without the others knowing. Then there was the proliferation of spies, agents and informers who declared their allegiance to any of these intelligence systems, the canniest of whom claimed to have worked for more than one of them. The coterie developed their own variants of intelligence systems structured on that from above.

For Tembo, the Young Pioneers, who were said to have been training with RENAMO at one time, formed a major component of his intelligence system with their own spies, agents and informers who reported to him directly. Given this framework of intelligence and counter-intelligence and the proliferation of agents, spies and informers for each intelligence system; given the fact that every citizen who mattered seemed to have been slotted into special zones for easy control; Banda and his inner circle could afford to threaten, at political gatherings, that they knew everything the people said and did even in private! How people survived these politically choking conditions is the ultimate miracle, for, to survive under Banda, to understand what was going on, one made extensive unlikely logical deductions from people's rumours about the relevance of the events that happened. What appeared in the local papers, what was heard on the radio, was often irrelevant to the meaning of the event, what mattered were the actions that the inner circle deduced from what they thought the people thought about Banda or them. If you wanted to survive under Banda, your faculty of speculation and quick perception of events had to be highly developed. If you did not like Banda's politics, several options opened up for you. You could fly into exile, which was subtly encouraged by the higher authorities: if you do not like our politics, join your rebel friends in exile!

Alternatively, you converted to "born-again" churches where you indulged in endless tearful prayers. If you were imprisoned, you developed phenomenal determination to survive and a passionate refusal to die in Banda's prisons. Otherwise you composed your surreptitious song, poetry, narrative, drama or choir, which you enjoyed privately or amongst trusted friends—always living in the hope that you would not be discovered. People's words and actions were given twists, turns and varying degrees of extension by Banda's inner circle and their security apparatus. Indeed those who were exiled, detained or imprisoned were either taken to Banda's traditional courts where they invariably lost their cases or where they were accused of subversion or treason by appeal to rumours drafted from agents, spies and informers, essentially about what they were presumed to have said against Banda or his coterie.

Sadly, with the Cold War still intact, the Western world looked away as Banda's violations of human rights and his indiscriminate arrest, detention, exile and elimination of his own people continued. Banda and his clique had created complex oral structures where it was not possible to take them to court after they had wronged any mortal. They could not be proved guilty for their involvement in the brutalities they inflicted on people because they made themselves above the law. Colonial legislation such as the Emergency Powers Act, the Prevention of Terrorism Act, the Censorship Act and other acts was "improved upon" in order to protect the already powerful from the powerless. No law, no judge, no jury could protect the ordinary people because Banda and his hench-persons had ingeniously muzzled even those traditional courts which were considered radical under British colonial rule. Those who opposed their despotic rule were recognised for and characterised by their invisibility and silence. Most people knew that this state of affairs obtained, although no one dared to declare it publicly for fear of being "accidentalised"—a term invented by the Chancellor College Writers' Group in 1983–84, meaning "to be eliminated by a well planned accident".

Only a few mad men and mad women occasionally challenged Banda's oral culture and provided implicit oral evidence, for instance, of his coterie's involvement in people's demise. Such eccentrics made desperate gestures to seek immediate justice and defend their dignity by publicly asking principally rhetorical questions whose implicit answers could be easily recovered. Why has no member of the self-styled royal family been imprisoned during Banda's entire life presidency? Why have Banda's own relatives languished in prisons and exile when the relatives of his concubine have not? Why must everyone be regarded as a potential rebel, potential prisoner, potential political opponent, except the self-styled royal family? Answers to these questions were arrived at by recourse to memory, logical moves or both, that is, by appeal to the listeners' inherent deductive mechanism which one used when one sought solutions, for instance, to conundrums. That is, if the inner circle were not imprisoned or exiled during Banda's presidency then the exiles and imprisonments that people suffered must be linked to them. The most effective war people could hope to wage against this thoughtless state of despotism was simply to think: to think about what was happening to the country; to think about what the country might have become; to think about how cultural change might have been brought about; to think about how political parties might have been organised; to think about how best to exploit the orality which Banda and his hench-persons so brilliantly exploited against innocent people. Thinking was the safest rebellion available for people to flush the despot, his hangers-on and their despotic apparatus out of their minds. One needed to think in order to survive; but to act on one's thoughts brought one in conflict with authority leading to one's imprisonment; one merely changed one's colours like the chameleon.

When multiparty democracy finally came to Malawi, it was brought about not only by Banda's and his coterie's own excessive political greed, but by the concerted thought, will and action of the thousands upon thousands of their victims at home and in exile. Indeed, the enormous greed and wealth of Life President Banda and his inner circle on the one hand, and the abject poverty of ordinary rural and urban Malawians on the other, were once brought into sharper focus by an unlikely source—the ABC channel television programme in the United States, "Prime Time Live" of September 1991, where Cecilia Kadzamira and her entourage were seen buying the richest and most expensive goods for their comfort from London's expensive shops, when the rest of Malawi was wallowing in untold physical suffering and material poverty. The divide between the rich and the poor was unbearable. No wonder there were brave foreigners who could no longer stomach the poverty and brutality which Banda and his inner circle inflicted on their own people. But as one veteran political prisoner declared after more than 14 years of his detention at Mikuyu Prison, without charge and without trial: what caused Banda's downfall and the downfall of Tembo and the Kadzamiras was God who must have got tired of hearing the tearful prayers of our children and decided to restore our dignity at long last!

Another New Malawi

Banda has been dead several years now. Muluzi is in total control and capable of changing the politics of Malawi in any direction he might prefer. Because multiparty politics is so malleable, people still need to be vigilant to protect their hard-won freedom. They need to watch particularly Banda's hangers-on who are ingeniously coming back. With Tembo and Kadzamira having been acquitted of the crimes everyone knows they committed under Banda, these people are encouraged to deny that they were ever responsible for the brutality of Banda's violent regime. With the advice which Muluzi seems to be getting from Tembo, people are already claiming that the Banda-Tembo-Kadzamira old oral culture of spies, informers and agents is returning to Malawi. If Muluzi thinks that he is taming Tembo by supporting his MCP wing and disregarding the other opposition political parties, he might be shocked to discover that it is he who eventually cowers under Tembo's wings.

We speak now because we want Muluzi to know that we do not want to return to Banda's autocratic rule. As Ntaba claims, everyone saw how Tembo caused Banda to fall; Tembo should not be allowed to destroy Muluzi, least of all by Muluzi himself. It is obvious why Banda, Tembo and Kadzamira were acquitted of the murders people like Ntaba know they committed. There was no documentary evidence, and none should be expected to be produced given the oral culture they created. These people who hate freedom and political opposition will continue to be acquitted for the reasons which clever lawyers offer in defending despots everywhere: the Bandas of the world will always be too senile to stand in court, there will never be enough evidence to convict the Tembos and Kadzamiras of the world. The irony of the situation is that it is the law itself which is the greatest monster today!

Banda's inner circle do not deny their being the most stubborn supporters of Banda's regime; but they cunningly repeat the reasons they invented to justify the violence they inflicted on innocent people under Banda; that it was Banda who was president for life and ruled Malawi; that everyone saw him on political platforms; that they were not responsible for the monstrosities which Banda inflicted on his people; and that they would not apologise. Under Banda's oral culture they were the law, judge and jury, today without the production of documentary evidence to prove them guilty, the law is on their side, they can afford to pay the lawyers large sums of money to defend them—no immorality of the legal system can be invoked on behalf of justice!

To Banda's inner circle the thousands and thousands of Malawians who were accidentalised by their hit squads; the people who are still starving in the villages today; the legacy of their confused and corrupt education system; the rampant lethal diseases and the health service which has no medicines, its inadequate doctors, nurses and lack of linen for patients—none of these issues matter. It is little wonder then that, robed in borrowed humility calculated to impress the ordinary people to vote them back to power, Cecilia Kadzamira, John Tembo and their extended family attend one village funeral after another these days. Banda must be turning in his grave, he must be wanting to rise to present his case, when he hears the denial of Tembo's involvement in the people's demise during his reign.

As already indicated, such denial of the truth was expected; almost everyone who lived under Banda's autocratic rule suspected that having created an oral culture, where evidence for the harm they inflicted on innocent people was cunningly erased from existence, Banda and his clique would deny that they ever caused anyone pain, hurt or harm. That is the whole point of creating an oral culture—to allow the perpetrators of justice in time to deny the injustice these people inflicted on the innocent! Nobody will be surprised at Tembo's acquittal in future cases which the courts might bring against him, least of all the law itself which is grievously flawed. It is absurd to expect documentary evidence to prove Tembo guilty when he made sure that such evidence was destroyed and that those who committed the crime on his behalf were eliminated after the event. Only oral evidence can prove Tembo guilty, which is impossible to bring to modern courts.

When Muluzi today declares at political gatherings, *Zinthu zatani?* and the people answer *Zasintha!* (Things have what?—Have changed!), we sincerely hope this dictum will be properly realised. It is our hope that Malawi does not allow another leader wearing robes of respectability and a huge smile to rule the country with another clique of power-hungry people. Should Muluzi throw people's hard-won freedom to Tembo and his extended family again, the people will not forgive him, history will laugh at him.

People will not allow themselves to live under another bunch of impostors in another oral world where the truth about anything that mattered was the privilege of those who suffered. We lament the fact that Malawi is having to start again where we left off at independence; Malawians are having to learn how to walk again, as it were. It is a shame that Banda never taught the people how to be democratic; that he eliminated Malawian "middle class"; that he never encouraged clever Malawians to form the country's think-tank which could help politicians rule the country without corruption and other vices; that he jealously silenced clever people and purged them from the government and parastatal machinery. We lament the fact that colonial legislation was never repealed and that the newspapers are still jingoistic about serious matters and unable to give the government constructive advice. We lament the fact that the government itself appears not to have learnt quickly how to take advice and exploit it for the benefit of the starving ordinary people. Some of those in power even proudly adopt Banda's bygone autocratic arrogance today—they still think that they know everything!

In the twenty-first century African politicians should not only consider filling the bellies of their extended families but the bellies of the people starving in the rural and urban communities who will vote for them as well. Is there any hope for the future? There is always hope. The future is in the people who are determined that there will not be another dictator. The first term of Muluzi's presidency has shown us what we should have known immediately after independence—what it means to be free. We are still fumbling though we will not be distracted from our ultimate goal – the preservation and consolidation of freedom and democracy achieved under difficult circumstances. We hope that Muluzi's second term—which, according to the pluralism that Malawians fought for, must also be his last—ends with the consolidation of the free and democratic culture achieved in the first term. If it is reconciliation and atonement that Malawi needs, let there be no illusions; the primary challenge for the UDF government today is whether they will embrace all opposition political parties as well as the rebels and other radicals whom they may not like within the fabric of Malawian society—that is the only test we have in order to measure the successful establishment of a free and democratic culture. We pray that Muluzi continues to listen to *all* linguistic, religious, ethnic communities, political parties, not only those that the UDF government has co-opted but even the dissidents he does not like. In his first term in office Muluzi treated political opponents with impartiality; Tembo and others should not stop him in the last term.

Recently a man who claimed to be my friend mocked me and suggested that those of us who got ourselves sacked, demoted, imprisoned, exiled or accidentalised in Banda's despotic times, had only ourselves to blame. Those who committed these atrocities were only doing their duty. And in these times of atonement, truth and reconciliation, we should bury the dark pages of our history and move on. Even if our torturers refuse to apologise, we should not allow ourselves to be forever trapped in the shame of our brutal past.

I do not think so. Such blatant dishonesty should not be accepted in the New Malawi. People who have suffered and endured silence, imprisonment, torture or exile should not be told to shut up about their incarceration, if they want to talk about it after they have been freed, especially when those who imprisoned them are now turning around to subvert ordinary people's hard-won freedom. People who have suffered find it difficult to both forgive and forget those who caused their hurt. I speak in defence of my country which does not need another despotic oral culture!

List of Contributors

Gerhard Anders was born in 1970 in Germany. He is completing his doctoral studies in the Department of International Law, University of Rotterdam. His research interests are legal anthropology; governance; social security and class formation in sub-Saharan Africa; and the reform programmes of the World Bank and the IMF.

Blessings Chinsinga was born in 1973 in Malawi. He lectures in the Department of Political and Administrative Studies at Chancellor College, University of Malawi. His research interests are rural development and poverty alleviation; institutions, governance and development; and globalisation and regional development.

Reuben Makayiko Chirambo was born in 1963 in Malawi. He is currently pursuing his doctoral studies in English Literature at the University of Minnesota. His research interests include contemporary popular music and politics in Malawi as well as folklore and literature in societies undergoing political changes.

Harri Englund was born in 1966 in Finland. He currently directs two research projects on political and cultural pluralism in Africa at the Universities of Helsinki and Uppsala. His research interests include ethnography; Chichewa/Chinyanja discourses on Human Rights and democratisation; rural-urban migration; and pentecostal Christianity.

Gregory H. Kamwendo was born in 1965 in Malawi. He is Deputy Director of the Centre for Language Studies at the University of Malawi. His research interests include sociolinguistics; language rights; communication in the delivery of health services in Northern Malawi; and language policies in Banda's Malawi.

Edrinnie Kayambazinthu was born in 1957 in Malawi. She teaches in the Department of English at Chancellor College, University of Malawi. Her research interests are sociolinguistics; language planning; language and gender; and language and Human Rights.

John Lwanda was born in 1949 in Malawi. Trained as a medical doctor, he is affiliated with the Department of General Practice at the University of Glasgow and with the Centre of African Studies at the University of Edinburgh. His research interests include HIV/AIDS, culture and medicine; the popular music of Malawi; and the epistemological boundaries of medical knowledge.

Jack Mapanje was born in 1944 in Malawi. He is Hon. Professorial Research Fellow in the School of English at the University of Leeds. His research interests are in the field of literary theory. Towards the end of Kamuzu Banda's regime, he was imprisoned without trial for almost four years. An acclaimed poet, he was given the Fonlon-Nichols Award at the annual conference of the African Literature Association in 2002. The Award—whose previous awardees include Ken Saro-Wiwa, Ngugi wa Thiong'o and Wole Soyinka—is given in recognition of excellence in creative writing and contributions to the struggles for freedom of expression.

Fulata Moyo was born in 1961 in Malawi. She teaches in the Department of Theology and Religious Studies at Chancellor College, University of Malawi. Her research interests include human sexuality and HIV/AIDS.

Clement Ng'ong'ola was born in 1955 in Malawi. He teaches in the Department of Law at the University of Botswana. His research interests are regional integration and international trade law in Africa; law and politics in Malawi; and labour law developments in Malawi.

Ulrika Ribohn was born in 1967 in Sweden. After studying Social Anthropology at the University of Oslo, she currently works for Grupos África de Súecia (Africa Groups of Sweden) in Northern Mozambique. Her research interest is conflict resolution in Northern Mozambique.

Peter VonDoepp was born in 1967 in the United States. He teaches in the Department of Political Science at the University of North Texas. His research interests are religion and politics; comparative democratisation processes in Africa; and judicial politics in African emerging democracies.

Appendix

Table 1:Parliamentary Seats by Party and Region, 1994

	North	Central	South	National
Alliance For Democracy	33	3	0	36
Malawi Congress Party	0	51	5	56
United Democratic Front	0	14	71	85
Total	33	68	76	177

Table 2: Parliamentary Seats by Party and Region, 1999

	Northern Region	Central Region	Southern Region	National
Alliance for Democracy	28	1	0	29
Malawi Congress Party	4	54	8	66
United Democratic Front	1	16	76	93
Independent Candidates	0	1	3	4
Total	33	72	87	192

Table 3:Presidential Election Results by Party and Region, 1994

Candidate	Party	North	Central	South	National	%
Kamuzu Banda	MCP	33,650	743,739	218,964	996,353	33.45
Chakufwa Chihana	AFORD	404,837	86,766	71,259	562,862	18.90
Kamlepo Kalua	MDP	1,754	5,161	8,709	15,624	0.52
Bakili Muluzi	UDF	20,837	321,581	1,062,336	1,404,754	47.16
Valid Votes		461,078	1,156,539	1,361,268	2,978,885	97.97
Votes Cast		467,419	1,185,516	1,387,730	3,040,665	80.54
Registered Voters		545,195	1,461,367	1,768,694	3,775,256	

Table 4:Presidential Election Results by Party and Region, 1999

Candidate	Party	North	Central	South	National	%
Gwanda Chakuamba	MCP	573,688	1,124,359	408,743	2,106,790	44.30
Bakili Muluzi	UDF	61,130	634,912	1,746,643	2,442,685	51.37
Kamlepo Kalua	MDP	5,673	27,240	34,943	67,856	1.43
Bingu Mutharika	UP	1,112	6,701	14,260	22,064	0.46
Daniel Nkhumbwe	CONU	5,806	8,004	10,537	24,347	0.51
Valid Votes		*647,409*	*1,801,209*	*2,215,126*	*4,663,751*	*98.07*
Votes Cast		*652,505*	*1,839,032*	*2,263,885*	*4,755,422*	
Registered Voters		*678,906*	*1,975,203*	*2,417,713*	*5,071,822*	

Sources: Electoral Commission, 1994 Parliamentary and Presidential Elections Report, Appendix XII, and Malawi Government Gazette Extraordinary, Vol. XXXVI, No. 44, 20 August 1999.

Bibliography

Achebe, C. 1966. *A Man of the People.* London: Heinemann.

Africa Watch 1990. *Where Silence Rules: The Suppresion of Dissent in Malawi.* New York: Human Rights Watch.

Agowi, K. 1989. "The Political Relevance of Ghanaian Highlife Songs since 1957", *Research in African Literature,* 20: 194–201.

Ahlberg, B. M. 1994. "Is There a Distinct African Sexuality?", *Africa* 64: 220–242.

Ake, C. 1995. "The Democratization of Disempowerment in Africa", in J. Hippler (ed.) *The Democratisation of Disempowerment: The Problem of Democracy in the Third World.* London: Pluto Press with Transnational Institute.

Ake, C. 2000. *The Possibility of Democracy in Africa.* Dakar: Codesria.

Aldelman, I. 1988. "A Poverty-Focused Approach to Development Policy", in C. Wilber (ed.) *The Political Economy of Under-Development,* 4th Edition. New York: Random House.

Ali, A. 1999. "The Challenge of Poverty Reduction in Africa", *Eastern Africa Social Science Review,* 15:60–89.

Alstyne, G. van 1993. "The Unvoiced Text: Allusion in Malawian Sung Poetry", *Journal of the Anthropological Society of Oxford* 24: 13–32.

Ammerman, N. 1981. "The Civil Rights Movement and the Clergy in a Southern Community", *Sociological Analysis* 41: 339–350.

Article 19 1993. *Malawi's Past: The Right to Truth.* Issue 29, 17 November 1993.

Article 19 2000. *At the Crossroads: Freedom of Expression in Malawi. The Final Report of the Article 19 Malawi Election Media Monitoring Project.* London: International Centre against Censorship.

Baker, C. 1972. "The Admininstrative Service of Malawi – A Case Study in Africanisation", *Journal of Modern African Studies* 10: 543–560.

Baker, C. 1988. "The Genesis of the Nyasaland Civil Service", *The Society of Malawi Journal* 41: 30–41.

Baker, C. 2001. *Revolt of the Ministers: The Malawi Cabinet Crisis, 1964–1965.* London: I.B. Tauris.

Banda, H. K. 1993. "Speeches for the Period 1964–1971 and 1989–1993", Malawi Broadcasting Corporation transcripts.

Banda, J. 1998. "The Constitutional Change Debate of 1993–1995", in K.M. Phiri and K.R. Ross (eds) *Democratization in Malawi: A Stocktaking.* Blantyre: CLAIM.

Barber, K. 1987. "Popular Arts in Africa", *African Studies Review* 30: 1–78.

Bayart, J.-F. 1993. *The State in Africa: The Politics of the Belly.* London: Longman.

Bayart, J.-F. 2000. "Africa in the World: A History of Extraversion", *African Affairs* 99: 217–267.

Benda-Beckmann, F. von and von Benda-Beckmann, K. 1994. "Coping with Insecurity", *Focaal: Tijdschrift voor Antropologie* 22 & 23: 7–31.

Benda-Beckmann, K. von and Strijbosch, F. (eds) 1986. *Anthropology of Law in the Netherlands: Essays on Legal Pluralism.* Dordrecht: Foris.

Benda-Beckmann, K. von, von Benda-Beckmann, F., Casino, E., Hirtz, F., Woodman G. and Zacher, H.F. (eds) 1988. *Between Kinship and the State: Social Security and Law in Developing Countries.* Dordrecht: Foris.

Best, B. 1997. "Over-the-Counter-Culture: Retheorizing Resistance in Popular Culture", in S. Redhead (ed.) *Clubcultures Reader: Readings in Popular Cultural Studies.* Cambridge, Mass.: Blackwell Publishers.

BLM, Banja la Mtsogolo 1997. *Annual Report.* Blantyre.

Boadi, G.E. 1996. "Civil Society in Africa", *Journal of Democracy* 7: 118–132.

Boeder, R.B. 1984. *Silent Majority: A History of the Lomwe in Malawi.* Pretoria: Africa Institute of South Africa.

Bork, S. 1970. *Mibbrauch der Sprache: Tendenzen Nationalsozialistischer Sprachregelung.* Bern: Francke.

Boyce, J. 1987. *Agrarian Impasse in Bengal: Institutional Constraints and Technological Change.* Oxford: Oxford University Press.

Brekle, H.E. 1989. "War with Words", in R. Wodak (ed.) *Language, Power and Ideology: Studies in Political Discourse*. Amsterdam: John Benjamins.

Brietze, P. 1974. "Murder and Manslaughter in Malawi's Traditional Courts", *Journal of African Law* 18: 37–38.

Brink, A. 1991. *An Act of Terror or the Crayfish Get Used to It*. London: Minerva.

Caldwell, J. and Caldwell, P. 1989. "The Social Context of Aids in Sub-Saharan Africa", *Population and Development Review* 15: 185–233.

Calhoun-Brown, A. 1996. "African-American Churches and Political Mobilization: The Psychological Impact of Organizational Resources", *Journal of Politics* 58: 935–953.

Carr, S. 1994. "Some Causes of Rural Poverty in Malawi", *Society of Malawi Journal* 47: 32–38.

Carr, S. and MacLachlan, M. 1993. "The Social Psychology of Development Work: The Double De-motivation Hypothesis", *Malawi Journal of Social Science* 16: 1–8.

Cassese, A. 1986. *International Law in a Divided World*. Oxford: Clarendon Press.

Catholic Church 1991. *AIDS: A Christian Response*. Balaka: Montfort Press.

CCAP, The Church of Central Africa, Presbyterian 2001. *Some Worrisome Trends Which Undermine the Nurturing of Our Young Democratic Culture*. Blantyre: CCAP General Synod.

Centre for Language Studies 1999. *Sociolinguistic Surveys of Four Malawian Languages: With Special Reference to Education*. Research Report Submitted to GTZ, Lilongwe.

Centre for Language Studies 2001. *Towards the Standardization of Chitumbuka Orthography*. Reseach Report Submitted to GTZ, Lilongwe.

Centre for Social Research 1999. *Two Decades of AIDS Research: A Directory*. Zomba: Centre for Social Research.

Chabal, P. and Daloz, J.-P. 1999. *Africa Works: Disorder as Political Instrument*. London: James Currey.

Chaima, C. 1994. "Knowledge, Attitudes, Beliefs and Behaviour Regarding the Sexual Activities of Girls in TA Kalolo, Lilongwe District", unpublished paper.

Cheesbrough, J. S. 1986. "Acquired Immuno-Deficiency Syndrome in Malawi", *Malawi Medical Journal* 3: 5–13.

Chilongozi, D. A., Costello, C., Daly, C., Liomba, N. G. and Dalibetta, G. 1996. "Sexually Transmitted Diseases: A Survey of Case Management in Malawi", *International Journal of STD and AIDS* 7: 269–275.

Chilowa, W. 2000. "Adjustment Impact on Social Policy Implementation in Malawi", a paper presented at the African Renaissance Conference, Pretoria, November 2000.

Chilowa, W. and Chirwa, E.W. 1997. "The Impact of Structural Adjustment Programmes and Human Development", *Bwalo: A Forum for Social Development* 1: 39–68.

Chilowa W., Milner, J., Chinsinga. B. and Mangani, R. 2000. *Social Policy in the Context of Economic Reforms: A Benchmark Survey Report*. Harare: SARIPS.

Chilowa, W. and Roe, G. 1987. *The Plight of the Urban Poor: Results from a Baseline Survey*. Zomba: Centre for Social Research.

Chimango, L.J. 1977. "Tradition and the Traditional Courts in Malawi", *Comparative and International Law Journal of South Africa* 10: 39–66.

Chimhundu, H. 1992. "Standard Shona: Myth and Reality", in N. Crawhall (ed.) *Democratically Speaking: International Perspectives on Language Planning*. Cape Town: National Language Project.

Chimombo, M. 1998. "Government Journalism: From Totalitarianism to Democracy?", in K.M. Phiri and K.R. Ross (eds) *Democratization in Malawi: A Stocktaking*. Blantyre: CLAIM.

Chimombo, M. 1999. "Language and Politics", *Annual Review of Applied Linguistics* 19: 215–232.

Chimombo, S. 1987. *Napolo Poems*. Zomba: Manchichi Publishers.

Chimombo, S. 1988. *Malawian Oral Literature: The Aesthetics of Indigenous Arts*. Zomba: Centre for Social Research.

Chimombo, S. 1993. *A Referendum of the Forest Creatures*. Zomba: WASI.

Chimombo, S. 1995. *Breaking the Beadstrings: A Long Poem*. Zomba: WASI.

Chimombo, S. and Chimombo, M. 1996. *The Culture of Democracy: Language, Literature, the Arts, and Politics in Malawi, 1992–1994*. Zomba: WASI.

Chinsinga, B. 1995. *The Poverty Alleviation Programme: A Formidable Policy Initiative*. BA Project Paper, Chancellor College, University of Malawi.

Chinsinga, B. 1999. "Unity and Diversity", *The Lamp* No. 19: 19.

Chipeta, C. 1993. "The Impact of Structural Adjustment on the People of Malawi" in A. Adepoju (ed.) *The Impact of Structural Adjustment on the Population of Africa*. London: James Currey.

Chiphangwi, J., Liomba, G, Ntaba, H. M., Schmidt, H., Deinhart, F., Eberle, J., Froner, G., Gurtler, L. and Zoulek, G. 1987. "Human Immunodeficency Virus Infection Is Prevalent in Malawi", *Infection*, 15: 363.

Chirambo, R. 2001. "Protesting Politics of 'Death and Darkness' in Malawi", *Journal of Folklore Research* 38: 205–227.

Chirwa, E.W. 1995. "Impact of Food Security and Nutrition Intervention Projects in Malawi", draft report submitted to the Food Security and Nutrition Unit, National Economic Council.

Chirwa, E.W. 1997. "Fostering Private Food Marketing and Food Supplies after Liberalisation in Sub-Saharan Africa: The Case of Malawi", draft report submitted to WIDER, the United Nations University.

Chirwa E.W., Mvula, P., Zgovu, E. and Namata, L. 1996. *Review of Credit Operations under Social Dimensions of Adjustment (SDA) Project and Other Programmes*, report by Wadonda Consult submitted to the Ministry of Economic Planning and Development.

Chirwa, W.C. 1998a. "Democracy, Ethnicity and Regionalism: The Malawian Experience, 1992–1996", in K.M. Phiri and K.R. Ross (eds) *Democratization in Malawi: A Stocktaking*. Blantyre: CLAIM.

Chirwa, W.C. 1998b. "Aliens and AIDS in Southern Africa: The Malawi-South Africa Debate", *African Affairs* 97: 53–79.

Chirwa, W.C. 2000. "Uses of the Past in Malawian Politics", a paper presented at the International Conference on Historical and Social Science Research in Malawi: Problems and Prospects, Zomba, June 2000.

Chisiza, D. 1961: *Africa: What Lies Ahead?* New Delhi: Indian Council for Africa.

Chisiza, D. 1962. "The Temper, Aspiration and Problems of Contemporary Africa", a paper presented at the Nyasaland Economic Symposium, July 1962.

Chiwaya, W.B. n.d. "Bar Girls: A Study in Mangochi District", unpublished paper.

Christiansen, R.E. and Stackhouse, L.A. 1989. "The Privatisation of Agricultural Trading in Malawi", *World Development* 17: 729–740.

Ciekawy, D. and Geschiere, P. 1998. "Containing Witchcraft: Conflicting Scenarios in Postcolonial Africa", *African Studies Review* 41: 1–14.

Comaroff, J. 1982. "Medicine: Symbol and Ideology", in P. Wright and A. Treacher (eds) *The Problem of Medical Knowledge: Examining the Social Construction of Medicine*. Edinburgh: Edinburgh University Press.

Comaroff, J. and Comaroff, J. (eds) 1993. *Modernity and Its Malcontents: Ritual and Power in Post-Colonial Africa*. Chicago: University of Chicago Press.

Comaroff, J. and Comaroff, J. (eds) 1999. *Civil Society and the Political Imagination in Africa: Critical Perspectives*. Chicago: University of Chicago Press.

Dallabeta, G.A, Odaka, N, Hoover, D, Chiphangwi, J.D, Liomba, G, Miotti, P. and Saah, A. 1993. "High Socio-Economic Status Is a Risk Factor for HIV-1 Infection, but Not for STDs in Women in Malawi", *Journal of Infectious Disease* 167: 36–42.

Davidson, V. 1973. "Malawi", in N. Rubin and E. Cotran (eds) *Annual Survey of African Law, Vol. III 1969*. London.

Dawson, M.C. 1992. "Socio-Economic Change and Disease: Smallpox in Colonial Kenya", in S. Feierman and J. M. Janzen (eds) *The Social Basis of Health and Healing in Africa*. Berkeley: University of California Press.

Diamond, L. 1994. "Rethinking Civil Society: Toward Democratic Consolidation", *Journal of Democracy* 5: 5–17.

Dijk, R. A. van 1992. "Young Puritan Preachers in Post-Independence Malawi", *Africa* 62: 160–180.

Donge, J.K. van 1995. "Kamuzu's Legacy: The Democratisation of Malawi or Searching for the Rules of the Game in African Politics", *African Affairs* 94: 227–257.

Donge, J.K. van 1998a. "The 1997 Civil Service Strike in Malawi: The Politics and Policy Making of Civil Service Remuneration and Reform", unpublished paper.

Donge, J.K. van 1998b. "The Mwanza Murder Case: A Search for a Usable Past", in K.M. Phiri and K.R. Ross (eds) *Democratization in Malawi: A Stocktaking*. Blantyre: CLAIM.

Drake, A.M. 1976. *Illness, Ritual, and Social Relations among the Chewa of Central Africa*. PhD Thesis, Duke University, Durham, N.C., USA.

Dunway, K.D. 1987. "Music as Political Communication in the United States", in J. Lull (ed.) *Popular Music and Communication*. Newbury Park, CA: Sage.

Dzimbiri, L.B. 1994. "Notes on Recent Elections: The Malawi Referendum of June 1993", *Election Studies* 13: 229–234.

Dzimbiri, L.B. 1998. "Democratic Politics and Chameleon-like Leaders", in K.M. Phiri and K.R. Ross (eds) *Democratization in Malawi: A Stocktaking*. Blantyre: CLAIM.

Dzimbiri, L.B. 1999. "Socio-Political Engineering and Chameleon Politics in Malawi: The Period of the Transition", *African Currents* 16: 24–45.

Edelman, M. 1977. *Political Language: Words That Succeed and Policies That Fail*. New York: Academic Press.

Ekeh, P.P. 1975. "Colonialism and the Two Publics in Africa: A Theoretical Statement", *Comparative Studies in Society and History* 17: 91–112.

Elkins, D.J. and Simeon, R. 1979. "A Cause in Search of Its Effect, or What Does Political Culture Explain?", *Comparative Politics* 11: 127–145.

Englund, H. 1996a. "Between God and Kamuzu: The Transition to Multiparty Politics in Central Malawi", in R. Werbner and T. Ranger (eds) *Postcolonial Identities in Africa*. London: Zed Books.

Englund, H. 1996b. "Witchcraft, Modernity and the Person: The Morality of Accumulation in Central Malawi", *Critique of Anthropology* 16: 257–279.

Englund, H. 2000. "The Dead Hand of Human Rights: Contrasting Christianities in Post-Transition Malawi", *Journal of Modern African Studies* 38: 579–603.

Englund, H. 2001a. "Winning Elections, Losing Legitimacy: Multipartyism and the Neopatrimonial State in Malawi", in M. Cowen and L. Laakso (eds) *Multiparty Elections in Africa*. Oxford: James Currey.

Englund, H. 2001b. "Chinyanja and the Language of Rights", *Nordic Journal of African Studies* 10: 299–319.

Englund, H. 2001c. "The Politics of Multiple Identities: The Making of a Home Villagers' Association in Lilongwe, Malawi", in A. Tostensen, I. Tvedten and M. Vaa (eds) *Associational Life in African Cities: Popular Responses to the Urban Crisis*. Uppsala: The Nordic Africa Institute.

Esho, H. 1999. "Development and Poverty", *Journal of Development Assistance* 5: 38–57.

Etounga-Manguelle, D. 2000. "Does Africa Need a Cultural Adjustment Program?", in L. Harrison and S. Huntington (eds) *Culture Matters: How Values Shape Human Progress*. New York: Basic Books.

Fabian, J. 1997. "Popular Culture in Africa: Findings and Conjectures", in K. Barber (ed.) *Readings in African Popular Culture*. London: James Currey.

Fabian, J. 1998. *Moments of Freedom: Anthropology and Popular Culture*. Charlotesville: University Press of Virginia.

Fatton, R. Jr. 1992. *Predatory Rule: State and Civil Society in Africa*. Boulder, CO: Lynne Rienner.

Feierman, S. and Janzen, J. M. (eds) 1992. *The Social Basis of Health and Healing in Africa*. Berkeley: University of California Press.

Fishman, J. 1972. *Language in Sociocultural Change*. Stanford: Stanford University Press.

Foreman, M. 1999. *Aids and Men: Taking Risks or Taking Responsibility?* London: PANOS/Zed Books.

Forster, P.G. 1994. "Culture, Nationalism, and the Invention of Tradition in Malawi", *Journal of Modern African Studies* 32: 477–497.

Forster, P.G. 1996. "AIDS, the Local Community and Traditional Health Practitioners in Malawi", unpublished report.

Forster, P.G. 1998. "Religion, Magic, Witchcraft, and AIDS in Malawi", *Anthropos* 93: 537–554.

Forster, P.G. 2000. "Democratisation in Malawi: Extended Review", *Journal of Southern African Studies* 26: 857–861.

Forsythe, S. 1992. "The Economic Impact of HIV and AIDS in Malawi", unpublished report.

Friedland, M. 1998. *Lift up Your Voice Like a Trumpet : White Clergy and the Civil Rights and Antiwar Movements, 1954–1973*. Chapel Hill: University of North Carolina Press.

Gerth, H.H. and Mills, W.C. (eds) 1948. *From Max Weber: Essays in Sociology*. London: Routledge.

Geschiere, P. 1996. "Witchcraft, Kinship and the Moral Economy of Ethnicity: Regional Variations in Cameroon", in L. de la Gorgendiere, K. King, and S. Vaughan (eds) *Ethnicity in Africa: Roots, Meanings and Implications*. Edinburgh: Centre of African Studies.

Geschiere, P. 1997. *The Modernity of Witchcraft: Politics and the Occult in Postcolonial Africa*. Charlottesville: University Press of Virginia.

Geschiere, P. and Gugler, J. 1998. "The Urban-Rural Connection: Changing Issues of Belonging and Identification", *Africa* 68: 309–319.

GOM, Government of Malawi 1991. *Malawi Public Service Regulations*. Zomba: Government Printer.

GOM, Government of Malawi 1994. "Implementation of the Poverty Alleviation Programme", *Poverty Alleviation Document No. 1*.

GOM, Government of Malawi 1995a. *Policy Framework for Poverty Alleviation*. Lilongwe: Ministry of Economic Planning and Development.

GOM, Government of Malawi 1995b. *Report of the Commission of Inquiry into the Conditions of Service for the Civil Servants (Chatsika-Report)*. Zomba: Government Printer.

GOM, Government of Malawi 1995, 1996, 1997, 1998, 1999b. *Economic Reports*. Zomba: Government Printer.

GOM, Government of Malawi 1999a. *Monthly Statistical Bulletin December 1999*. Zomba: National Statistical Office.

GOM, Government of Malawi 2001. *Malawi National Land Policy*. Lilongwe: Ministry of Lands and Housing.

GOM/UN 1993. *Situation Analysis of Poverty in Malawi*. Zomba: Government Printer.

Griffiths, J. 1986. "What Is Legal Pluralism?", *Journal of Legal Pluralism* 24: 1–55.

Guth, J., Green, J., Smidt, C., Kellstedt, L. and Poloma, M. 1997. *The Bully Pulpit: The Politics of Protestant Clergy*. Lawrence, KS: University Press of Kansas.

Gwengwe, J.W. 1986. *Kukula ndi mwambo*. Blantyre: Dzuka Publishing Company.

Hadenius, A. and Uggla, F. 1996. "Making Civil Society Work, Promoting Democratic Development: What Can Donors Do?", *World Development* 24: 1621–1639.

Harbeson, J. 1994. "Civil Society and Political Renaissance in Africa", in J. Harbeson, N. Chazan and D. Rothchild (eds) *Civil Society and the State in Africa*. Boulder, CO: Lynne Rienner.

Harrison, L. and Huntington, S. (eds) 2000. *Culture Matters: How Values Shape Human Progress*. New York: Basic Books.

Harriss, J., Hunter, J. and Lewis, C. (eds) 1995. *The New Institutional Economics and Third World Development*. London: Routledge.

Haynes, J. 1996. *Religion and Politics in Africa*. London: Zed Books.

Hedges, D. 1989. "Some Notes on Malawi-Mozambique Relations 1961–87", *Journal of Southern African Studies* 15: 617–644.

Helitzer-Allen, D. and Allen, H. 1992. "Focused Ethnographic Study of Sexually Transmitted Illnesses in Thyolo, Malawi", unpublished paper.

Helitzer-Allen, D. and Mankhambera, M. 1993. "How Can We Help Adolescent Girls Avoid HIV Infection?", unpublished study report.

Hentschel, J. 2000. "Combining Census and Survey Data to Trace the Spatial Dimensions of Poverty: A Case Study of Ecuador", *The World Bank Economic Review* 14: 147–165.

Herring, R. 1999. "Persistent Poverty and Path Dependency in Agrarian Reforms: Lessons from the United States and India", *IDS Bulletin* 30: 13–22.

Hodder-Williams, R. 1974. "Dr Banda's Malawi", *Journal of Commonwealth and Comparative Politics* 12: 91–114.

Holly, W. 1989. "Credibility and Political Language", in R. Wodak (ed.) *Language, Power and Ideology: Studies in Political Discourse*. Amsterdam: John Benjamins.

Hours, B. 1986. "African Medicine as an Alibi and Reality", in U. Maclean and C. Fyfe (eds) *African Medicine in the Modern World*. Edinburgh: Edinburgh University Press.

Hyden, G. 1983. *No Shortcuts to Progress: African Development Management in Perspective*. London: Heinemann.

Hyden, G. 1999. "Rethinking the Study of African Politics", in D. Olowu, A. Williams and K. Boremekun (eds) *Governance and Democratization in West Africa*. Dakar: Codesria.

Inglehart, R. 1988. "The Renaissance of Political Culture", *American Political Science Review* 82: 1203–1230.

International Labour Organisation 1984. *Introduction to Social Security*. Geneva: International Labour Organisation.

Jambo, I.W. 1993. *Face to Face with AIDS: A True Life Story*. Balaka: Montfort Press.

Jensen, M. and Poulsen, K. 1993. *Human Rights and Cultural Change – Women in Africa*. Copenhagen: The Danish Centre for Human Rights.

Johannessen, L. 1997. "A Critical View of the Constitutional Hate Speech Provision", *South African Journal of Human Rights* 13: 135–150.

Jones, A. 1992. *Like a Knife: Ideology and Genre in Contemporary Chinese Popular Music*. New York: Cornell University Press.

Kadzamira, Z.D. 2000. "Management of the Electoral Process during the Second Multi-Party Elections", in M. Ott, K.M. Phiri and N. Patel (eds) *Malawi's Second Democratic Elections: Process, Problems, and Prospects*. Blantyre: CLAIM.

Kadzamira, Z.D., Mawaya, A.G. and Patel, N. 1998. *Profiles and Views of Political Parties in Malawi*, a study commissioned by the Public Affairs Committee and the Malawi-German Programme for Democracy.

Kakhongwe, P. 1997. *Directory of AIDS Service Organisations in Malawi*. Zomba: Centre for Social Research.

Kalipeni, E. 1997. "Population Pressure, Social Change, Culture and Malawi's Pattern of Fertility Transition", *African Studies Review* 40: 173–208.

Kaluwa, B.M. 1992. "Malawi Industry: Policies, Performance and Problems" in G.C.Z. Mhone (ed.) *Malawi at the Crossroads: The Post-Colonial Political Economy*. Harare: SAPES.

Kaluwa, B.M., Silumbu, E., Banda, E.S. and Chilowa, W. 1992. *The Structural Adjustment Programmes in Malawi: A Case of Successful Adjustment?* Harare: SAPES.

Kaluwa, O. L., Feluzi, H. G., Songwe, A. C. and Zingani, A. M. 1995. *1995 Sentinel Surveillance Report*. Lilongwe: Ministry of Health.

Kamwendo, G.H. 1997. "Language Policy in Malawi", *Zimbabwe Journal of Educational Research* 9: 202–215.

Kamwendo, G.H. 1999a. "Inflammatory Political Language: A Threat to Democracy in Malawi", a paper presented at the 21st Southern African Universities Social Science Conference (SAUSSC), Zomba, November –December, 1999.

Kamwendo, G.H. 1999b. "Empowering an Embarrassing Language: The Case of Chilomwe in Malawi", a paper presented at the Workshop on the Empowerment of Khoesan Languages, Gaberone, 1999.

Kamwendo, G.H. 1999c. "Centre for Language Studies: An Overview", *Malilime: Malawian Journal of Linguistics* 1: 41–46.

Kamwendo, G.H. 2000. "The Use and Abuse of Language during Election Campaigns", in M. Ott, K.M. Phiri and N. Patel (eds) *Malawi's Second Democratic Elections: Process, Problems, and Prospects*. Blantyre: CLAIM.

Kamwendo, G.H. and Kamowa, O. 1999. "HIV/AIDS and a Return to Traditional Cultural Practices in Malawi", in R.H. Kempe (ed.) *AIDS and Development in Africa: A Social Science Perspective*. New York: The Haworth Press.

Kangwere, P. 1998. "Private Investment: An Alternative Means to Poverty Reduction: A Case of Malawi", a paper presented at the National Economics Conference on Policies, Performance and Prospects, Mangochi, October 1998.

Kanyongolo, F.E. 1998. "The Limits of Liberal Democratic Constitutionalism in Malawi", in K.M. Phiri and K.R. Ross (eds), *Democratization in Malawi: A Stocktaking*. Blantyre: CLAIM.

Kanyongolo, F.E. 1999. *Human Rights Jurisprudence in Polarised Societies: A Comparative Analysis of Malawi and South Africa*. PhD thesis, University of East Anglia.

Karlen, A. 1995. *Plague's Progress: A Social History of Man and Disease*. London: Victor Gollancz.

Karlström, M. 1996. "Imagining Democracy: Political Culture and Democratisation in Buganda", *Africa* 66: 485–505.

Kasfir, N. 1998. "The Conventional Notion of Civil Society: A Critique", *Journal of Commonwealth and Comparative Politics* 36: 1–20.

Kaspin, D. 1993. "Chewa Visions and Revisions of Power: Transformations of the Nyau Dance in Central Malawi", in J. Comaroff and J. Comaroff (eds) *Modernity and Its Malcontents: Ritual and Power in Post-Colonial Africa*. Chicago: University of Chicago Press.

Kaspin, D. 1995. "The Politics of Ethnicity in Malawi's Democratic Transition", *Journal of Modern African Studies* 33: 595–620.

Kayambazinthu, E. 1989. "Patterns of Language Use in Malawi: A Sociolinguistic Investigation in Domasi and Malindi Areas of Southern Malawi", *Journal of Contemporary African Studies* 8 & 9: 109–131.

Khaila, S.W. 1995. *The Cultural Determinants of Violence against Women: A Basis for Policy Intervention.* Zomba: Centre for Social Research.

King, M. and King, E. 1992. *The Story of Medicine and Disease in Malawi.* Blantyre: Montfort Press.

King, M. and King, E. 2000. *The Great Rift: Africa, Surgery, Aids, Aid.* Cambridge: ARCO Books.

Kishindo, P.A.K. 1985. "Sexual Behaviour in the Face of Risk: The Case of Bar Girls in Malawi's Major Cities", *Health Transition Review, Supplement, 5:* 153–160.

Kishindo, P.A.K. 1990. "Knowledge, Attitudes and Beliefs on AIDS", unpublished manuscript.

Kishindo, P.A.K. 1994. "Land Tenure: The Case of the Salima District, Central Malawi", *Malawi Journal of Social Science* 16: 57–67.

Kishindo, P.A.K. 1995. "High Risk Behaviour in the Face of the AIDS Epidemic: The Case of the Bar Girls in the Municipality of Zomba", *Eastern Africa Social Science Research Review* 11: 35–43.

Kishindo, P.A.K. 1997. "Malawi's Social Development Policies: A Historical Review", *Bwalo: A Forum for Social Development*, 1: 11–20.

Kishindo, P.J. 1993. "Linguistic Diversity and National Unity", *UDF News* 1, No. 44: 8.

Kishindo, P.J. 1998. "On the Standardization of Citumbuka and Ciyao Orthographies: Some Observations", *South African Journal of African Languages* 18: 85–92.

Kool, H. E., Bloemkolk, D., Reeve, P.A. and Danner, S. A. 1990. "HIV Seropositivity and Tuberculosis in a Large General Hospital in Malawi", *Tropical Geographical Medicine* 42: 128 – 132.

Kydd, J. and Christiansen, R.E. 1982. "Structural Change in Malawi since Independence: Consequences of a Development Strategy Based on Large-Scale Agriculture", *World Development* 10: 355–375.

Laitin, D. 1978. "Religion, Political Culture, and the Weberian Tradition", *World Politics* 30: 563–592.

Landell-Mills, P. 1992. "Governance, Cultural Change, and Empowerment", *Journal of Modern African Studies* 30: 543–567.

Levine, D. 1981. *Religion and Politics in Latin America: The Catholic Church in Venezuela and Colombia.* Princeton: Princeton University Press.

Levine, D. 1992. *Popular Voices in Latin American Catholicism.* Princeton: Princeton University Press.

Levine, D. and Wilde, A. 1977. "The Catholic Church, 'Politics' and Violence: The Colombian Case", *Review of Politics* 39: 220–249.

L'Herminez, R.H., Hofs, M.A.G. and Chiwaya, W.B. 1992. "Aids in Mangochi District", *Malawi Medical Journal* 8: 113–117.

Liomba, G., Kandulu, M. and Kandiyado, V. 1993. "Family and Community Care Situation Analysis", unpublished report for the National Aids Coordination Programme, Lilongwe.

Lwanda, J.L. 1993. *Kamuzu Banda of Malawi: A Study in Promise, Power and Paralysis.* Glasgow: Dudu Nsomba Publications.

Lwanda, J.L. 1996. *Promises, Power, Politics and Poverty: The Democratic Transition in Malawi 1961 to 1999.* Glasgow: Dudu Nsomba Publications.

MacGaffey, W. 1990. "Religion, Class, and Social Pluralism in Zaire", *Canadian Journal of African Studies* 24: 249–264.

Mainwaring, S. 1986. *The Catholic Church and Politics in Brazil, 1916–1985.* Stanford: Stanford University Press.

Malawi AIDS Control Programme Manual, 1989. Lilongwe: Ministry of Heath.

Malawi Demographic and Health Survey 1992. Zomba: National Statistical Office.

Malawi Electoral Commission 1994. *1994 Parliamentary and Presidential Elections Report.* Zomba: Government Printer.

Malawi Electoral Commission 1999. *1999 Parliamentary and Presidential Elections Report.* Zomba: Government Printer.

Malawi National AIDS Control Programme Sentinel Survey Report, 1999. Lilongwe: Ministry of Health.

Malawi National Family Planning Strategy, 1994–1998. Zomba: Government Printer.

Malawi Vision 2020 Draft. Lilongwe: UNDP/Malawi Government.

Maluwa, T. 1996. "The Role of International Law in the Protection of Human Rights in the Constitution of Malawi", in A.A. Yusuf (ed.) *African Yearbook of International Law*. Amsterdam: Kluwer Law International.

Maluwa-Banda, D.W. 2000. "HIV/AIDS-Related Knowledge and Self-Reported Sexual Behaviour of Secondary School Students in Southern Malawi: Implications for AIDS Education and Counselling", a paper presented at the International Conference on Historical and Social Science Research in Malawi: Problems and Prospects, Zomba, June 2000.

Mamdani, M. 1996. *Citizen and Subject: Contemporary Africa and the Legacy of Late Colonialism*. Princeton: Princeton University Press.

Mapanje, J. 1981. *Of Chameleons and Gods*. London: Heinemann.

Marshall, R. 1995. "'God is not a Democrat': Pentecostalism and Democratization in Nigeria", in P. Gifford (ed.) *The Christian Churches and Democratization in Africa*. Leiden: Brill.

Matiki, A. 1996. "Language Shift and Maintenance: Socio-economic Determinants of Linguistic Change among the Lomwe People", *Journal of Humanities* 10 & 11: 1–25.

Mattern, M. 1998. "Cajun Music, Cultural Revival: Theorizing Political Action in Popular Music", *Popular Music and Society* 22: 31–47.

Mazrui, A. 1990. *Cultural Forces in World Politics*. London: James Currey.

M'Bama, J.M.A. 1991. "Re: Qualities of Frequent Injection Prescribers and Injection Seekers", *Moyo Journal* 24: 11–13.

Mbembe, A. 2001. *On the Postcolony*. Berkeley: University of California Press.

Mburu, F. M. 1992. "The Social Production of Health in Kenya", in S. Feierman and J.M. Janzen (eds) *The Social Basis of Health and Healing in Africa*. Berkeley: University of California Press.

McAuliffe, E. 1994. "AIDS: The Barriers to Behaviour Change", unpublished paper.

McCracken, J. 1999. "New Perspectives on the History of Christianity in Malawi", *Journal of Religion in Africa* 24: 486–493.

Médard, J.-F. 1982. "The Underdeveloped State in Tropical Africa: Political Clientelism or Neo-Patrimonialism?", in C. Clapham (ed.) *Private Patronage and Public Power: Political Clientelism in the Modern State*. London: Frances Pinter.

Mhiri, C. 1992. "The Slim Disease in Patients with AIDS", *Transactions of the Royal Society of Tropical Medicine & Hygiene* 86: 303–306.

Mhone, G.C.Z. (ed.) 1992a. *Malawi at the Crossroads: The Post-Colonial Political Economy*. Harare: SAPES Books.

Mhone, G.C.Z. 1992b. "The Political Economy of Malawi: An Overview", in G.C.Z. Mhone (ed.) *Malawi at the Crossroads: The Post-Colonial Political Economy*. Harare: SAPES Books.

Migdal, J.S. 1988. *Strong Societies and Weak States: State-Society Relations and State Capabilities in the Third World*. Princeton: Princeton University Press.

Mikkelsen, B. 1995. *Methods for Development Work and Research: A Guide for Practitioners*. New Delhi: Sage.

Mkamanga, E. 2000. *Suffering in Silence: Malawi Women's 30 Year Dance with Dr Banda*. Glasgow: Dudu Nsomba Publications.

Mkandawire, R. 1992. "The Land Question and Agrarian Change in Malawi", in G.C.Z. Mhone (ed.) *Malawi at the Crossroads: The Post-Colonial Political Economy*. Harare: SAPES.

MOH, Ministry of Health 1978. *Report of the National Seminar on Primary Health Care*. Lilongwe.

MOH, Ministry of Health 1991. *Bibliography of Health Information in Malawi*. Lilongwe.

MOH, Ministry of Health 1994. *The Malawi National Family Planning Strategy* (NFPS). Lilongwe.

Moore, H.L. 1994. *A Passion for Difference: Essays in Anthropology and Gender*. Cambridge: Polity Press.

Moore, M. 1999. "Politics against Poverty: Global Pessimism and National Optimism", *IDS Bulletin* 30: 30–45.

Moto, F. 2000. "The Semantics of Poetic and Dramatic Works: The Case of Mapanje and Chimombo", a paper presented at the International Conference on Historical and Social Science Research in Malawi: Problems and Prospects, Zomba, June 2000.

Mpasu, S. 1995. *Political Prisoner 3/75 of Dr. H. Kamuzu Banda of Malawi*. Harare: African Publishing Group.

Msapato, K. M., Kumwenda, K. M., Chirwa, B. Z, Chalira, A. M. and Mzembe, C. P. 1990. *Study of Knowledge and Aspects of Attitudes of School Teenagers in Mzimba District about HIV Infection/AIDS*. Lilongwe: Ministry of Health.

Msonthi, J. 1982. "Herbal Medicines Used by Traditional Birth Attendants in Malawi", *Tropical Geography* 34: 81–85.

Msonthi, J. 1984. "The Herbalists Association of Malawi as a Profession", *The Society of Malawi Journal* 37: 45–53.

Msonthi, J. 1986. "Government, Associations and the University: Liason in Malawi", in M. Last and G.L. Chavunduka (eds) *The Professionalisation of African Medicine*. Manchester: Manchester University Press.

Msukwa, L.A.H. 1981. *Meeting the Basic Health Needs of Rural Malawi: An Alternative Strategy*. Norwich: Geo Books.

Msukwa, L.A.H., Kanyoni, S.E. and Bamusi, N.S. 1994. *Poverty in Malawi: A Review of Literature*. Zomba: Centre for Social Research.

Muluzi, B, Juwayeyi, Y.M., Makhambera, M. and Phiri, D.D. 1999. *Democracy with a Price: The History of Malawi since 1900*. Blantyre: Jhango/Heinemann.

Mutharika, P.A. 1996. "The 1995 Democratic Constitution of Malawi", *Journal of African Law* 40: 205–220.

Mwangulube, K., Simgogo, P. and Nowa, S. 1997. "Baseline Survey for Malawi Prisons AIDS Interventions Report", unpublished report for UNAIDS.

Nagengast, C. 1997. "Women, Minorities and Indigenous Peoples: Universalism and Cultural Relativity", *Journal of Anthropological Research* 53: 349–370.

Nahirny, V. and Fishman, J. 1965. "American Immigrant Groups: Ethnic Identification and the Problems of Generations", *Sociolinguistic Review* 13: 311–326.

Namate, D. E. and Kornfield, R. 1997. "Condom Use among Urban Workers and Their Wives", unpublished report for UNFPA/MOH.

National Aids Control Programme Strategy Planning Unit 1999. *A Decade of AIDS Research in Malawi*. Lilongwe: NACP.

Nazombe, A.J.M. 1995. "Malawian Poetry of the Transition: Steve Chimombo's 'A Referendum of the Forest Creatures' and Jack Mapanje's 'The Chattering Wagtails of Mikuyu Prison'", in M.S. Nzunda and K.R. Ross (eds) *Church, Law and Political Transition in Malawi 1992–94*. Gweru: Mambo Press.

NEC, National Economic Council 1998. *Qualitative Impact Monitoring of Poverty Alleviation Policies and Programmes in Malawi, Volume 1 Research Findings*. Lilongwe: NEC.

NEC, National Economic Council 2000. *A Study to Develop Research Policy and Operational Definition of Poverty in Malawi*. Lilongwe: NEC

Neisser, E. 1994. "Hate Speech in the New South Africa: Constitutional Considerations for a Land Recovering from Decades of Racial Repression and Violence", *South African Journal of Human Rights* 10: 336–356.

Nelsen, H., Yokley, R. and Madron, T. 1973. "Ministerial Roles and Social Actionist Stance: Protestant Clergy and Protest in the Sixties", *American Sociological Review* 38: 375–386.

Newell, J. 1995. "'A Moment of Truth'? The Church and Political Change in Malawi, 1992", *Journal of Modern African Studies* 33: 243–262.

Ng'ong'ola, C. 1996. "Managing the Transition to Political Pluralism in Malawi: Legal and Constitutional Arrangements", *Journal of Commonwealth and Comparative Politics* 34: 85–110.

Ngwira, N., Kayambazinthu, E. and Kamchedzera, E. 2000. "Double Jeopardy: Vulnerable Children's Access to Basic Education", unpublished research report for UNICEF-Malawi.

Nkosi, K. 1999. "Men, the Military and HIV/AIDS in Malawi", in M. Foreman (ed.) *AIDS and Men: Taking Risks or Responsibility?* London: Zed Books.

NSO, National Statistical Office 1999. *1999 African Statistics Day Special Report*. Zomba.

Nurse, G.T. 1964. "Popular Songs and National Identity in Malawi", *African Music Society Journal* 3: 101–106.

Nyangulu, D. 1990. "Tuberculosis and HIV Infection", *Malawi Medical Journal* 6: 7–8.

Nzunda, M.S. and Ross, K.R. (eds) 1995. *Church, Law and Political Transition in Malawi 1992–94*. Gweru: Mambo Press.

Obeng, S.G. 1997. "Language and Politics: Indirectness in Political Discourse", *Discourse and Society* 8: 49–83.

Ogden, J.A. 1996. "Producing Respect: The 'Proper Woman' in Postcolonial Kampala", in R. Werbner and T. Ranger (eds) *Postcolonial Identities in Africa*. London: Zed Books.

O'Malley, P. 1999. *Living Dangerously: A Memoir of Political Change in Malawi*. Glasgow: Dudu Nsomba Publications.

Orubuloye, I. O., Caldwell, J. C., Santow, G., Caldwell, P. and Anarfi, J. (eds) 1994. *Sexual Networking and AIDS in Sub-Saharan Africa: Behavioural Research and the Social Context*. Canberra: Australian National University.

Otanez, M. 2000. "Public Anthropology and Social Engagement: Labor Advocacy in Malawi", a paper presented at the Annual Meeting of the American Anthropological Association, San Francisco, November 2000.

Ott, M. 2000. "The Role of Christian Churches in Democratic Malawi", in M. Ott, K.M. Phiri and N. Patel (eds) *Malawi's Second Democratic Elections: Process, Problems, and Prospects*. Blantyre: CLAIM.

Ott, M., Phiri, K.M. and Patel, N. (eds) 2000. *Malawi's Second Democratic Elections: Process, Problems, and Prospects*. Blantyre: CLAIM.

Packard, R. 1989. *White Plague, Black Labour: Tuberculosis and the Political Economy of Health and Disease in South Africa*. Pietermaritzburg: University of Natal Press.

Patel, N. 2000. "The 1999 Elections: Challenges and Reforms", in M. Ott, K.M. Phiri and N. Patel (eds) *Malawi's Second Democratic Elections: Process, Problems, and Prospects*. Blantyre: CLAIM.

Pearce J., Ngwira A. and Chimseu, J. 1996. *Living on the Edge: A Study of the Rural Food Economy in Mchinji and Salima Districts*. Lilongwe: Save the Children Fund (UK).

Peltzer, K. 1986. *Some Contributions of Traditional Healing Practices towards Psychosocial Healthcare in Malawi*. PhD thesis, University of Hannover.

Pfaffe, J. (ed.) 2000. *Local Languages in Education, Science and Technology: Proceedings of the Second National Symposium on Language Policy Formulation*. Zomba: Centre for Language Studies.

Phiri, I.A. 1996. "Marching, Suspended and Stoned: Christian Women in Malawi 1995", in K.R. Ross (ed.) *God, People and Power in Malawi: Democratization in Theological Perspective*. Blantyre: CLAIM.

Phiri, K.M. 1998. "Dr Banda's Cultural Legacy and Its Implications for a Democratic Malawi", in K.M. Phiri and K.R. Ross (eds) *Democratization in Malawi: A Stocktaking*. Blantyre: CLAIM.

Phiri, K.M. and Ross, K.R. (eds) 1998. *Democratization in Malawi: A Stocktaking*. Blantyre: CLAIM.

Posner, D. 1995. "Malawi's New Dawn", *Journal of Democracy* 6: 131–145.

Preston, B. 1995. *Chiefs: Traditional Authority and Democratic Governance in Malawi, A Report on NDI Program Activities with Malawi Chiefs in Preparation for the National Constitutional Conference*. Blantyre: NDI.

Probst, P. 1999. "Mchape 95, or the Sudden Fame of Billy Goodson Chisupe: Healing, Social Memory and the Enigma of the Public Sphere in Post-Banda Malawi", *Africa* 69: 109–137.

Pye, L. and Verba, S. 1965. *Political Culture and Political Development*. Princeton: Princeton University Press.

Ranger, T. 1989. "Missionaries, Migrants and the Manyika: The Invention of Ethnicity in Zimbabwe", in L. Vail (ed.) *The Creation of Tribalism in Southern Africa*. Berkeley: University of California Press.

Roberts, S. 1966. "The Malawi Forfeiture Act – A Surfeit of Discretion", *Journal of African Law* 10: 131–134.

Roe, G. and Chilowa, W.R. 1989. *A Study on the Effects of Macro-Economic Adjustment Policies on Urban Poor Households: First Stage*. Zomba: Centre for Social Research.

Ross, K.R. (ed.) 1996. *God, People and Power in Malawi: Democratization in Theological Perspective*. Blantyre: CLAIM.

Ross, K.R. 1998. "Does Malawi 'Still' Need a Truth Commission?", in K.M. Phiri and K.R. Ross (eds), *Democratization in Malawi: A Stocktaking*. Blantyre: CLAIM.

Sahn, D. and Sarris, A. 1990. "The Political Economy of Decline and Reforms in Africa: The Role of the State, Markets and Civil Organisations", in A. de Janvry (ed.) *State, Market and Civil Organisations*. Berkeley: California University Press.

Schoffeleers, M. 1999a. *In Search of Truth and Justice: Confrontations between Church and State in Malawi 1960–1994*. Blantyre: CLAIM.

Schoffeleers, M. 1999b. "The AIDS Pandemic, the Prophet Billy Chisupe, and the Democratization Process in Malawi", *Journal of Religion in Africa* 24: 406–441.

Schoffeleers, M. and Roscoe, A.A. (eds) 1987. *Land of Fire: Oral Literature from Malawi*. Limbe: Popular Publications.

Semu, L. and Kadzamira, E. 1995. "Peace, Violence against Women, the Girl Child and Economic Empowerment: Final Report", unpublished report.

Serwada, D. 1985. "Slim Disease: A New Disease in Uganda and Its Association with HTLV-III Infection", *Lancet* 2: 849–852.

Skinner, T.M. 1963. *Report of the Nyasaland Local Civil Service Commission of Inquiry*. Document at the National Archives of Malawi.

Sornig, K. 1989. "Some Remarks on Linguistic Strategies of Persuasion", in R. Wodak (ed.) *Language, Power and Ideology: Studies in Political Discourse*. Amsterdam: John Benjamins.

Stannus, H. S. 1910. "Notes on Some Tribes of British Central Africa", *Journal of the Royal Anthropological Institute* 40: 285–334.

Strathern, M. 1995. "The Nice Thing about Culture Is That Everybody Has It", in M. Strathern (ed.) *Shifting Contexts: Transformations in Anthropological Knowledge*. London: Routledge.

Sverrison, A. 1997. "The Politics and Governance of Poverty Alleviation: Comparative Case Studies in Sub-Saharan Africa and Latin America", *The European Journal of Development Research* 8: 129–156.

Szemere, A. 1996. "Subcultural Politics and Social Change: Alternative Music in Postcommunist Hungary", *Popular Music and Society* Summer 1996: 19–41.

Taffet, J. 1997. "'My Guitar Is Not for the Rich': The Chilean Song Movement and the Politics of Culture", *Journal of American Culture* 20: 91–103.

Taha, T.E., Canner, J.K., Chiphangwi, J.D., Dallabeta, G.A., Mtimavalye, L.A.R. and Miotti, P.G. n.d.. "Condom Use among Infected and Uninfected Women in Malawi", unpublished paper.

Taha, T.E., Canner, J.K., Wangel, A.M., Chiphangwi, J.D., Liomba, N.G., Miotti, P.G., Dallabetta, G.A. and Saah, A.J. 1994. "Research on HIV in Malawi: The John Hopkins University/Ministry of Health (JHU-MOH) Project", *Malawi Medical Journal* 10: 6–11.

Taha, T.E., Dallabeta, G.A., Chiphangwi, J.D., Mtimavalye, L.A.R., Liomba, N.G., Kumwenda, N., Hoover, D. and Miotti, P.G. 1998. "Trends of HIV-1 and Sexually Transmitted Diseases among Pregnant and Postpartum Women in Urban Malawi", *AIDS* 12: 197–203.

Tembo, K.C. 1993. "Village Health Committees as Instruments for Primary Health Care Promotion", *Society of Malawi Journal* 46: 38–42.

Tembo, K.C. and Phiri, T.B. 1993. "Sexually Based Cultural Practices Implicated in the Transmission of HIV/AIDS", *Society of Malawi Journal* 46: 43–48.

Tenthani, R. 2001. "Torture Victims Want Truth Out, Ministers Say Too Late", *PANAPRESS* Online, June 29, 2001.

Thorne, S. 1997. *Mastering Advanced English Language*. London: Macmillan.

Thornton, J. 1992. *Africa and the Africans in the Making of the Atlantic World, 1400–1680*. Cambridge: Cambridge University Press.

Timpunza-Mvula, E. 1992. "Language Policies in Africa: The Case for Chichewa in Malawi", in R. Herbert (ed.) *Language and Society in Africa: The Theory and Practice of Sociolinguistics*. Johannesburg: University of Witvatersrand Press.

Toye, J. 1999. "Nationalising the Anti-Poverty Agenda", *IDS Bulletin* 30: 6–13.

Tygart, C. 1977. "The Role of Theology among Other Belief Variables for Clergy Civil Rights Activism", *Review of Religious Research* 18: 271–278.

Vail, L. 1978. "Religion, Language and the Tribal Myth: The Tumbuka and Chewa of Malawi", in J.M. Schoffeleers (ed.) *Guardians of the Land: Essays on Central African Territorial Cults*. Gwelo: Mambo Press.

Vail, L. and White, L. 1989. "Tribalism in the Political History of Malawi", in L. Vail (ed.) *The Creation of Tribalism in Southern Africa*. London: James Currey.

Vail, L. and White, L. 1991. *Power and the Praise Poem: Southern African Voices in History*. London: James Currey.

Venter, D. 1995. "Malawi: The Transition to Multi-Party Politics", in D. Venter (ed.) *Democracy and Political Change in Sub-Saharan Africa*. London: Routledge.

Verderber, R.F. 1989. *The Challenge of Effective Speaking*. California: Wardsworth Publishing Company.

VonDoepp, P. 1998. "The Kingdom beyond Zasintha: Churches and Political Life in Malawi's Post-Authoritarian Era", in K.M. Phiri and K.R. Ross (eds) *Democratization in Malawi: A Stocktaking*. Blantyre: CLAIM.

Wald, K. 1997. *Religion and Politics in the United States*. Third Edition. Washington, DC: Congressional Quarterly Press.

Wangel, A.M. 1995. *AIDS in Malawi – A Case Study: A Conspiracy of Silence?* MSc thesis, London School of Hygiene and Tropical Medicine.

Werbner, R. (ed.) 1998. *Memory and the Postcolony: African Anthropology and the Critique of Power.* London: Zed Books.

Werbner, R. (ed.) 2002. *Postcolonial Subjectivities in Africa.* London: Zed Books.

Werbner, R. and Ranger, T. (eds) 1996. *Postcolonial Identities in Africa.* London: Zed Books.

White, L. 1987. *Magomero: Portrait of an African Village.* Cambridge: Cambridge University Press.

WHO/MOH 1989. "A Five-Year Medium-Term Plan for the Prevention and Control of AIDS in Malawi (1989–1993)", Ministry of Health.

Williams, T.D. 1978. *Malawi: The Politics of Despair.* Cornell: Cornell University Press.

Winter, J. A. 1973. "Political Activism among the Clergy: Sources of a Deviant Role", *Review of Religious Research* 14: 178–186.

Wodak, R. (ed.) 1989. *Language, Power and Ideology: Studies in Political Discourse.* Amsterdam: John Benjamins.

World Bank 1990a. *Malawi Public Sector Review.* Washington DC.

World Bank 1990b. *Malawi: Agriculture Sector Adjustment Credit.* Washington DC.

World Bank 1994. "Malawi Public Service Pay and Employment Study", *World Bank Southern Africa Department. Report No. 13071-MAI.*

World Bank 1995. *A Profile of Human Resources and Poverty in Malawi.* Washington DC.

World Bank 2000a. *Helping Countries Combat Corruption: Progress at the World Bank since 1997.* Washington DC.

World Bank 2000b. *Reforming Public Institutions and Strengthening Governance.* Washington DC.

Yamba, B. 1997. "Cosmologies in Turmoil: Witchfinding and AIDS in Chiawa, Zambia", *Africa* 67: 200–223.

Zeleza, T.P. 1997. "Visions of Freedom and Democracy in Postcolonial African Literature", *Women's Studies Quarterly* 25: 10–35.

Index